Problem-Solving Technologies

Philosophy, Technology and Society

Series editor: Sven Ove Hansson

Technological change has deep and often unexpected impacts on our societies. Sometimes new technologies liberate us and improve our quality of life, sometimes they bring severe social and environmental problems, sometimes they do both. This book series reflects philosophically on what new and emerging technologies do to our lives and how we can use them more wisely. It provides new insights on how technology continuously changes the basic conditions of human existence: relationships among ourselves, our relations to nature, the knowledge we can obtain, our thought patterns, our ethical difficulties, and our views of the world.

Titles in the Series:

The Ethics of Technology: Methods and Approaches, edited by Sven Ove Hansson
Nanotechnology: Regulation and Public Discourse, edited by Iris Eisenberger, Angela Kallhoff and Claudia Schwarz-Plaschg
Water Ethics: An Introduction, Neelke Doorn
Humans and Robots: Ethics, Agency, and Anthropomorphism, Sven Nyholm
Interpreting Technology: Ricœur on Questions Concerning Ethics and Philosophy of Technology, edited by Mark Coeckelbergh; Alberto Romele and Wessel Reijers
The Morality of Urban Mobility: Technology and Philosophy of the City, Shane Epting
Problem-Solving Technologies: A User-Friendly Philosophy, Sadjad Soltanzadeh
Test-Driving the Future: Autonomous Vehicles and the Ethics of Technological Change, edited by Diane Michelfelder (forthcoming)
The Ethics of Behaviour Change Technologies, edited by Joel Anderson, Lily Frank and Andreas Spahn (forthcoming)

Problem-Solving Technologies

A User-Friendly Philosophy

Sadjad Soltanzadeh

ROWMAN & LITTLEFIELD
Lanham • Boulder • New York • London

Published by Rowman & Littlefield
An imprint of The Rowman & Littlefield Publishing Group, Inc.
4501 Forbes Boulevard, Suite 200, Lanham, Maryland 20706
www.rowman.com

86-90 Paul Street, London EC2A 4NE, United Kingdom

Copyright © 2021 The Rowman & Littlefield Publishing Company, Inc.

All rights reserved. No part of this book may be reproduced in any form or by any electronic or mechanical means, including information storage and retrieval systems, without written permission from the publisher, except by a reviewer who may quote passages in a review.

British Library Cataloguing in Publication Information Available

Library of Congress Cataloging-in-Publication Data Available

ISBN 9781538157879 (cloth) | ISBN 9781538157893 (paperback) | ISBN 9781538157886 (epub)

LCCN 2021945107

*To my students at Lyneham High School and
Narrabundah College*

Contents

Preface		xi
1	Introduction	1
	Historical Context	2
	Metaphysical Context	6
	Anthropological Context	9
	Outline	14

PART I: THE GENERAL CATEGORISATION

2	Artificial Categorisations	19
	Usefulness	20
	Artefacts	21
	The Modification Condition	21
	The Intention Condition	23
	Assessing the Artefact/Non-artefact Distinction	25
	Entity Realism	29
	Assessing the Entity Realist Approach	30
	Summary	32
3	A User-Friendly Metaphysics	33
	Activity Realism	33
	The Usefulness of the Activity Realist Approach	35
	Comparing the Two Approaches	38
	Final Pushbacks	40
	Summary	44
4	Problem-Solving Technologies	45
	Defining Technology	45
	Degrees of Technological-ness	48

Responding to Objections	51
Summary	54

5 The Conditions for the Possibility of Technologies — 55
  The Humanism/Non-humanism Debate — 56
  Humanism and Non-humanism in Philosophy of Technology — 57
    The Metaphysical Dimensions — 59
  Non-humanist Conditions — 61
  Humanist Conditions — 63
    Revisiting Problem-Solving Activities — 63
    Human Users — 64
    The Mind-Dependence of Problems — 67
    Human Evaluators — 67
  Cognitive Objects in Problem-Solving Activities — 69
  Summary — 73

PART II: THE PARTICULAR CATEGORISATION

6 A Taxonomy of Function Theories — 77
  Ways of Studying Function — 78
  Sources of Function — 79
    Intentional Theories — 79
    Capacity-based and Causal-Role Theories — 81
    Evolutionary Theories — 82
  Justification of Function Ascriptions — 84
  Linguistic Categorisation of Objects — 86
    Creative Use — 87
    Linguistic Values of Evolutionary Theories — 90
  Summary — 91

7 Conservative Functions vs. Authentic Functions — 93
  Entity Realism and Function Essentialism — 94
    Preston's Theory — 95
  Assessing Entity Realist Theories of Function — 98
  Entity Realism, the Causal Theory of Reference and the
      Study of Kinds — 100
  From Internalist to Externalist Theories — 103
  From Intentional to Belief-based Theories — 105
  Summary — 108

8 A User-Friendly Theory of Function — 111
  The Belief-based Consequentialist Theory — 113
  Justified Beliefs vs. Truth — 116
  Black Boxes and Non-material Consequences — 121
  Summary — 124

PART III: ONTOLOGY

9 Existence of Artefacts — 129
   An Entity Realist Notion of Being — 130
   Entity Realism and the Ontology of Artefacts — 131
   How to Assign Existence to Artefacts — 134
   Summary — 138

10 Reality of Technologies — 141
   An Activity Realist Notion of Being — 142
   The Problem-based Reality of Technologies — 146
   Existing Realities — 148
   Language and Reality — 150
   Summary — 152

PART IV: ACTIVITY REALISM IN PRACTICE

11 Scientific Reality — 157
   Clarifying Terminology — 158
   The Reality of Scientific Entities — 160
   The Technology-Dependent Reality of Unobservable Entities — 162
   Comparing the Three Activities — 164
   Conservatism and Degrees of the Technology-Dependence of Sciences — 167
   Summary — 171

12 The Human, the Technological and the Limitations of Autonomous Systems — 173
   Activity Realism and Autonomous Systems — 174
   Norms and Goals of Activities — 175
   Replaceable Activities — 178
   Irreplaceable Activities — 182
      The Epistemic Condition of Performance — 182
      The Logical Condition of Engagement — 184
   Design Ramifications — 187
   Summary — 189

References — 191

Index — 199

About the Author — 205

Preface

We had some unorthodox artworks in our shared house. Among these was a painting which was predominantly black, another 'painting' which was just a plain white canvas and then . . . there was a hammer. Someone had hung a hammer on the wall, with a little piece of paper next to it which read 'This is not a technological object'. Some of us found the way the hammer was hanging from the wall aesthetically pleasing, and some others thought the artist was trying to communicate a message, perhaps something in between Rene Magritte's *The Treachery of Images* and Marcel Duchamp's *Bicycle Wheel*.

Every now and then, we grabbed the hammer and used it for different purposes before hanging it back onto the wall. Occasionally, I used it as a weight to make sure that the puncture patch which I had glued to my bike's inner tube stayed stable until the glue dried. On one summer day, we used the hammer as a mallet in our homemade game of croquet. Sometimes, before we had house inspections, we used the hammer to hit and cut thick weeds growing in our backyard, hoping that the result would be satisfactory to the property manager. Once we used the hammer to smash away the parts of an old washing machine so that we could use the drum as a firepit. We organised a backyard bonfire party that evening with our new firepit.

Despite the different ways in which most of the housemates used the hammer, some of us did not care much about it. This was particularly the case with a housemate who was a flight captain. He barely spent time with us. In fact, he owned a decent house in a warmer town, and was renting a bedroom in our house only because most of his flights were scheduled to depart from, or land in, our city, Canberra. The flight captain never joined our conversations about the hanging hammer or ever used it for any purpose. The divine existence of the hammer never entered the captain's reality.

The hammer of our old shared house is only one example of the various ways that we approach and integrate objects into our everyday activities. These various ways cannot be explained by universal claims about objects. This is because at the level of personal experiences, each individual interaction with an object establishes the ground for a different identification of the object. It is true that the atoms and molecules which made up the hammer existed independently of what we thought about it. But this truism is insufficient and irrelevant to explain how the hammer played important roles for some of us, and was as insignificant and unreal as an ancient civilisation's god for some others. It is true that the hammer was a creation of a manufacturing process, and its production history can be linked back to the first versions of hammers produced by our ancestors. But these universally valid points cannot explain how, in reality, each individual housemate interacted with the hammer, and how the hammer acquired dynamic identities, sometimes as an artwork, sometimes as a technological tool and sometimes as an object of entertainment.

This book is about the identification and categorisation of objects, particularly technologies, at the level of personal experiences. At the level which matters to us. At the level where we connect to objects and use them for varied purposes. The book accepts the fluid identity of objects to argue that we need to stop asking 'What is this object?' and expect to hear a universal truth about the object's identity or the category to which it belongs. An object is simply an object. Nothing more. Any further identification of the object is temporal and depends on its role in the activities in which it is used. Although this book is primarily a work in the philosophy of technology, it can also be seen as a work in the loosely real field of the philosophy of identifications and categorisations. Considering the novelty of its approach, you, the reader, may notice some unexplored territories. For most of you, the book will function as a thought-provoking work, rather than an answer-providing one.

I thank Sarah Greet for her feedback and editing assistance. Thanks also to Eloise Menzies for editing an earlier draft of the book. Thanks to the Asser Institute for giving me the opportunity to finalise the writing of this manuscript.

Sadjad Soltanzadeh
May 2021
Canberra, Australia

Chapter 1

Introduction

The question 'what is technology?' can be answered through different perspectives. One way of viewing technology is to include modern electronic devices and advanced systems, such as smartphones, drones, smart vehicles and robots, and exclude mundane objects such as hammers, tables, sewing needles and sandals. This way of viewing technology might be concerned with the social status of material possessions. Technology is associated with being modern, and being modern is seen as a class marker. The more technological, the more modern a person or a society is regarded to be.

But functioning as a material expression of social identity is only one among various functions that technologies can assume. Technologies can be used in scientific laboratories, as clothing items, as means of transportation, as kitchen utensils and appliances, as navigational tools or as tools to achieve simple tasks, such as fixing a punctured tube, cutting thick garden weeds or smashing the electronic parts of an old washing machine to build a firepit out of the drum.

To get a better understanding of what technology is, we turn to the discipline which studies technology and its impact on people's daily lives, namely, philosophy of technology. Philosophers of technology study the various functions that technological objects assume and the moral issues concerning technological objects. The specific question, 'what is technology?' is studied by one particular branch of philosophy of technology: metaphysics of technology. In addition to this question, metaphysics of technology deals with questions such as 'what gives objects their function?' and 'what place do technologies have in reality?' These questions require philosophising about the nature of technology and that of reality. Historically, however, the general attitude of philosophers of technology towards these metaphysical questions has not been the same.

HISTORICAL CONTEXT

The majority of current philosophers of technology associate themselves with the 'empirical turn'. The empirical turn, which began towards the end of the Twentieth century, is a movement which avoids general theories about technology. Instead, it aims to understand technologies by studying the different interactions that users and designers have with specific technological products. Philosophers of the empirical turn study technologies without necessarily answering metaphysical questions, such as 'what makes something a technology?' and 'what are the conditions of possibility of technology?' In fact, some of them explicitly state that the philosophy of technology should avoid these questions (Hickman, 2008; Verbeek, 2005).

There are historical reasons why these and similar metaphysical questions concerning technology have been largely avoided by philosophers of the empirical turn. The empirical turn was a response to *essentialist* theories of technology, which were characterised by predominantly metaphysical approaches towards technology.

Essentialism in relation to any subject matter, say X, is the idea that all instances of X have a property, which is the essence of X, and it is this essence which makes them instances of X (as opposed to instances of Y or Z). For example, identifying gold as a chemical element with the atomic number 79 is an essentialist identification of gold. Being a chemical element with the atomic number 79 is taken as the essential property of all instances of gold. And it is this essence which makes any instance of gold an instance of *gold*. Essence is context-independent. Things carry their essences in all contexts, including in isolation. Being a chemical element with the atomic number 79, for example, is a property which all instances of gold necessarily have, regardless of whether or how they are used.

Essentialism can be interpreted in a narrow or a broad sense. In its narrow sense, essence is considered to be an intrinsic property. Identifying an individual based on their genetic information is an essentialist identification of the individual in the narrow sense of essentialism. This is because genetic information is an intrinsic property of the individual. In the broad sense of essentialism, essence can be an intrinsic or an extrinsic property. Identifying an individual in relation to their biological parents is an essentialist identification in the broad sense of essentialism. This definition relies on the relational properties of the individual with their biological parents. Relational properties are extrinsic properties. But in this case, they are also context-independent, because the biological parents of an individual never change, regardless of what the individual does. This context-insensitivity is what the narrow and the broad senses of essentialism have in common. Once an entity acquires its essential property, the property stays with the entity regardless of the future contexts in which the entity appears.

Essentialism about technology is the idea that all technologies have a shared property which they carry in all contexts. One of the most historically influential examples of essentialist theories of technology is that of Martin Heidegger. According to Heidegger, the essence of technology is extrinsic, non-technological and non-material: it is a form of revealing; it is the way in which technology reveals the world to us (Heidegger, 1977). We may use different technologies for different purposes, but we do not have control over the way technology reveals the world to us. This essence transcends particular instances of technologies, which is why essentialist philosophies of technology, such as Heidegger's, are sometimes described as 'transcendental' theories. Essentialist theories paint all technologies with the same brush. They are not context-sensitive and lack the conceptual tools to analyse technologies at the practical level.

The empirical turn should be understood in contrast to essentialist and transcendentalist conceptions of technology. As a result of the empirical turn, philosophy of technology has moved away from identifying the essence of technology as manifested in, yet distinct from, specific technological objects. Instead, contemporary philosophy of technology mostly focuses on how users and designers interact with artefacts; how specific technologies influence, and are shaped by, social norms, values and objectives; and how different technologies impact individuals' relations with each other and with the world. The motivations behind the empirical turn were mainly pragmatic: a philosophy of technology was needed that would enable us to address normative and social issues at the contextual levels of use and design. As such, this movement is often described as 'engineering-oriented' and 'society-oriented' (Brey, 2010; Franssen et al., 2016).

In the past decade, to progress the empirical turn, some philosophers of technology have identified and recommended other 'turns' in the field. Almost all of these subsequent turns are motivated to make philosophy of technology more practically relevant. Peter-Paul Verbeek, for instance, has called for a change of focus which he refers to as 'accompanying technology' (2010). Verbeek believes that ethical evaluations of technology often focus on 'technology assessment' with the aim of merely approving or disapproving of a technology. Such assessments, according to him, rely on the assumption that there is a gap between what is social and what is technological. Technology accompaniment is an approach which takes into account the interrelatedness between humans and technology at the normative, anthropological and metaphysical levels. It requires close engagement with designers and equipping users with frameworks to understand the impact of technology on their quality of life.

Rafaela Hillerbrand and Sabine Roeser, on the other hand, have identified a third 'practice turn' in philosophy of technology (2016). According to Hillerbrand and Roeser, the first and second practice turns recognised the social significance of technologies and examined the philosophical issues related to technology and the engineering practice. The third practice turn, they argue, requires close collaboration of philosophers of technology with engineers. This practice turn is compatible with a similar call from Peter Kroes and Anthonie Meijers for an 'axiological turn' (2016). The axiological turn aims to understand the role of values in the design, development and use of technology. It also aims to critically reflect on the role which philosophers of technology can play as possible actors in developing technology.

Similarly, and more critically, Adam Briggle calls for a 'policy turn' in the field (2016). When we consider *whom* philosophers of technology speak to, Briggle believes that the empirical turn and the classical (essentialist) philosophy of technology belong to the same camp. The empirical turn, according to Briggle, has at best provided a more satisfactory *description* of technologies, compared to the essentialist theories. This, in itself, does not make the empirical turn more useful, as philosophers of the empirical turn still only speak to philosophers. Instead, a policy turn is needed in philosophy of technology, in order to make the field socially relevant. The policy turn requires philosophers to start from real-world problems as debated by engineers, policymakers and stakeholders. A common theme in these subsequent turns is the recommendation for philosophers to closely collaborate with engineers and policymakers.

The empirical turn and its subsequent 'turns' have led to the emergence of two trends in the field of philosophy of technology. This book addresses, challenges and redirects both. The first trend is the development of distinct and focused subfields in philosophy of technology that can be broadly categorised into two groups: theoretical and applied. At the theoretical level, philosophers of technology study the nature of artefacts, technical functions and the ontological questions concerning technology. These theoretical discussions belong to the metaphysics of technology. At the applied level, there are an ever-increasing number of philosophers who examine the social, moral and regulatory aspects of specific fields such as nanotechnology, biotechnology, artificial intelligence and autonomous systems.

However, there is an obvious gap between the theoretical and practical subfields of philosophy of technology. Rarely do we see philosophical theories of technology, technical function and technological reality inform an ethical, regulatory or epistemic study of a particular scientific or technological field. Nor do we find studies whose metaphysical definitions and distinctions take into account the practical problems that technological objects are meant to solve. Theoretical definitions of technology, technical function and technological reality have remained disconnected from applied studies of particular technologies.

Problem-Solving Technologies dissolves this gap by taking the practicality of technologies as the starting point of its metaphysical explorations. Technologies are useful objects; we need a useful conceptualisation of these objects. This book develops a metaphysical approach that can help us to address practical and normative issues. This book, in a nutshell, creates a philosophy of technology whose pragmatic values are richer than an anti-essentialist stance.

In a sense, *Problem-Solving Technologies* revision of the metaphysics of technology is motivated by what a number of philosophers have also suggested in the past few decades: making the field more practically relevant. While to achieve this goal, others have recommended further engagement with engineers and policymakers, this book finds another area of improvement. Here it is argued that the gap between the theoretical and applied branches of the philosophy of technology is partly a result of practically irrelevant theories and approaches which have dominated the metaphysics of technology. The metaphysical foundations of philosophy of technology impact the practical relevance of the field through the categorisations and distinctions that they generate. A number of central concepts and distinctions currently used in the metaphysics of technology are not fruitful to guide decision-making and normative analyses of technologies. They simply are the wrong tools for such practical purposes. To create a more useful philosophy of technology, current metaphysics needs to be revised in the same way that, at a different level, the institutional relationships between philosophers, engineers and policymakers need to be revised.

However, *Problem-Solving Technologies* does not merely call for a revised metaphysics of technology. It develops a practically useful approach, uses this approach to build new concepts and theories in different subfields of the metaphysics of technology and shows how these concepts and theories can be implemented to examine concrete philosophical and applied problems.

To develop a user-friendly philosophy of technology, this book also addresses the second trend which has followed the empirical turn. The second trend is the focus on artefacts, which, as demonstrated in the next chapter, are intentionally modified objects, such as kitchen appliances, sculptures, sewing needles, toothbrushes, buildings and musical instruments. As argued elsewhere, in the past few decades, and as a result of the empirical turn, philosophy of technology has been identified and pursued as the field which predominantly studies artefacts (Soltanzadeh, 2019). The tendency to identify artefacts as the subject matter of philosophy of technology is evident in different branches of the field. Philosophers interested in the metaphysics of technology investigate the ontological status of artefacts and artefact kinds (Franssen et al., 2016; Meijers, 2009), and develop theories of artefact functions (Houkes & Vermaas, 2010; Preston, 2009, 2013; Vermaas & Houkes, 2006). Normative branches of philosophy of technology are replete with references to the moral and political aspects of artefacts (Franssen, 2006; Joerges, 1999; Kroes & Verbeek, 2014; Winner, 1980). Some journals have dedicated full issues exclusively to the study of artefacts in philosophy and metaphysics of technology (Houkes & Vermaas, 2009a; Kroes & Meijers, 2006). Peer-reviewed encyclopaedia articles, such as the 'Philosophy of Technology' and the 'Artifact' entries on the Stanford Encyclopaedia of Philosophy have set the study of artefacts as the task of philosophy of technology (Franssen et al., 2018; Preston, 2018). *Problem-Solving Technologies* challenges the commonly held assumption that artefacts are philosophically significant in ways that non-artefacts are not. By doing so, it argues that the focus on artefacts is misplaced and misleading. Instead, the book re-examines the metaphysical question of 'what is technology?' to reshape the subject matter of philosophy of technology.

Problem-Solving Technologies goes on to show that the two trends which have overshadowed the current philosophy of technology have common roots. This common root is the metaphysical approach which has generated them both. Philosophers of the empirical turn have ironically, and perhaps unwittingly, assumed a metaphysical approach which is not practically useful. In fact, although philosophy of technology after the empirical turn identified itself with an anti-essentialist position, new forms of essentialism were adopted, particularly in the analytic metaphysics of technology. The field's focus on artefacts is linked to the disconnection between the theoretical and applied subfields of philosophy of technology. The approach which underlies the artefact/non-artefact distinction in metaphysics of technology makes theoretical discussions irrelevant for practical decision-making and evaluative purposes.

This book develops an approach which redefines the approach and focus of philosophy of technology, and results in theoretical distinctions and definitions which are informed by, and can contribute to, decision-making and evaluative practices. This approach is named *activity realism*, as contrasted with *entity realism* in light of which the subject matter of philosophy of technology is currently defined.

METAPHYSICAL CONTEXT

To develop the activity realist approach, this book provides a separate and systematic treatment of the three distinct subfields of the metaphysics of technology. These lines of research include the general categorisation of technology, the particular categorisation of technologies and the ontology of technology.

The general categorisation of technology differentiates between technological objects, as a group, and non-technological objects. It provides an answer to the question 'what is technology?' What we use as kitchen appliances, for example, all fit into the general category of technological objects. But the picture that we may hang in our bedrooms or the chalice that priests use during their religious ceremonies can be categorised as artistic and religious objects. The general categorisation of technology defines technology and by doing so, it specifies what objects philosophy of *technology* should be about.

The field of the general categorisation of technology has not received much attention from philosophers after the empirical turn. Two historical reasons can explain this inattentiveness. First, the empirical turn in philosophy of technology was inspired by similar developments in philosophy of science. During the first half of the twentieth century, philosophy of science dealt with questions regarding the nature of science and scientific activity. Philosophers of science were interested in the general categorisation of science; they were interested in identifying criteria that would demarcate between scientific knowledge and other belief systems, which were often draconically labelled as *pseudo*-science. The mainstream approach in philosophy of science, however, changed over time. The field moved away from general questions on demarcating between science and pseudo-science, and became more interested in following conceptual and normative issues in relation to particular fields of science. This led to the emergence of focused fields of research, such as philosophy of physics, philosophy of economics and philosophy of biology. Each of these fields now has their own subfields with their own specific research questions. The reluctance of the contemporary philosophy of technology to engage in the topic of the general categorisation of technology may be partly caused by a historical trend which affected other philosophical fields as well.

The second historical reason to avoid the general categorisation of technology can be found in the anti-essentialist motivations behind the empirical turn, which were mentioned earlier. The general categorisation of technology requires identification of a property, or a set of properties, that all technologies have in common. This property can be used to define technology as a general. One way to define technology would be through identifying the essence of technology, as a property which all technologies have in common in a context-independent way. As discussed earlier, modern philosophy of technology consciously distances itself from essentialism. So, one could say that a reason why modern philosophy of technology avoids the general categorisation of technology is due to the connection drawn between the general categorisation and essentialism: essentialism leads to the general categorisation of technology, and defining technology as a general group can easily be interpreted as believing in the existence of a technological essence, which should be avoided.

However, one needs to be wary of a fallacy here. The fallacy is in the form of affirming the consequent. Although essentialism implies the presence of a property that all technologies have in common, this does not mean that the identification of *any* property that all technologies have in common leads to essentialism. It is possible to identify a common property which characterises all technologies, without appealing to essence. This common characteristic can be a derived property that technologies acquire from the type of activity in which they are used. The activity realist approach defines technology through such a derived property.

The activity realist metaphysics formulates technological-ness as a property which objects acquire from *problem-solving activities*. As such, activity realism leads to a fluid identification of technological objects. An object may be a technological object at one point and not be a technological object at another. Nevertheless, this derived fluid property is something that all technologies have in common by virtue of being used in the same type of activities.

The second subfield of the metaphysics of technology is the particular categorisation of technologies. Particular categorisation makes distinctions between different types of objects, in a more specific way than the general categorisation. The particular categorisation is often pursued through developing theories of function. Each object is put in the same category as others with similar functions. For example, all objects which are used as means of transport can be put into the category of vehicles. These objects can of course be further grouped in more particular categories, depending, for example, on whether they travel in the air, on earth or in the water.

The particular categorisation is independent of the general categorisation. In other words, the requirements for an object to belong to a general category are different from the requirements for it to belong to a particular category. What makes a particular hammer a technological object, for example, is different from what makes it belong to the particular category of objects that can be used for smashing the electronic parts of an old washing machine. Given the independence of the general and particular categorisations, objects of different general categories can belong to the same particular category. For example, an artistic and a technological object can both be identified with the same function. Consider a knife which is used in an artwork to send an anti-violence message to its viewers. This knife, according to the arguments of the first part of this book, would belong to the general category of artistic objects. However, for the knife to convey its anti-violence meaning in the artwork, it should be grouped in the particular category of weapons. The particular category of weapons includes, among other things, this knife and other objects which can be used to harm others.

The third subfield of the metaphysics of technology addresses the ontological status of technologies. Ontology is the study of being, and most ontological theories determine what exists and what does not exist. Currently, given the field's focus on artefacts, ontological investigations of technologies are often pursued as the study of the ontological status of artefacts and artefact kinds. But these theories also assume a universal and binary notion of being, much like that of existence. Most discussions of the current ontological theories of technologies, therefore, are around the existential status of artefacts and artefact kinds. They are concerned with whether artefacts, as distinct from their constituents, exist or not.

To develop a useful metaphysics of technology, activity realism replaces the notion of 'existence' with that of 'reality'. The notion of reality as developed in this book is akin to, and can be seen as an elaborated version of, William James' notion of 'practical reality' (1981) or John Dewey's notion of 'experienced reality' (1905). Reality is defined based on what is significant to us, not based on what may or may not exist 'out there'.

ANTHROPOLOGICAL CONTEXT

Problem-Solving Technologies defines technologies in the context of problem-solving activities. But what are problem-solving activities? And what place do they have in the general context of human activities?

Appealing to disparate means to solve problems shapes a widespread range of human activities. Every day, from the time we get up until when we go to bed we think about what to put on, where, when and how to satisfy our hunger and thirst, how to get to places we want to go, how to talk to our managers, what to take to a friend's board game night and so on. Of course, individuals differ in what concerns them, what they plan to do in order to solve a given problem, and how they enact those plans; but regardless of whether one is attempting to solve global poverty issues or is deciding whether to use a tablespoon or a soup spoon, there is a generic pattern behind many human activities. This generic pattern is in not being at ease with one's perception of the status quo, desiring something or wanting a different state of affairs to be the case and using certain means to achieve the desired situation. These means take different forms, such as orders, policies and bureaucracies, activities and body movements. But whatever form these means take, these activities can be represented by this scheme:

current (problematic) situation ----- (means/instruments) → desired situation

Activities which follow this scheme can be called *problem-solving activities*. Each problem-solving activity, as Jan Schmidt has clarified, consists of three elements: an undesired (initial) state, including an anticipation of prospective futures, a desired (goal) state and the barriers in getting from the current situation to the desired one (Schmidt, 2011).

In this way, problem-solving activities are related, but not identical, to goal-oriented activities. Depending on how 'problem' and 'goal' are defined, there is not necessarily a one-to-one relation between problem-solving activities and goal-oriented ones. One problem-solving activity may involve multiple goal-oriented activities. For instance, a person may realise their house gets too cold in winter. They decide that one way to solve this problem would be to insulate their house. They become ambitious and decide to build a house with zero amount of energy loss. Building a house with zero amount of energy loss becomes their goal. After a bit of studying, they realise that such a house would be working against the laws of thermodynamics. So, to show respect to the second law of thermodynamics, they reset their goal to build a house with energy loss of 1 per cent; building a house with energy loss of 1 per cent becomes their new goal. Later on, they discover that due to the quality of the materials available in the market, the best they can expect to achieve would be a house with energy loss of 10 per cent. So, they set a new goal which suits the new expectations. This means that although the problem-solving activity which the person has been engaging in has remained the same, they have switched from one goal-oriented activity to others. As is discussed in chapter 5, solutions to problems are open to evaluative judgements. If one plan is deemed to fail, new goals can be set to solve the problem.

Problem-solving activities can also be seen as a subspecies of goal-oriented activities. By examining goal-oriented activities, we can identify at least three subgroups of this kind, although sometimes a practice can be an instance of more than one of these three subgroups simultaneously. First, there are those activities in which the goal of the activity is to define or to modify the rules of another activity. These activities can be referred to as *rule-setting activities*. In rule-setting activities, the goal or the desired situation is not clear prior to the activity because it is not necessarily known in advance what the rules of the activity will turn out to be. Designing new games and making policies are examples of rule-setting activities. When parliamentarians discuss a social or economic issue to establish a law, they are engaged in rule-setting activities.

Second, there are goal-oriented activities in which both the end and the means are clear. These activities can be called *habitual goal-oriented activities*. Arguably, most goal-oriented activities that reflective beings engage in fall into this category. When we engage in these activities, we do not often need to think about how we can achieve our goal; we just do it. Hence, the word 'habitual'. Think about someone who feels thirsty, and to quench their thirst, they just go to the kitchen and pour themselves some water. The person would automatically take these actions without consciously thinking how to solve the problem of feeling thirsty. Such habitual activities are the most common forms of goal-oriented activities.

Third, there are activities which can be referred to as *problem-solving activities*. In problem-solving activities, the goal is clear, but the means to achieve the goal are not always clear. The whole point of engaging in problem-solving activities is to plan and use different means to solve the perceived problems. Of course, there is not always a sharp distinction between habitual goal-oriented activities and problem-solving activities. The distinction fades over time both at the social level and at the individual level. Most, if not all, activities which are now performed habitually have formerly been problem-solving activities. Someone or a group of people had to initially solve a problem to tell us how it is done. Others also had to learn how to solve the problem before they could perform it out of habit.

In any problem-solving activity, the current and the desired situations can be interpreted in two different ways. One is interpreting them as worldly facts – existing in a mind-independent way – and the other is interpreting them as reflective beings' perceptions of worldly situations. It is the latter interpretation which is used here, not the former. This is because it is a necessary condition for any problem to be *perceived* as a problem and for any solution of a problem to be *perceived* as the solution to a problem. In other words, the reality of problems requires the existence of a perceiving subject. There is no problem in nature in and by itself. It is the minds of reflective beings that find certain situations problematic. And thus, what happens in the process of problem-solving activities from the time they are initiated until they are completed is that a subject's perception of a problem is replaced by their sense of satisfaction of achieving a desired situation.

The reality of problems is partly conditioned by the reflective beings who have the mental capacities to perceive certain states of affairs as problematic. There is nothing intrinsically problematic about a worldly situation. For example, increasing the level of greenhouse gases in the atmosphere is perceived as a problem by those who believe that it will cause climate change and find climate change to be a problem. However, the so-called 'climate deniers' do not find it problematic. When we have different sets of values and beliefs, our perceptions of what is problematic and what is unproblematic are different. The mind-dependence of problems will be extensively discussed in chapter 5.

This last point on the mind-dependence of problems leads to an important clarification: primarily, about how reflective beings address problematic situations, and secondarily, about the scope of this book. A problem arises as a result of a mismatch between the states of affairs (i.e. the world) and reflective beings' needs, values and desires (i.e. the mind). Overall, two generic and distinct strategies can be used to address this mismatch. One strategy manipulates the world to match the mind; the other manipulates the mind to match the world. The former can be called 'externalist', and the latter 'internalist', although the terminology is not crucial here. In appealing to externalist strategies, we protect our internal beliefs, our world of ideas. The instability caused by the mismatch between our needs, values and desires, on the one hand, and the environment, on the other, is remedied by modifying the environment.

Problem-*solving* activities are a species of externalist strategies to address problems. Solving a problem means making changes to the world until the world matches the mind to a satisfactory level. These changes can be made to the physical or the social world. Examples of changes made to the physical world are building a dam, inventing and using medical imaging technologies, hammering a nail into the wall or drawing graffiti in public places. But externalist strategies have also been the drive of many social movements and interpersonal power relations – for better or worse. By demanding better work conditions, abolition of slavery, destruction of nuclear weapons or, by using force, implementing anti-immigration policies, giving orders or censorship, people attempt to make changes to the social world so that it matches their desires and values.

Internalist strategies, on the contrary, involve acceptance and adaptation. To use these strategies, we need to first identify the mental component of the problem, which can be needs, values or desires which have conditioned and shaped our perception of certain states of affairs as problematic. And second, alter or remove those needs, values and desires so that they do not make us feel unease with the states of affairs. In internalist strategies, we protect the external world, our environment. The mismatch between our beliefs and ideas, on the one hand, and the external world, on the other, is remedied by modifying the former.

Stoicism, as a school of thought, is a good example of philosophies that promote internalist strategies. Stoics would argue that instead of becoming slaves to our passions, letting them control us and constantly feeding them, we need to seek wisdom and develop virtues to acquire an internal peace. This is how, according to the stoics, we can develop genuine happiness and tranquillity and *dissolve* problems that we face.

Here it is worth mentioning that internalist strategies can and have been used to bring social changes as well. Think about the change of norms and values in relation to racial identity or the expression of sexual identity in the past few decades. For a long time, racial identity has been a source of conflict in many parts of the world. Different externalist practices were in play to solve the problem of some people being uneasy with, and hostile towards, persons belonging to certain racial groups. These practices included building borders or bridges, establishing laws, staging wars and committing genocides. However, although racially motivated crimes are still prevalent, the ideologies around race, at least in some societies, have changed. As a result, a lot of people do not perceive people of other races as sources of problems anymore. The mismatch between the mind and the world is resolved by changing mental attitudes towards race. Similarly, our general attitude towards sexual minorities has changed from designing institutions, legislations, medical practices and punitive measures to 'correct' or punish individuals who express non-mainstream sexual identities, into accepting sexual minorities and diverse expressions of sexual identities. We no longer constantly invest in changing the behaviours of others. Instead, we have changed *our* value system to not perceive minority groups as sources of problems.

The focus of this book is on problem-solving activities and the material means, or in other words, technologies, which reflective beings use to solve problems. In other words, this book conceptualises technologies in the context of externalist strategies to solve problems. This is in line with José Ortega y Gasset's attitude towards technology. Technology, as he writes, is not 'the adaptation of the individual to the medium' but 'the adaptation of the medium to the individual' (Gasset, 1961, 96).

Nevertheless, neither the classification of coping strategies into internalist and externalist ones, nor the externalist focus of this book, mean that there is a unilateral relationship between our needs, values and desires, on the one hand, and technological developments, on the other. Although technological developments follow individuals' beliefs and ideas, technology can itself influence our preferences and perceptions of values as well. Problem-solving activities belong to externalist strategies as they require us to make changes to the world; however, the changes that we make to the world influence the goals that we pursue in life as well. This issue will be further discussed in chapter 5.

It should also be noted that not all human activities can be reduced to problem-solving activities. As social psychologists have argued, the vast majority of our actions and decision-makings occur at the subconscious level of our brains (Haidt, 2001). John Bargh and Tanya Chartrand have also challenged the widely accepted assumption that 'people are consciously and systematically processing incoming information in order to construe and interpret their world and to plan and to engage in courses of action' (Bargh & Chartrand, 1999). Other researchers have argued that our mental life is overshadowed by unconscious passive decision making (Goleman, 2006; Hauser, 2006; Smythe & Evans, 2007). These empirical findings mean that problem-solving activities shape only a small fraction of our everyday life and practices.

Nevertheless, problem-solving activities are one of the distinctive features of reflective beings, especially humans. The fact that conscious problem-solving activities make up a small fraction of humans' everyday life does not mean that studying this fraction is unnecessary or uninteresting. In fact, it would be a fallacy to judge the importance of an activity by the amount of time spent on it. It is the mental capacity of humans to engage in problem-solving activities and make changes to the outside world which has led to significant differences between the human species and other animals. What may be interpreted as the progress and prosperity of humans is partly brought by humans' engagement in problem-solving activities.

OUTLINE

The first part of this book, which consists of the next four chapters, addresses the topic of the general categorisation of technology. Chapter 2 defines *usefulness* and demonstrates that the artefact/non-artefact distinction is not practically useful. The chapter argues that what makes this distinction not useful is the metaphysical approach which is used to generate this distinction. This metaphysical approach is dubbed 'entity realism', and any other distinction developed through this approach is argued to be equally practically irrelevant. Excerpts of chapters 2 and 3 are taken from Soltanzadeh (2019). Chapter 3 proposes and explores an alternative metaphysical approach, named 'activity realism'. By demonstrating the usefulness of this approach, the chapter argues for the practical advantages of activity realism over entity realism. Chapter 4 uses the activity realist approach to redefine the subject matter of philosophy of technology. After conceptualising technologies in the context of problem-solving activities, the chapter examines some implications of this definition. In this definition, the status of objects as technologies is determined subjectively, and technological-ness is argued to be a matter of degree. Some sections of chapter 4 are based on (Soltanzadeh, 2016). Chapter 5 explores the conditions of possibility of technology, which, similar to the definition of technology, is a topic which philosophers of the empirical turn have explicitly avoided. When technologies are understood in relation to problem-solving activities, the conditions of the possibility of technologies can be determined by identifying the conditions of the possibility of problem-solving activities. This chapter breaks up these conditions of possibility into two groups: those which are internal and those which are external to problem solvers. The chapter identifies external conditions as worldly factors that motivate problem solvers to engage in problem-solving activities, and internal conditions as capacities that enable entities to comprehend problems and use technologies in problem-solving activities. Chapter 5 is a revised version of Soltanzadeh (2015).

The second part of this book addresses the topic of the particular categorisation of technologies. Chapter 6 provides a taxonomy of function theories, showing that the topic of function can be studied from three different dimensions. These dimensions include metaphysical, epistemological and linguistic. Metaphysical theories of function define function and explain how objects acquire their functional identities. Epistemological theories are concerned with the ways people can justify their beliefs about objects' functions. And linguistic theories investigate the way speakers of language use different terms to refer to different types of objects. Chapter 7 analyses the existing metaphysical theories of function to show how most of these theories are generated through an entity realist approach. The chapter draws connections between the entity realist, metaphysical theories and the linguistic study of function, showing how they complement each other. The conclusion drawn from these discussions is that the entity realist theories of function, similar to mainstream linguistic theories, result in static and universal categorisations of objects. A practically useful metaphysical theory of function, on the other hand, must be able to capture the personal and fluid functional identification of objects. The final chapter of part two, Chapter 8 develops and explores an activity realist theory of function. This theory is called 'the belief-based consequentialist theory' and defines an object's function in relation to the intended impacts of its use. The belief-based consequentialist theory shows how objects can acquire dynamic functional identities, and how one object can be identified with different functions by different people. This theory is also able to conceptualise the function of a black box and non-material functions of objects. Non-material functions include, among other things, the function of objects as class markers or as material expressions of social identity.

The third part of this book is composed of two chapters and focuses on the ontology of technologies. Chapter 9 critically examines current ontological theories. It identifies existence as the entity realist notion of being. Existence is considered as a universal and binary meta-property of objects. By revisiting the definition of artefacts, this chapter highlights arguments both against and in favour of the existence of artefacts and artefact kinds. Chapter 10 conceptualises 'reality' as an activity realist notion of being. Reality of objects is defined in relation to their roles in the activities of reflective beings. Unlike existence, reality is dynamic, subjective, and is defined in a non-binary manner. In addition to defining the ontology of technologies in terms of their problem-based reality, this chapter argues that technologies can be real to different degrees for different people.

The fourth and final part of this book consists of two chapters on the practical applications of the activity realist approach. Chapter 11 applies the activity realist notion of reality to conceptualise the reality of scientific entities. It identifies experimental observations, theoretical descriptions and practical applications as three main activities that shape the reality of scientific entities. Considering the role of technologies in these activities, the chapter illustrates the extent to which scientific reality is shaped by technologies. Chapter 12 is a revised version of a journal paper (Soltanzadeh, 2021). It investigates the structure of different human activities to argue that autonomous systems can only be employed as *technological* systems, characterised by solving practical problems and making changes to the outside world. The epistemic condition of performance or the logical condition of engagement may restrict delegation of non-problem-solving activities to machines.

Part I

THE GENERAL CATEGORISATION

Chapter 2

Artificial Categorisations

One of the main roles of any metaphysical theory, say, of X, is to define X and provide criteria for X-ness. This role is often referred to as 'the general categorisation of X' or 'the demarcation of X from non-X's'. Demarcation is philosophically important because it can feed into other dimensions of our analysis of X; it defines the subject matter of the philosophy of X. Investigating the ethics of X, the rationality of actions that involve X, regulatory aspects of X or X's social and political consequences, all presuppose and interact with how X is defined and what entities are included in the general category of X.

In philosophy of technology, the general categorisation of technology demarcates between what is and what is not a technology. It defines the subject matter of philosophy of technology. As discussed in the introduction, in the past few decades, there has been a tendency to identify the study of artefacts as one of the central subject matters of philosophy of technology. This subject identification relies on a metaphysical distinction between artefacts and non-artefacts, and rests on the assumption that artefacts are philosophically significant in ways that non-artefacts are not. As a result, a large number of philosophers of technology discuss the conceptual and normative issues of artefacts. This chapter argues that if we want philosophy of technology to be practically useful, the artefact/non-artefact distinction is a misleading place to start, as this distinction is developed through a metaphysical approach which is of little use for practical decisions and evaluations. One of the central concepts in this chapter and throughout this book is that of usefulness.

USEFULNESS

Something is useful when it has desired impacts in the activities in which it is used. An object, for instance, is useful if its users can make changes to their surroundings by using it. A border is useful if people are expected to behave differently on either side of it. A categorisation is useful if our practical decisions are sensitive to whether we are dealing with objects that belong to the category or those which do not.

Usefulness is a relational property. Something can be useful for one purpose, but not so useful for other purposes. The distinction between words that contain the letter 'B' and those which do not can be useful in word games such as Scrabble or Bananagrams. But this distinction is not useful when we need to decide the most eloquent way of expressing our emotions.

Therefore, things which do not have any impacts are not useful. Moreover, things which do have impacts, but their impacts are not desired are also not useful. For example, the former planet of the solar system Pluto has gravitational impacts on Neptune and its adjacent celestial bodies. But unless someone intends to achieve something with it, Pluto's gravitational pull remains not useful.

What makes a general categorisation of, say, X, useful? The general categorisation of X is useful if some of our practical decisions discriminate between Xs and non-Xs. It is useful when we use different normative criteria and decision-making frameworks to deal with cases that involve X as opposed to those that involve non-Xs. The general categorisation of planets, for example, which demarcates between planets and other objects (including dwarf planets), is not scientifically very useful. The scientific theories that are used to explain the behaviour of planets are the same as those used to explain the behaviour of non-planets. The fact that the status of Pluto changed from a planet to a dwarf planet, for instance, did not change Pluto's properties, its gravitational pull on Neptune or the theories that scientists use to study Pluto as opposed to 'fully fledged' planets. A metaphysical theory of humanity, on the other hand, would be useful, because many of our moral, regulatory, rational and social decisions are sensitive to the distinction between humans and non-humans. Whether something is a human, as opposed to a horse, a creek or a planet, changes our normative duties and general attitudes towards that thing.

In this book, the notion of usefulness is employed to articulate arguments at two levels: the level of categorisations and the level of approaches. At the first level, we identify and categorise objects in relation to their properties. At this level, this chapter examines the usefulness of the artefact/non-artefact distinction. At the second level, we use philosophical approaches in order to generate conceptual distinctions and worldly categorisations. At this level, this chapter examines the usefulness of the approach which underlies the artefact/non-artefact distinction. The following chapters adopt the alternative, user-friendly approach to generate useful categorisations and distinctions in the metaphysics of technology.

Metaphysical approaches and conceptual distinctions are considered to be useful for philosophy of technology if they help us understand technologies, or if they influence the normative criteria that we use to evaluate the use of technological objects, as opposed to other types of objects, such as entertaining, religious or artistic objects. Here, the argument is that if we want the metaphysics of technology to be practically useful, then we need to rethink certain conceptual distinctions and metaphysical approaches which have dominated the field.

In addition to two levels at which the usefulness of categorisations and approaches is analysed, there are other contexts in which the term 'usefulness' is employed in this chapter and throughout this book. For example, technological objects are considered to be useful for solving practical problems. This claim is used as a criterion to assess the usefulness of metaphysical approaches. If an approach cannot capture the usefulness of technologies, it is not useful for conceptualising technologies.

However, the fact that the notion of usefulness is employed at different levels and in different contexts should not create any confusion. This is because there is only one sense in which the term 'usefulness' is used throughout this book. Two important characteristics of this notion of usefulness, as discussed earlier, are that usefulness is relational and that usefulness requires desired impact. As we see, the notion of usefulness will shape all proposed definitions in this book, across all subfields of the metaphysics of technology.

ARTEFACTS

Different definitions of artefacts have been proposed, among others, by Daniel Devereux (1977), Randall Dipert (1993), Risto Hilpinen (1993, 2011) and Amie Thomasson (2007, 2009). These definitions acknowledge that two general conditions need to be met for something to be an artefact. These conditions can be referred to as the *modification condition* and the *intention condition*.

The Modification Condition

According to the modification condition, it is necessary for an object to undergo some modifications in order to become an artefact. The reason why umbrellas, hammers or security cameras are artefacts, but clouds, rocks or planets are not artefacts is that the former group are modified objects whereas the latter group are not.

However, modifications come in different forms and degrees. Carving, painting, cleaning, casting, breaking, burning, moving are all different forms of modification. Do these procedures all satisfy the modification condition? Or is there a minimum level of modification required for an object to become an artefact? Is moving an object from one corner to another a form of modification? How about breaking it apart or painting it? Here we need to clarify what forms of physical changes can satisfy the modification condition.

Daniel Devereux has clarified the types of physical changes which can turn an object into an artefact. According to Devereux,

> a natural object cannot become an artifact without undergoing some internal change. By 'internal change' I mean a change in the thing itself and not just in its relationship to other things. Changes in size, shape, or colour, would count as internal changes; a change in physical location would not. (Devereux, 1977, 135)

According to Hilpinen, too, objects need to undergo at least a minimum form of manipulation to become genuine artefacts. The simplest form of manipulation that Hilpinen accepts is separation. It involves 'the separation of an object from another object so that one (or both) of the resulting objects can be used for some purpose' (Hilpinen, 2011). Cutting a branch from a tree trunk and trimming off the side branches and leaves is a procedure which creates an artefact by the act of separation. But picking up a piece of rock from the ground is not an artefact-creating procedure because it does not involve sufficient modifications of the object. Hilpinen refers to objects like a piece of rock picked up from the ground to be used as a hammer or as a paperweight as 'naturefacts' which according to him are not genuine artefacts (Hilpinen, 2011).

So, based on Devereux's conception of internal change or Hilpinen's distinction between artefacts and naturefacts, regardless of the way and the types of activities in which they are subsequently used, natural objects that are collected from the ground do not satisfy the modification condition and do not qualify as artefacts. However, carving, painting, casting, breaking or burning would all satisfy the modification condition. Some other forms of manipulation, such as cleaning, become hard cases for the conditions set by Devereux or Hilpinen. Does an object go through an internal change when it is being cleaned? Is cleaning a simpler or a more complex form of manipulation than separation? The answer is at best ambiguous. The ambiguity of such cases, however, does not influence our current discussions. For the sake of the arguments of this chapter, all we need is the existence of a modification condition, even though this condition does not draw a sharp distinction between processes that satisfy this condition and those that do not.

Other more interesting cases would be those that satisfy the modification condition, but the modification is purely natural. Given that modification is taken here to be synonymous with 'change', the process of modification does not have to be done by reflective beings. A tree may fall because of a storm or because humans cut it down. In either case, the fallen tree satisfies the modification condition. But we may want to make a distinction between a deliberately cut tree and the one that is knocked down by the storm. This point takes us to the second condition, namely, the intention condition.

The Intention Condition

In addition to having to be modified to qualify as an artefact, it is also necessary for an object to satisfy the intention condition. The intention condition stipulates that what the artefact turns out to be must be intended by its makers. Satisfying the modification condition alone does not turn an object into an artefact if its makers does not intend it to be what it is. Even though the tree knocked down by heavy wind has undergone enough changes to satisfy the modification condition, it is not an artefact because it was not intended to be what it now is – a fallen tree. A screwdriver that is used to tighten screws satisfies the intention condition because it was intended to be what it is. As Amie Thomasson would say, artefacts are not only the products of human physical activity, they are also the products of human mental activity (Thomasson, 2009, 194–196). This mental activity is marked by the intention to bring about an object with certain qualities. Similarly, Lynne Baker has argued that the existence of artefacts depends on the intentions of their designers and the execution of those intentions (Baker, 2004, 103). Other authors such as Randall Dipert (1993) and Hilpinen (2011) have also acknowledged that a correct description of an artefact must include the makers' intentions.

Artefacts which are used to achieve certain goals are physical structures with specific functions defined in reaction to those goals. As such, artefacts can be approached based on either their pure physicality or based on their functionality (or both). This is often referred to as the dual nature of artefacts: 'technical artefacts can be said to have a dual nature: they are (i) designed physical structures, which realize (ii) functions, which refer to human intentionality' (Kroes & Meijers, 2006, 2).

Considering the fact that artefacts can be approached from two different perspectives, the intention condition can be interpreted in two different ways. On one interpretation, it is necessary for an artefact to have the same physical properties that its makers intended. On the other interpretation, it is necessary for an artefact to have the same function that its makers intended. The first interpretation of the intention condition is built upon the modification condition, such that if an object violates the modification condition it would automatically violate the intention condition. That is, if an object is not modified at all, it does not make sense to talk about its intentional modification. But the second interpretation is independent of the modification condition, and the violation or satisfaction of the modification condition would not say anything about the violation and satisfaction of the intention condition. For example, a piece of rock that is simply collected from the ground to be used as a hammer does not satisfy the modification condition, but it may indeed assume the function of a hammer, which is what the person who collected the rock intended it to be. These interpretations of the intention condition can be further clarified with some examples.

A person may use a lighter to open beer bottles. Here the lighter would still have the same physical properties intended by its makers, but its function would be different from the makers' intentions. On the physical interpretation of the intention condition, the lighter would be an artefact, but according to the functional interpretation, it would not be. Now imagine a case where the person throws a glass bottle to the ground to break it into small pieces so that they can use one of the pieces to cut through some thick paper. In this case, the small pieces of glass will have the function which the person intends them to have, but they may not have the exact intended physical properties. In fact, it is almost impossible to plan the shape and the size of objects which are created by smashing another object onto the ground. Here, whether any of those glass pieces would be an artefact or not depends on how the intention condition is interpreted. On the functional interpretation of the intention condition, those pieces will be artefacts, but on the physical interpretation of the condition, they will not be.

However, excluding the broken glass pieces from our conception of artefacts can make the physical interpretation of the intention condition very demanding. We may rule out those broken glass pieces as artefacts because the maker did not plan or intend their exact shape, but many objects do not turn out to have the exact same shape that their makers intend. Even the lighter used in the previous example may be ever so slightly smaller, bigger, heavier or lighter than what the designers intended. Would these differences exclude the lighter from the category of artefacts?

One way to defend this physical interpretation of the intention condition is to make it less demanding. Instead of requiring the designer to have an exact construction plan and execute that plan perfectly, we can allow deviations from a loose construction plan as long as the necessary physical properties of the object are created. Here it would not matter if the lighter is slightly bigger or heavier than the designers' plan. As long as the lighter has the necessary physical structure to be a 'lighter', it would satisfy the intention condition.

By this modified standard, the broken glass pieces would also be artefacts because they do have the sharp edges required to cut through paper.

This modified standard, however, relies on the functional interpretation of the intention condition: the necessary physical properties of a lighter are determined by its function as a lighter, and the necessary physical properties of a cutting tool are determined by its function as a cutting tool. So, if we accept the modified version of the physical interpretation of the intention condition, we need to also add the functional interpretation of the intention condition. This means that the lighter which was used to open up a bottle would not be an artefact anymore. A modification that was made to make the intention condition less demanding has had the opposite effect.

One final suggestion here is to separate the context of use from the context of design (i.e. modification). As long as an object has a designer who has intentionally modified it in ways that would make it suitable for particular purposes, then it is an artefact. And it will remain an artefact even if the intentions of the users do not match the intentions of the makers. In this way, the lighter that is used to open bottles would still be an artefact because it has designed features that make it suitable to be used as a lighter. The lighter would remain an artefact even if it is used in an artwork, as a religious object, or buried underground. Whatever happens to the object after it has become an artefact does not change the status of the object as an artefact. However, as shown in the rest of this chapter, the separation between the contexts of use and design impacts the practical relevance of the artefact/non-artefact distinction.

ASSESSING THE ARTEFACT/NON-ARTEFACT DISTINCTION

There are numerous ways in which we can categorise objects in the world. Some categorisations may be based on very clear distinctions, but clarity does not automatically render the distinction useful. Although the clarity of a distinction (expressed in terms of necessary and sufficient conditions) is often regarded as philosophically valuable, this value is only instrumental to the purpose for which the distinction is made. We should first consider what we want to achieve by making a distinction, and only after that can we celebrate the clear-cut definitions we have developed. By adhering to the reality of artefacts, we divide worldly objects into two categories: objects that satisfy the intention and modification conditions and those that do not. This distinction is expressed in terms of necessary and sufficient conditions, but it is not clear what can be achieved by this distinciton.

The metaphysics of artefacts and the distinction between artefacts and non-artefacts is useful for fields of study such as archaeology, history and anthropology. This is because the line drawn between objects that are intentionally modified and those that are not can provide clues about the needs, skills, manufacturing techniques and commonly used raw materials of old as well as current civilisations. If an object belongs to the category of artefacts, it can provide clues about the culture from which it originated. When an object is excavated, for example, it is significant to know whether it is an artefact or not; because if we believe the object is intentionally modified for a particular purpose, we can make inferences about the needs, skills, manufacturing methods and commonly used raw materials of past civilisations. Artefacts also indicate the creativity of humans in comparison to other animal species. Other animals mostly use natural unmodified objects as tools to achieve their goals, and while some animals may make small modifications to objects before using them, no other known species exhibits the same level of dedication as humans to design new objects for artistic, religious, instrumental or entertainment purposes.

However, in philosophy of technology, the majority of concerns revolve around social, moral, rational and regulatory issues. For the focus on artefacts to be impactful, the artefact/non-artefact distinction should influence the functional and normative frameworks that we use to investigate and evaluate the use of objects. As is argued here, our practical decisions and normative evaluations are indifferent to the artefact/non-artefact distinction or to any other distinction that is generated from the same metaphysical approach.

Consider (1) a mass-produced camping hammer, (2) a rock and (3) a small object lying on a river bank. This third object, which we believe is a piece of sandstone, was in fact purposefully carved and regularly used by members of a past civilisation. Both the first and the third objects are artefacts, but we believe that only the first object is an artefact. Now, consider these objects being used to (1) hit tent pegs into the ground, (2) break a window to escape from a building which is on fire or (3) threaten someone in order to take their money. Do our evaluations of any of these actions depend on whether the first, the second or the third object is used? Does the artefact/non-artefact distinction require us to use different decision-making or normative frameworks for actions done with the second object as opposed to the other two? Not really.

The rational assessment of an action considers the efficiency and effectiveness of the means and the methods chosen to achieve the ends. To assess the first action (1), we need to ask questions such as: did the pegs get into the ground? Was it easy to use the object? Our moral evaluations consider the rightness or wrongness of actions and their consequences on sentient beings. To morally evaluate the second action (2), we would question the impacts of breaking the window and escaping from the room on people's well-being and note the number of people who were saved and whether anyone was harmed in the process of escaping from the building. Legal evaluations consider the consequences of actions on those who are protected by the law. In the third example (3), we need to know the extent to which the person was harmed and the intentions and the mental states of the person who committed the crime. These evaluations should not discriminate between the three objects mentioned earlier. The metaphysical distinction between the piece of rock (non-artefact), on the one hand, and the hammer and the sandstone (artefacts), on the other, as well as the epistemic distinction between the hammer (believed to be an artefact), on the one hand, and the rock and the sandstone (believed to be non-artefacts), on the other, do not change the decision to use the objects or to evaluate their effectiveness or their impacts on the user and others. As Franssen rhetorically asks, 'How much do we gain by claiming that bottles – our bottles, made of glass or plastic – essentially are for containing liquids and that gourds essentially are natural objects that, accidentally, can be used for containing liquids?' (Franssen, 2008, 29).

As another example, think about the person who is walking in the rain and decides to keep an object on top of her head to stay dry. Now, if that person picks up a big leaf from the ground to keep it above her head, the person is not using an artefact because the leaf does not satisfy the modification or the intention condition. But if she separates a similar leaf from a branch and does exactly the same thing with it, she would be using an artefact. This is because (1) separation is a procedure that satisfies the modification condition, and (2) she has intended for the separated leaf to have the size it has, and for it to be used for staying dry.

The question is: what is the distinction between artefacts and non-artefacts doing for us or for our subject in this case? If the distinction between artefacts and non-artefacts was relevant, then the function of the first leaf would have been different from that of the second leaf. If this distinction was relevant, the rationality of a person's act of holding a leaf above her head to stay dry in the rain would have depended on whether the person has separated the leaf from the tree or has picked it up from the ground. However, the function of those leaves and the rationality of the acts of using them to stay dry in the rain are independent of whether or not the leaves satisfy the modification and intention conditions. In fact, when we want to analyse the function of these objects or the rationality of using them, we need to shift our focus from their intrinsic properties to the reasons for which they are used, and the roles that they are meant to play.

In general, neither the metaphysical status of an object as an artefact or a non-artefact nor our beliefs about this metaphysical status affect the planning or evaluation of actions. Assuming that the consequences remain the same, no action becomes legally acceptable, morally permissible or rationally sound if we exchange artefacts used in the course of the action with non-artefacts (or vice versa). It is of course true that after we find an action problematic, we can hold different social groups, such as the users, the regulators or the makers responsible. However, this responsibility distribution comes after determining the moral worth of the action, which itself is independent of the status of the object as an artefact or a non-artefact.

This is not to say that artefacts are not useful – we use artefacts on a daily basis. Rather, the metaphysical distinction between artefacts and non-artefacts is not useful. To repeat, a categorisation is useful if our practical decisions are sensitive to whether we are dealing with objects that belong to the category or those which do not. The artefact/non-artefact distinction does not require us to use different decision-making or evaluatory frameworks, and is thus not impactful. It is of little to no use in guiding practical actions.

It should be acknowledged that other philosophers have also doubted (Heersmink, 2013) or indeed extensively argued against (Baker, 2004, 2008) the philosophical significance of the distinction between artefacts and non-artefacts. However, these philosophers either have concluded that the history of artefacts' production and evolution makes them more important than natural objects (Heersmink, 2013) or have argued that artefacts and natural objects fit into one and the same ontological category (Baker, 2008). The reason provided by Baker is that humans should be approached as a part of nature and for this reason, human products should not be seen as different from other natural phenomena, including animal constructs (Baker, 2004, 2008).

Other philosophers have also suggested that metaphysical studies of artefacts are not always practically significant. As Wybo Houkes and Pieter Vermaas (2009b) explain, the metaphysics of artefacts is often pursued in a 'detached' way, through investigating those features of artefacts that only interest metaphysicians. As such, Houkes and Vermaas propose a more 'involved' treatment of artefacts by taking into account the fact that artefacts are intentionally designed and that they play roles as means to achieve human ends (ibid.). This approach has led some to ground the philosophical study of artefacts on action theories and consider the actions of design and use as crucial for the study of these entities (Houkes & Vermaas, 2004, 2010; Preston, 2013). However, not all artefacts are used to achieve ends. In addition, as demonstrated in the example of the hammer, the rock and the sandstone above, when artefacts *are* used as means to achieve human ends, they do not become practically significant because they are artefacts; rather, because they play roles as means to achieve ends. The fact that they are artefacts is irrelevant. The problem of the irrelevance of the artefact/non-artefact distinction for practical decisions and evaluations cannot be resolved by a more involved treatment of artefacts. The problem is rooted in the philosophical approach that has produced the artefact/non-artefact distinction.

ENTITY REALISM

What renders the artefact/non-artefact distinction of little use for practical decisions and evaluations? The artefact/non-artefact distinction is rooted in a metaphysical approach that can be called 'entity realism'. Entity realism is an approach which identifies objects by properties which they maintain in isolation, independently of what happens to the rest of the world. We hold an entity realist approach towards the subject matter X, if we are able to imagine a temporal possible world where at least at one point in that world's timeline, nothing exists except for X.

Note that entity realism, as defined here and used in the general arguments of this book as an approach to identify and categorise entities, is distinct from, and should not be confused with, realism about entities (Hacking, 1983) or, simply, entity realism used in philosophy of science in discussions on the ontological status of unobservable entities. Here entity realism is introduced as a more fundamental metaphysical approach which can be used in any sub-field of metaphysics.

Entity realism not only defines but also categorises objects based on their isolated properties. This approach gave rise to the study of kinds in metaphysics and philosophy of science, with kind membership being assessed by properties that members have in isolation. Belonging to the natural kind of water, for instance, requires H_2O molecules. A substance will be a member of the kind if it consists of H_2O molecules. To develop and sharpen our definition of a kind from an entity realist point of view, we need to examine properties that all members of the kind carry along in all contexts and purify our definition from contingent factors. If, for example, we want to define the general category of swans, we examine properties that all swans have in common. This would include swans' common genetic characteristics and exclude, for example, their feather colour or the size of their neck.

Entity realism is not the only philosophical approach that identifies and categorises objects based on properties which they have in isolation. Substance metaphysics rests on a similar principle. Substance metaphysics considers reality to be fundamentally made of discrete substances (Winters, 2017). Substances exist in their own right, rather than being contingent on other things. In substance metaphysics, relations do not fundamentally exist because substances are not relational (Oderberg, 2012). Being someone else's offspring, for instance, is not a substance because it is a relation.

Entity realism results in a more expanded metaphysics than substance metaphysics because the former permits some derived and relational properties. Properties that are defined through the entity realist approach are often intrinsic properties which are exhausted by physical, chemical and biological descriptions of entities. However, we can hold the entity realist view even if our definitions rely on relational properties. Being an offspring of another person, for example, is a property which is defined through the entity realist approach, even though it is a relational property. Once someone acquires the property of being someone else's offspring, they will keep it independently of what happens to the rest of the world. It becomes a part of who they are.

As such, entity realism can be taken synonymous with essentialism in the broad sense of the term. As explained in the introduction of this book, essentialism has a narrow and a broad sense. In its narrow sense, essence is considered to be an intrinsic property, while in the broad sense, essence can include relational properties. In an entity realist definition, as in essentialism, once an object is grouped in a particular category, it retains its membership in that category regardless of its context.

The artefact/non-artefact distinction is rooted in the entity realist approach because once an object becomes an artefact, it remains so, independently of the context in which it is used. After an object is intentionally modified, it keeps its status as an artefact even if it does not get used at all, or is used for purposes that deviate from those that the makers had in mind. The conceptualisation of artefacts as a general category of objects, and the distinction between artefacts and non-artefacts, therefore, are rooted in an entity realist approach.

ASSESSING THE ENTITY REALIST APPROACH

Metaphysical categorisations made on the basis of an entity realist approach can be epistemically impactful. A significant portion of scientific activity, especially in the case of the natural sciences, such as physics, chemistry and biology, is devoted to understanding intrinsic properties of entities and categorising them into smaller groups of subatomic particles, molecules, rocks, organisms, species and so on. Entity realism is impactful here as it guides research and our understanding of the world.

Entity realism also guides our evaluations and decisions in domains where we assign non-instrumental values to objects. Whether an object is actually made out of gold or not, for instance, can make a big difference in the value that we give to it. Original artworks, too, carry the inseparable property of being created by renowned artists, and this property distinguishes them from copies. We value them because of what they are and not whether or how they are used.

However, entity realism is not impactful in philosophy of technology, which is concerned with objects that have instrumental value. Our practical decisions to use technologies to achieve certain goals are indifferent to the properties that objects have in isolation. It is not important what technologies are when they have no impact in their context of use.

In general, three related arguments can demonstrate the irrelevance of entity realist categorisations, such as the artefact/non-artefact distinction for philosophy of technology. The first argument rests on the property of being useful and the relational nature of this property. Technologies have practical values in our lives and are used to make changes to our surroundings. The use of an object indicates a need or a desire to bring about those changes. As noted earlier, usefulness is a relational property. It is defined in relation to the purpose and the context of use. Context-independent properties such as the material from which an object is made, its creators or their intentions, do not, on their own, indicate anything about how useful an object can be. Since the entity realist approach defines objects based on these isolated properties, this approach cannot reliably capture the relational nature of technologies as useful objects.

The second argument relies on the irrelevance of entity realist distinctions for our decision-making frameworks. Decision-making frameworks are developed around the goals that we want to achieve. Decision-making frameworks are not developed around the use of any particular type of object defined in an entity realist way. For example, we do not make our decisions about using purple objects, objects made before 2016 or objects heavier than 2.1 kg, which are categories of objects defined through the entity realist approach. Rather, we consider our goals, develop selection criteria based on these goals and only then we will choose the objects or methods that can help us achieve our goals. Depending on the goals, we may indeed decide to use a purple object, an object made before 2016 or an object which is heavier than 2.1 kg. However, the chosen object's properties would be useful for an activity *because* they match the goals that we want to achieve. Objects' usefulness cannot be assessed independently of what we want to do. Decision-making frameworks cannot be built around isolated properties of objects.

The third argument demonstrates the irrelevance of entity realist distinctions for normative evaluation of our actions. As discussed in the example of the hammer, the rock and the sandstone earlier, the norms that we use to evaluate our actions do not alter based on the objects that we use. We do not use different norms for evaluation of actions that involve the use of purple objects, objects made before 2016 or objects heavier than 2.1 kg, as opposed to actions which do not involve the use of these objects. Properties and distinctions that are developed through the entity realist approach do not require us to use different norms for using different types of objects. These reasons render the entity realist distinctions not impactful and of little to no practical use in the sense developed earlier in the first section.

The impracticality of entity realism and especially the artefact/non-artefact distinction implies that the fields of study defined as 'artefact functions', 'the ethics of artefacts' and 'the rationality of artefact use' have their focus misplaced. Their focus is misplaced in the same way that the focus of non-existing fields such as 'the function of purple objects', 'the ethics of using objects made before 2016' or 'the rationality of using objects that are heavier than 2.1 kg' would be misplaced.

What renders the artefact/non-artefact distinction irrelevant for philosophy of technology is the entity realist approach from which it originates. Satisfying the modification and intention conditions does not say anything about the usefulness of objects. The modification and intention conditions categorise objects based on properties that should not affect our decision-making and evaluative frameworks. Any other distinction generated by entity realism faces similar problems in meeting what is required of a practically relevant philosophy of technology; that is, developing definitions and distinctions which have the use of objects in mind, and are relevant to our practical decision-making.

SUMMARY

This chapter defined the concept of usefulness and used this concept to assess the practical usefulness of the artefact/non-artefact distinction and the metaphysical approach which has generated it. Usefulness is a relational property: something may be useful for one purpose but not for another. Moreover, usefulness implies desired impact. Things which do not have any impacts, or those whose impacts are not desired are not useful. This notion of usefulness can be used to assess the usefulness of entities, categorisations and approaches.

Despite the implicit identification of artefacts as the subject matter of philosophy of technology, the artefact/non-artefact distinction is not useful and cannot capture the usefulness of technologies. This is because neither the metaphysical status of an object as an artefact nor people's beliefs about this metaphysical status would affect the practical decision-making and normative frameworks applied in assessing its use. The artefact/non-artefact distinction is generated through a metaphysical approach which is called "entity realism." Entity realism is similar to the broad sense of essentialism. This approach identifies objects based on universal properties which, once acquired, objects keep in all contexts.

If we wish to build a useful metaphysics of technology, we need to reinvent its underlying metaphysical approach. The next chapter creates and explores a useful metaphysical approach which can be used to redefine the subject matter of philosophy of technology and generate useful concepts and distinctions in all three subfields of the metaphysics of technology.

Chapter 3

A User-Friendly Metaphysics

As discussed in the previous chapter, entity realism is a philosophical approach that conceptualises and categorises objects based on features that they have in isolation. This approach, which is used to generate the artefact/non-artefact distinction, does not provide a foundation for a useful metaphysics of technology. An alternative approach can be called *activity realism*, which conceptualises and categorises objects on the basis of their relation to purposeful activities of reflective beings. This chapter introduces activity realism, explores the usefulness of this approach and compares activity realism with entity realism. The chapter concludes by responding to some objections which argue for the usefulness of the entity realist approach and the artefact/non-artefact distinction.

ACTIVITY REALISM

Activity realism provides an alternative, context-sensitive approach for the identification and categorisation of objects. The context which it considers to be central in its identification and categorisation of objects is the activities of reflective beings. Each activity is in turn understood in terms of the broad purpose which it pursues. Storytelling, religious, game-playing, artistic and problem-solving are examples of some activities that reflective beings engage in.

Activity realism identifies and categorises objects based on dynamic and derived properties which they obtain from their use in different activities. Each object is put in the same category as other objects which play similar roles in similar activities. Vivaldi's *Four Seasons*, for instance, is a piece of music which is understood and valued in the context of human aesthetic activities. As such, it is grouped in the same general category as other musical works such as Beethoven's *Moonlight Sonata* or Chopin's *Nocturnes*. A chalice, on the other hand, can have a religious identity when it is used in Christian ceremonies. It can also have an instrumental identity when it is used for drinking wine or other liquids. As a religious object, it is categorised together with other religious objects, such as the cross and prayer beads. As a tool, it is categorised with other tools, such as spoons and screwdrivers.

The activity-dependent conceptualisation of objects in activity realism implies that if an activity in which an object is used ceases to be real, the object would also lose *that* dimension of its reality. For example, if humans do not engage in aesthetic activities, and stop listening to or producing music, or reading or telling stories about music, the *Four Seasons* will also lose its current significance and its classification as a piece of music. If people stop following Christianity and performing Christian ceremonies, or reading or writing or talking about Christianity, the chalice will also lose its religious significance and its classification as a religious object. It can of course retain its identity as a tool as long as it is used in practical problem-solving activities, such as drinking wine or other liquids.

Although activity realism is contrasted with entity realism, activity realism is not the only non-entity realist approach. Another seemingly non-entity realist approach is 'process philosophy' which, similar to activity realism, considers reality to be dynamic. Process philosophy is based on the premise that being is a dynamic phenomenon, and that 'the actual world is a process, and that the process is the becoming of actual entities' (Whitehead, 1967, 33).

A main difference between process philosophy and activity realism is that, in regard to being real, process philosophy does not discriminate between what *we* consciously perceive and/or act upon, and occasions that have no place in our activities: '"Actual entities" – also termed "actual occasions" – are the final real things of which the world is made up . . . God is an actual entity, and so is the most trivial puff of existence in far-off empty space' (Whitehead, 1967, 27–28). In activity realism, a puff of existence in far-off empty space is not real as it plays little to no role in the activities of reflective beings. God's reality, too, is dependent on religious activities in a similar way that the reality of *Four Seasons* is dependent on musical activities. As argued in chapter 10, in activity realism, reality has a practical significance and is defined based on things which are interesting and important.

The categorisation of objects in the activity realist approach is not concerned with properties that objects retain in isolation. Objects, when approached in isolation and independently of their relevance for reflective beings, do not belong to any category. Instead, an activity realist categorisation is concerned with dynamic properties which objects derive from the activities in which they are used. Objects can be employed in different capacities in different types of activities. Due to the dynamic nature of activities and the various roles that objects can play in different activities at different points in time, activity realist demarcations made between different types of objects are dynamic. The dynamic categorisation of objects in activity realism will be further clarified in the next section.

Although in activity realism, objects are identified in relation to their role in purposeful activities, the identification of an object as the product of an activity is not an activity realist identification. Artefacts are the products of the activities of makers. As noted earlier, more 'involved' metaphysics of artefacts have considered the role of the activity of design in their study of artefacts. However, identification of an object as an artefact remains an entity realist identification because artefacts remain artefacts independently of contextual factors. The artefactual property is similar to the derived property of being someone's offspring. The activity of mating or the use of In Vitro Fertilisation (IVF) can result in new offspring. However, identification of someone as another person's offspring is an entity realist identification because the offspring retains this property independently of how they came to be, what they do or how successful or miserable they become.

Defining an object using the activity realist approach entails, but is not entailed by, the mind-dependence of that object. A chalice, for instance, defined as a religious object, has a mind-dependent existence because the reality of religious activities depends on human intentions to engage in those activities. However, we can believe that some objects are mind-dependent and yet approach them through an entity realist perspective. Artefacts are mind-dependent. This mind-dependence is stipulated in the intention condition: artefacts are what they are because someone has intended them to be so. However, as discussed earlier, the definition of artefacts is an example of an entity realist approach. An object's status as an artefact does not change, even if the makers are spatially or temporally absent from the activities in which the object is used. Activity realism, therefore, generates mind-dependent realities, but not all objects which are mind-dependent are defined from the activity realist approach; entity realism can also generate mind-dependent definitions of objects.

THE USEFULNESS OF THE ACTIVITY REALIST APPROACH

To understand why activity realism can provide a useful metaphysical foundation for philosophy of technology, we need to examine the way in which this approach demarcates between different types of objects. In activity realism, the general categorisation of objects is made through the activities in which they are used. In other words, in an activity realist philosophy, description of activities precedes identification and categorisation of objects. An object becomes an artistic object when it is used in a work of art; it becomes a religious object when it is used to connect with divine beings; it becomes an object of entertainment when it is used for playing games or other forms of entertainment; and it becomes a technological object when it helps users solve practical problems by virtue of its physical properties.

A bicycle wheel, for instance, can be a technological object when it is used to help us ride smoothly and with minimal friction. But it can also be installed in an artwork, as it was by Marcel Duchamp (1913), to assume an artistic identity. A small piece of stone can be an object of entertainment if it is used in a rock tossing game. But it can also become a religious object when used to connect with God, as it is by Shiite Muslims. The hammer referred to in the preface of this book becomes a technological object when it is used in activities such as hitting a nail into a wall, keeping a puncture patch on a bike's inner tube until the glue dries or breaking a washing machine into pieces. It becomes an artistic object when it is hung at a pleasing angle and is shone in a spotlight. And it becomes an object of entertainment when it is used as a mallet in an improvised game of croquet.

In activity realism, therefore, no object counts as a technology on its own. It is classed as a technology in relation to the purpose for which it is used. Technological-ness is a property which objects derive from the problem-solving activities in which they are used (Hickman, 2001; Ortega y Gasset, 1961; Soltanzadeh, 2015, 2016). In this general categorisation, technologies are not contrasted with natural objects; rather with other types of objects which are also defined through the activity realist view, such as artistic, religious or entertainment objects. Since technological objects are defined in relation to problem-solving activities, the distinction between problem-solving activities and other types of activities translates into the distinction between technologies and other types of objects whose identification is dependent on the activities in which they are used. Other types of activities do not follow the structure of problem-solving activities explained in the introduction of this book – their goal is not to solve practical problems.

So, in activity realism, the general categorisation of technology is a temporal categorisation. Different sets of objects at different points may enter or leave this general category, and the number of objects which belong to this category frequently expands and shrinks. Moreover, since the general categorisation of objects as technological, entertaining, artistic, educational, religious and so on is solely dependent on the type of activities in which the objects are used, a single object may belong to two or more categories at the same time, depending on how it is approached and perceived.

TVs, for instance, are both technological and entertainment objects. They are objects of entertainment because most people use them for the sake of entertainment. But they can also be approached as technologies when they are seen as solving particular problems. TVs are parts of our devised solution to broadcasting and receiving sounds and images between two places which are not geographically close. Musical instruments, as another example, are necessary to carry out most musical performances. However, designing something that can produce melodic sounds is a problem in need of a practical solution. Seen as objects used at concerts to make music, musical instruments have artistic identities and become artistic objects; but seen as objects that solve the problem of producing sounds that musicians want to make, musical instruments acquire technological identities and become technological objects. As artistic objects, we evaluate musical instruments based on their place in the piece in which they are used and make statements such as 'a drum set is inappropriate for playing Chopin's *Nocturnes*'; but as technological objects, we evaluate them based on the extent to which they produce the sounds which musicians want them to, and make statements like 'this violin is out of tune'.

In activity realism, as discussed in chapter 8, the particular categorisations of objects are made based on what is believed to be the intended impacts of their use. A piece of cloth, for example, wrapped around a person would acquire the identity of a cloak. If the cloth is attached to a long stick and hung somewhere conspicuous, it may acquire the identity of a flag. The flag itself may be a symbol of peace, a sociopolitical ideology or a sports team. The same piece of fabric can be wrapped around a mop to clean the floor, or taken to a religious site and, as a result, be considered to have become sacred. Each cloth belongs to a distinct category of objects. The first cloth belongs to the category of cloaks, the second to that of flags, the third to mop pads and the fourth to the category of sacred objects.

The cloth, the entity realist would argue, is the same cloth, no matter where it is used and what we do with it. Its properties as an entity remain the same. However, from the activity realist point of view, each time that we use it for a different purpose, it acquires different properties in relation to the purpose for which it is used. And it is these properties that matter in practice.

The properties defined, and the categorisations made, through the activity realist perspective are useful because they shape the decision-making and the evaluative frameworks that we use. The decision to use the cloth as a cloak and the evaluation of its performance as a cloak take similar decision-making and normative frameworks as the decision-making and evaluative frameworks that we use for other potential cloaks, such as curtains, sheets and designer cloaks. These decision-making and evaluative frameworks are different from the decision-making and evaluative frameworks that we use to decide to use the cloth as a flag, a mop pad or a sacred object.

It is true that in each case, some intrinsic physical properties of the cloth make it useful for the purpose for which it is used. But each case requires a different set of these physical properties. In each case, the usefulness of the cloth is assessed in relation to different standards. Describing the cloth as an entity, independently of whether and how it is used, does not help us with our decision-making or evaluations; the activity in which we want to use the cloth does. We need to first consider the purpose for which we want to use an object and then look for physical properties that can help us with that task. The decision-making and evaluative frameworks are built around what is required in the activity, not around objects' isolated properties.

Activity realist distinctions are practically useful, because decisions whether to use an object, moral evaluations of its use and assessments of efficiency and effectiveness are sensitive to the type of activity in which objects are used and the intended consequences of their use. Practical decisions about an object are made in order to control its interactions with its surroundings. A decision to use an object is made by reflecting on what that object can help to bring about. Rational, moral and regulatory evaluations of an object are guided by its function within, and its influence on, the context in which it is used. Considering the contextual sensitivity of practical decisions and evaluations, a useful philosophical approach needs to conceptualise and categorise technologies based on their usefulness in purposeful actions. Activity realism opens up the possibility for this conceptualisation.

COMPARING THE TWO APPROACHES

As discussed in the previous chapter, artefacts are defined from an entity realist perspective, and are often (misguidedly) treated as the subject matter of philosophy of technology. For something to be an artefact, it needs to satisfy the modification and the intention conditions; that is to say, it needs to undergo some alterations in its physical properties, and the product of those alterations need to be intended. However, understood from an activity realist perspective, technologies may not need to satisfy the modification or the intention conditions. This point can be substantiated with some examples.

Consider (1) a tree knocked down by a heavy wind and (2) the glass pieces of a broken window. These objects do not satisfy the intention condition because no one has intended them to be what they are. But this does not mean that they cannot be used as technological objects. The broken tree can be moved, placed across a river and used as a bridge. This solves the problem of walking from one side of the river to the other without getting wet. Here we have a technological object that does not satisfy the intention condition: it has a problem-solving instrumentality, but it is not what it is because someone has intended it to be so. A similar argument can be used about the glass pieces of a broken window. One can use one of the broken pieces to cut through objects. No one intended for the physical properties of the glass piece to be what they are. No one even intended the window to break. The modification has been accidental. But the glass pieces can help solve the problem of cutting through objects, and as such will be technological objects. So, the fallen tree and the broken glass are technological objects, but they are not artefacts because they do not satisfy the intention condition. Therefore, satisfying the intention condition is not necessary for something to be a technology because some technologies may not have any makers.

In addition to not being necessary, the makers' intentions are also not sufficient for something to be a technology. Think about the work of art *Fountain* attributed to Marcel Duchamp (1917). *Fountain* is a work of art which contains one and only one urinal. The urinal had been produced by a urinal-making company and was intended by its makers to function as a normal urinal, solving the problem of urinating while standing without making a mess. But the urinal in *Fountain* is not used to solve anyone's problems. It is a work of art displayed at an art exhibition. An artist signed it and placed it in an art museum. Here we have a case of an object which was intended by its makers to be used in particular contexts, but it has ended up in a totally different context. This shows that the intentions of the makers are not sufficient for an object to become a technological object.

Let us now turn to the modification condition and examine whether being modified is necessary or sufficient for something to be a technology. We can use two examples to show why modification is not a necessary condition for something to be a technological object. First, imagine a distant planet on which complex chemical and physical reactions produce objects which resemble technological objects that humans use on earth. Although it is hard to imagine naturally produced computers or airplanes, for the current argument even naturally produced wooden sandals or chairs would do. These objects do not satisfy the modification condition because they have not undergone any changes. However, the intelligent inhabitants of that planet may use the objects in similar types of activities as humans use their earthly counterparts; that is, as technological objects to achieve certain goals. As a second example, consider a piece of rock picked up and used to hit nails into the wall or a broken branch, which has fallen on the ground, used as a walking stick. Such objects do not satisfy the modification condition because, as Risto Hilpinen (2011) and Daniel Devereux (1977) would argue, picking up an object from the ground is not a sufficient artefact-making form of modification. However, the rock and the broken branch are used as problem-solving instruments. They may even get passed down from one person to person and be used for similar purposes for a long time. These cases show that it is not necessary for technological objects to undergo any artefact-making modifications.

In addition, undergoing modification is not sufficient for something to be a technological object. Duchamp's *Fountain*, the hammer discussed in the preface of the book, or the exhaust gas emitted from a car's tailpipe would be good examples here. In spite of being modified, none of these objects is a technological object because none of them have any practical problem-solving instrumentality. Undergoing modifications does not necessarily turn something into a technological object.

The contrast between technologies and artefacts can be further examined to highlight the deep metaphysical distinction between the entity realist and activity realist approaches.

Artefacts, which are defined through the entity realist approach, can be contrasted with natural objects. Technological objects, on the other hand, should be compared to artistic, religious, educational or entertainment objects. The entity realist approach which supports the distinction between artefacts and non-artefacts categorises objects by properties that they possess in all contexts. The activity realist approach that supports the distinction between technological objects and non-technological objects categorises objects by what occurs *around* them. The line between artefacts and non-artefacts is drawn on the basis of the events which have happened to the object in the past; the line between technological and non-technological objects is drawn on the basis of the purpose for which an object is used in the present. Turning an object into an artefact gives the object a metaphysical status that it keeps in all contexts. Once an object has entered the category of artefacts, its membership in that category becomes independent of what reflective beings intend to do with it in the future. Once acquired, artefactual properties cannot be lost. Technological properties, on the other hand, are derived and dynamic, because their reality is contingent on reflective beings' problem-solving activities. If the problem for which a technology has been used is dissolved, the object will lose its technological identity.

FINAL PUSHBACKS

Discussions of the previous chapter and this chapter have questioned the practical and normative relevance of the entity realist approach and proposed an alternative, practically useful activity realist approach. However, there are still some arguments that seem to support the view that the distinction between artefacts and non-artefacts and the entity realist manner of identifying and categorising objects can be normatively relevant.

The first argument of this kind rests on the assumption that we often value natural environments and objects, as opposed to artificial ones. National parks, for example, are usually only declared where areas are relatively untouched by humans. Areas that have been intentionally changed are thought to be less valuable. Not all changed areas are artefacts of course. A logged forest might not be an artefact because its state after logging might not be intentional in the strict sense of the word. But pristine and untouched places are still valued. This preference for the natural over the artificial goes to the point that sometimes we make intentional modifications in order to make something 'appear' untouched. Think about restoring an old mining site to make it look like it did before being mined. Are these not normative issues raised by the artefact/non-artefact distinction?

We often ascribe higher value to national parks compared to plantation forests or restored mining sites. However, rather than ascribing value to the parks because they are not artefactual, the reason we value national parks may be because they are authentic; that is, since achieving the state of being a forest, they have remained intact. Ascribing higher value to national parks compared to restored mining sites can be compared to ascribing higher value to authentic artworks compared to their replicas. Similarly, we also value old buildings or artefacts crafted by ancient civilisations. We do not want these objects to undergo further changes because they would lose their authenticity, even though their authenticity might be artefactual. It would be psychologically interesting to explore why authenticity is valued, and whether authenticity is valued for different reasons in different contexts. In some cases, it may not be much more than a way of romanticising an object or an experience (think about keeping the personal items of a former loved one or keeping intact the office of a deceased Nobel laureate). And in some cases, valuing authenticity is instrumental; for example, the value given to the authenticity of an animal or a plant with pure genes or the value in preserving a crime scene. But in these and similar cases, the authenticity of objects and places is valued independently of whether those objects or places are artefacts or not.

Another example where it may be tempting to see the distinction between artefacts and non-artefacts as axiologically relevant relates to the value that we give to artworks. Compare a case in which cans of paint drop from a shelf, breaking open and colouring a piece of fabric on the floor, with another case in which an abstract artist pours different colours of paint randomly on fabric creating a similar pattern of colours. Aside from the fact that the second painted fabric would be an artefact but the first one would not, we also give a much higher value to the painted fabric in the second case compared to the first. Does the distinction between artefact and non-artefact justify the value difference between these two cases?

Again, while it is true that we value an abstract painting more highly than fabric which has been accidentally painted, this value difference can be justified without reference to the artefact/non-artefact distinction. The value difference can be justified by the fact that the intentionally painted fabric is seen as an *artwork*. It is the artistic property of the painted fabric which is valued, not its artefactual property. For the same reason, if an accident results in a similar pattern of colours on a piece of fabric, people are unlikely to stare at the fabric and discuss the meaning behind its colours. Similarly, if a non-artist gets a few cans of paint and creates a similar pattern of colours on a piece of fabric, people may not ascribe the same value to the resulting product. If, however, in the future, the 'non-artist' becomes recognised as an artist, people may go back to their old painted fabrics and suddenly ascribe higher value to them because now they have acquired artistic values. This shows that the artist's painted fabric is not valued because it is artefactual, but because it is perceived to be artistic. Otherwise an ordinary person's painted fabric would be similarly valued. Of course, the question of what makes something an artwork is a separate question.

Interestingly enough, for something to be an artwork it does not necessarily need to be modified by its artist. Marcel Duchamp's *Fountain* is an object which is not modified by its artist: it shares its physical properties with many other objects in the world, but they are still regarded and valued as artworks. Here we could conduct an analysis, as we did earlier for technological objects, to show that the category of artworks and that of artefacts is not the same because the modification and the intention conditions are neither necessary nor sufficient for something to be an artwork. Artworks, unlike artefacts, are defined through an activity realist approach. The distinction between artistic and non-artistic objects, similar to the distinction between technological and non-technological objects, is made on the basis of the reason for which and the types of activities in which the object is used. This distinction is a practically relevant one. Similar distinctions can be made between religious and non-religious objects, between entertaining and non-entertaining objects, or between legally significant and legally insignificant objects.

Third, there are cases where we may seem to be interested in entity realist categorisations and the context-independent properties of some objects that define them as entities. Think about the properties that make something a drug or a weapon. We seem to rely on their context-independent properties to permit or prohibit their trade or use. However, our concern here is not the context-independent properties per se. We are interested in identifying those properties because they are likely to be used in certain ways and generate morally loaded outcomes. It is the potential impacts of the drugs and the weapons on their surroundings, not what they are in isolation, which justifies us to permit or prohibit them. In the case of some technologies, such as weapons of mass destruction, given that there is so much harm that can be done with them, we try to ban them altogether. We may even hold the makers responsible for manufacturing technologies which cause harm. With some others, such as certain biotechnological products, we regulate them by allowing their medical or humanitarian use, and prohibiting malicious applications. These decisions are rooted in relational properties of technologies, and the justification for such decisions is made with the context of use in mind. If those artefacts stayed in the hands of scientists who were after cures for deadly viruses, we would not have been concerned about them.

Finally, one may appeal to the distinction between the context of use and the context of design to argue why philosophising about artefacts is not and should not remain disconnected from our normative discussions. It may be argued that although in the context of use it does not matter whether an object satisfies the modification and intention conditions, in the context of design it does matter because designers deal specifically with artefacts: they modify objects and intend them to have specific functions. As such, the modern philosophy of technology may justify its focus on artefacts by saying that the people who interest them are engineers and designers, and considering the fact that these groups deal with artefacts, it makes sense for our philosophy to deal with the normative and regulatory aspects of artefacts.

However, saying that 'designers deal with artefacts, as opposed to non-artefacts, and for this reason the distinction between artefacts and non-artefacts should be normatively relevant' is similar to saying that 'Toyota workers produce Toyotas, as opposed to other cars, and for this reason the distinction between Toyota cars and non-Toyota cars should be normatively important'. An object becomes an artefact for the very reason that it has undergone a design process. The statement 'designers deal with artefacts' is a tautology. It does not in itself justify the relevance of the line drawn between artefacts and non-artefacts. Technical artefacts are indeed philosophically important, but that is not because they are artefactual, rather it is because they are used as technological objects. They are philosophically important for the same reasons that non-artefactual technological objects can be important.

In general, the reason why we need to pay attention to the ethics of design is not because the manufactured products satisfy the intention and the modification conditions. It is the ways and the contexts in which we envision the manufactured products to be used that urge us to discuss the ethics of design. Our worry about gun ownership, for example, is not because guns are *artefacts*. We discuss the ethics of gun ownership because we have moral concerns about using guns in specific contexts as means to achieve (morally wrong) goals. In fact, if guns were only used in museums as parts of artworks, we would not have problems with them. But the fact that guns are likely to be used as technological objects for morally wrong actions becomes important in our normative and regulatory discussions. Our discussions are aimed at regulating the contexts in which these products are used. It is the activities in which they would be used that affect our moral judgements, not their metaphysical status as an artefact.

SUMMARY

As discussed in the introductory chapter, one of the roles of the general categorisation of technology is to define the subject matter of the field of philosophy of technology to clarify what we are philosophising about when we are philosophising about technology. The change in the subject matter of philosophy of technology that has been argued for in this and the previous chapter does not merely require an expansion or reduction of the definition of artefacts, or a slight shift to include or exclude some objects which were mistakenly included or left out. Rather, this change requires a change in perspective in the general metaphysical approach.

The metaphysical foundations of philosophy of technology impact its practical relevance through the categorisations and distinctions that they generate. A practically useful metaphysics is one whose definitions and categorisations can play a role in decision-making and normative frameworks that we use. However, an object's artefactual status does not require us to use different decision-making frameworks or different normative standards to evaluate its use. This renders the artefact/non-artefact distinction not impactful and of little to no practical use. The irrelevance of the artefact/non-artefact distinction is shared by other distinctions made from the entity realist approach. The concepts developed, and the distinctions made, by the entity realist approach do not equip us with useful tools to make or evaluate practical decisions and actions. As such, the metaphysics of technology needs to separate itself from the entity realist approach.

Technologies are useful objects, and usefulness is a relational property. The metaphysics of technology should be able to capture this relational property. Activity realism constructs a useful metaphysics because the categorisations made on the basis of this approach influence our decision-making and evaluative frameworks. We use different normative rules and decision-making criteria to deal with objects that are used in one activity rather than another. An activity realist metaphysics liberates the metaphysics of technology from its artificial focus, and opens up the possibility of identifying and categorising objects based on their relation to purposeful activities of reflective beings.

Chapter 4

Problem-Solving Technologies

The practically useful, activity realist approach introduced in the previous chapter can be used to develop an activity-dependent definition of technology. This chapter defines technologies in the context of problem-solving activities, and discusses some relevant features of this definition. In this definition, technologies are understood as problem-solving physical instruments.

This definition redefines the subject matter of philosophy of technology. The subject matter of philosophy of technology is no longer objects which are manufactured through an intentional design process (i.e. artefacts); rather, it is objects that are used in problem-solving activities: philosophy of technology should be concerned with problem-solving physical instruments.

This definition of technologies is an activity realist definition. This is because the technological-ness of objects is derived from the type of activities in which they are used. Objects become technologies because they are used in problem-solving activities, as opposed to other types of activities. Hence, here technologies are not contrasted with natural objects, which artefacts are contrasted with. Rather, technologies are contrasted with objects that are used in other, non-problem-solving activities, such as artistic, religious and entertainment objects.

This chapter first presents the activity realist definition of technologies, and after illuminating the key features of this definition, it responds to some objections and hard cases.

DEFINING TECHNOLOGY

In the definition of technology as problem-solving physical instrument, technologies are structures which have instrumental, problem-solving values. In this definition:

something is a technology if and only if it is considered to help its user(s) to solve a problem by virtue of its physical characteristics.

A few points should be clarified in relation to this definition.

First, the word 'help' used in the definition may sound anthropomorphic. However, here helping is similar to contributing, and the anthropomorphic connotation is not part of the definition. Moreover, an object does not always have to flawlessly contribute to the solution in order for it to be a technology. A person might believe that they can open a can with a screwdriver. Even if they do not satisfactorily succeed in their act of opening a can with a screwdriver, the screwdriver will still be a technological object for them. A screwdriver may indeed not be a particularly suitable tool for opening cans. But whether something is a good or a bad technology is a different question from whether it is a technology or not. As long as an object is used with the intention that its physical properties will help its user solve a given problem, it is a technology.

Second, and to add to the first point, technologies are inherently subject to evaluative and comparative judgements. Maarten Franssen (2006) has elaborated on this feature of the normativity of technologies: some technologies may be good or bad technologies and some technologies may be better than some others. Here, given that technologies are defined in relation to problem-solving activities, their evaluative and comparative judgements need to be made in relation to the problem-solving roles that they play. Some hammers, for example, do a better job of hammering nails than other hammers; some others may function better as paperweights; some may be more suitable for smashing household objects into pieces. What determines whether a technology is good or bad is the degree to which its user(s) feel the problem which they intended to solve has actually been solved.

The *instrumental* evaluations of technologies, however, should not be confused with aesthetic, economic or other forms of evaluation. When we say an object is ugly/beautiful or expensive/cheap, we make evaluative judgements of the object, but these non-instrumental evaluations have nothing to do with what we expect the technology to do at the level of practical problem-solving. The main difference between instrumental and non-instrumental evaluations is that the former are inherent in technologies, whereas the latter are not. Technologies are open to instrumental evaluations by virtue of being technologies. Non-instrumental evaluations are contingent on other types of activities and other non-technological approaches towards the object. As mentioned in the previous chapter, in the activity realist philosophy, one object can acquire different identities when approached through the lens of different activities. Each of these activities can create a new dimension to evaluate the object from the perspective of that activity.

Third, the status of objects as technologies is assessed subjectively. Something which is a technology for some people may not be a technology for others. There are different types of circumstances in which this could happen. The first is ignorance. If someone uses an object for a particular purpose, that object becomes a technology for that person. At the same time, if others are not aware of the existence of that object or the particular problem-solving activity it is used in, it will not be a technology for them. For example, some objects that are used for particular problem-solving purposes in a society in a rainforest may be meaningless for a society which lives in the arctic because they may not be aware of those objects or the problems they are used for. The second type of circumstance in which an object may be a technology for some people but not for others is the absence of intention to use that object. This could itself be due to disinterest or difference in lifestyles. Even if the arctic people are aware of some objects used for particular problem-solving purposes in a rainforest, they may never intend to use such objects because they never face such problems. This makes those objects technological for rainforest society members, but not for people in the arctic regions.

Fourth, the activity realist approach that has been used to conceptualise the general category of technology can be used to conceptualise other types of objects and differentiate between technological and non-technological objects as well. For example, assigning activity-dependent identities to objects can be used to conceptualise artworks and differentiate between technologies and works of art. To repeat, nothing essentially technological can be found in the physicality of things. It is playing a problem-solving role that turns a physical object into a technology. A similar point can be made about works of art. What makes an object an artwork is not the physical characteristics of the object. It is the type of activities in which an object is used which turns it into an artwork. The philosopher of art George Dickie has suggested a similar definition of art. He defends a cultural anthropological definition of art in which artworks are artworks only in reference to the roles they play in an art world (Dickie, 2004). There is nothing inherently artful about objects, in the same way that there is nothing inherently technological, religious or entertaining about objects. What differentiates between different general categories of objects, then, is not the difference between the structures of the material objects. The difference is in the type of activities in which they are used.

Therefore, as long as the types of activities in which reflective beings engage remain the same, the types of objects to which technologies are contrasted remain the same. If reflective beings always stay engaged in similar types of activities, then technological objects are always contrasted to the same categories of objects, such as artistic, religious and entertainment objects. However, the set of objects which belong to each general category changes over time. An object may be a technological object at one point and later become a work of art. This means that determining which objects belong to the general category of technologies cannot be done in a timeless manner. In this approach, we cannot draw an unchanging line between what is a technology and what is not.

And finally, in this activity realist definition, there is a close relationship between technological-ness, use and autonomy: whether an object is a technology or not, whether it is being used or not and whether it is autonomous or not are definitionally related. This is because being intentionally used is a part of what makes something a technology. This point can be discussed with some examples.

Consider a bicycle which is ridden for its rider to go from point A to point B. This bicycle is a technology as it is used for practical problem-solving purposes. Now consider a horse which is ridden to take its rider from point A to point B. Is the horse a technology? Some may argue that the horse is a technology for the same reason that the bicycle is: it is a physical entity and it is used as a part of the solution to the problem of getting from A to B. However, in riding a horse, we do not use the horse in the same way that we would use a bicycle or a car (Soltanzadeh, 2015). This is because entities that have a certain level of autonomy which allows them to act according to their own decisions are not *used* in the same sense that objects such as bicycles are. Bicycles are used because they cannot refuse to do what their users want them to do. They do not have any level of autonomy; users have a high degree of control over what they do. But horses 'used' to take their riders from one point to another, agents 'used' by some organisations for spying purposes and forward players 'used' in sport teams to score goals are used only in a loose sense of the word because they have a level of autonomy which allows them to decide not to perform what is expected of them (ibid.).

There is, therefore, a close relationship between technological-ness, use, control and autonomy. The more autonomy an entity has, the less meaningfully it is used, the less control others have over it and the less technological the entity would be. Similarly, the more technological an entity becomes, the more it is being used, the more control others have over it and the less autonomy it will have.

DEGREES OF TECHNOLOGICAL-NESS

In the previous section, it was demonstrated that technological-ness can come in different degrees which reversely correlate with degrees of autonomy. This section elaborates a different sense in which technological-ness comes in degrees.

After defining technological objects as problem-solving physical instruments, we can define *problem-solving properties* of an object in terms of the properties that the object needs to have in order to help their users to solve a particular problem. Problem-solving properties of an object, like a hammer, to be used for hitting nails into the wall, for example, are having a hard end and being able to be held and used by one hand. Problem-solving properties of an object to be used for keeping people dry in the rain are having a waterproof material which can cover people's bodies from the raindrops. Problem-solving properties defined in this way are, therefore, context-, or more precisely, solution-dependent: depending on the solution devised to address a particular problem, technologies need to have different problem-solving properties.

The notion of 'problem-solving property' can be used to provide a different argument for the claim that objects can be technological to different degrees: solutions with different degrees of complexity require objects with different degrees of problem-solving properties. Given that objects are defined in relation to their problem-solving properties, objects with different degrees of problem-solving properties would be technological to different degrees. An object which requires very specific problem-solving properties to fulfil its function is more technological than an object which does not require specific problem-solving properties to fulfil its function.

A few examples can be used to elaborate this point further. First, consider a tree chosen as a meeting point. Is a tree used as a meeting point a technology? It obviously solves the problem of specifying a location to meet with someone. But does it solve it by virtue of its physical properties? At first glance it may seem that a tree's physical properties do not matter in its functioning as a meeting point: regardless of how big a tree is or how its trunk or leaves look, a tree can be chosen as a meeting point. However, if we think more carefully, we notice, for instance, that the shade cast by a cloud or the Amazon rainforests cannot be chosen as meeting points. And this is particularly due to the physical properties of the shade of the cloud and the Amazon rainforests. One is neither spatially, nor temporally stable, and the other is way too vast. This means that the tree's physical properties – in its having roots that stabilise it at one specific point on the ground – are relevant when we choose it as a part of the solution to the problem of specifying a location to meet with someone. It is, notwithstanding, true that this particular solution to the problem does not impose a significant burden on the physical properties that a possible meeting point needs to have. The solution only requires possible meeting points to be accessible and recognisable, which are problem-solving properties that many objects can have. To fulfil these requirements, the size of the tree, the colour of the trunk and the appearance of the leaves do not matter. Moreover, a meeting point does not need to be where a tree is growing. A building, a bridge or a statue can all be meeting points. Such loose requirements imply that if an object is used as a meeting point, it would be technological, but only to a minimal degree.

The problem-solving properties for an object to be used to hit nails into the wall, however, are more specific. Such an object needs to have at least one hard end and also be easy to grab and carry. So, the solution to the problem of getting nails into the wall poses more complex requirements on the physical properties of the problem-solving object compared to our solution for the problem of specifying a meeting point. Therefore, a hammer, a piece of rock a metal water bottle or anything else used to hit nails into the wall is more technological than a tree, a building or anything else chosen as a meeting point.

Similarly, the solution to the problem of hitting nails into the wall imposes fewer and less complex problem-solving properties compared to the solution to the problem of having dirty clothes automatically cleaned. Therefore, a hammer, a piece of rock, a metal water bottle or anything else used to hit nails into the wall is less technological than a washing machine, a dishwasher or anything else used to get clothes automatically washed. And the same comparison can be made between technologies used to wash dirty clothes and those used for air travel, and between technologies used for air travel and those used to accelerate subatomic particles. Thus, depending on their problem-solving properties, some objects can be more technological than others. It is the complexity of the requirements imposed by the relevant solution on problem-solving objects that determines the degree to which an object is technological.

Three other points need to be highlighted here. First, the argument that objects can be technological to different degrees relies on the concept of complexity: the more complex problem-solving properties the object needs to have, the more technological that object will be. Complexity, however, can be defined in different ways, and unless defined precisely, it remains an ambiguous concept. The important point here is that the ambiguity of this concept does not influence the conclusion made in this section, namely, that objects can be technological to different degrees. Complexity may be an ambiguous concept, but the fact that it is ambiguous does not mean that it is vacuous. We have an understanding of the notion of complexity, and based on this understanding we can refer to some plans and some objects as more complex than others. Regardless of how we define complexity, accepting that complexity is a matter of degree entails that things can be technological to different degrees. The argument that objects can be technological to different degrees does not need a precise definition of complexity. To accept the argument, we only need to accept that complexity is a relative concept and that some solutions can be more complex than others.

Secondly, problem-solving properties are solution-dependent, not problem-dependent. Different solutions may be used to solve a single problem. However, depending on the complexity of each solution, the objects used to solve the problem may not be equally technological. The more complex the solution, the more technological the object would be. For instance, think about solving the problem of getting nails into the wall to hang a picture. If the solution to this problem is *hitting* the nails with a hard object, then this solution requires a much less complex material object than when the solution involves designing a robot which climbs up the wall and uses a concentrated water jet to make holes in the wall before inserting nails into the holes.

Finally, because a particular physical object can be used to solve different problems, a physical object can be more technological when used for one particular purpose compared to another. A mobile phone, for example, is more technological when used to send text messages than when it is used as a flashlight. This is because the problem-solving properties which the mobile phone needs to have in order to send a text message are more complex than the problem-solving properties which it needs to have in order to function as a flashlight. The same object is also more technological when used as a flashlight compared to when it is used to open beer bottles. So a single object can be technological to different degrees depending on the complexities of the particular solutions to problems it is helping its users to achieve.

RESPONDING TO OBJECTIONS

Before concluding this chapter, it is worthwhile to discuss some objections and hard cases for the definition of technology developed here. These discussions will shed further light on the activity realist conception of technology.

One of the objections to the definition of technological objects as problem-solving physical instruments is that not all instances of human–technology relations are clear examples of problem-solving activities. Rather, the use of technology seems to be performed out of habit. For example, when we fill up a water bottle and put it on our desk, we do not really consciously think that we have now found a solution to the problem of keeping drinking water nearby while we are at our desk. When we enter our houses, we do not always get the impression that we have solved the problem of using a shelter to keep us secure against predators and harsh weather conditions. There are many instances of human–technology relations which may not appear as examples of problem-solving activities. We simply do them habitually. How does the definition of technologies as problem-solving physical instruments explain this?

Even though not all instances of human–technology relations are paradigmatic cases of problem-solving activities, all technology is introduced as a form of problem-solving physical instrument. As discussed in the introduction of this book, there is continuity between problem-solving activities and habitual goal-oriented activities. Many habitual goal-oriented activities start as problem-solving activities. It is only after becoming accustomed to the solution that we no longer consider the activities as problem-solving activities. When we find a shelter or use a water bottle for the first time, we do feel that we have satisfied a need or a desire and that some practical problems have been solved. But simply because we become accustomed to the presence of the solution over time does not mean that the objects cease to perform their problem-solving roles.

The other objections to this definition of technologies as problem-solving physical instruments are in the form of hard cases. In particular, there are at least two groups of objects which challenge this definition. These cases are natural objects which are not strictly used, but play roles in problem-solving activities and structures built and simple tools used by animals.

Consider activities like constructing a watermill on a river or sitting in the moonlight to study. Are the river and the moon technologies in these examples? The reason to think that the moon and the river are technologies is that they are physical objects that help us solve practical problems. The river plays an instrumental role in solving the problem of generating power and the moonlight enables us to read a book at night. If we compare the river and the moon against the definition of technology given earlier, we notice that they both help us solve practical problems, and both objects do so by virtue of their physical properties. It, therefore, seems that in this account the moon and the river qualify as technologies. But do they?

Although the objects in the examples above have instrumental values, the moon and the river do not qualify as technologies. This is because what these objects do does not depend on human intentions, and the interactions that humans have with them do not qualify as acts of *use*. In the definition of technologies as problem-solving physical instruments, a physical object which has instrumental values needs to be (intended to be) *used* by problem solvers in order to qualify as a technological object. As explained earlier, intentional use is an integral part of the definition.

Wybo Houkes and Pieter Vermaas (2004) have provided an account of use which is useful to mention here. Their account is based on the concept of 'use plan' and requires the manipulation of a given object as a part of goal-oriented series of actions: 'Defining a plan somewhat loosely as a goal-directed series of considered actions, a use plan of object x is a series of such actions in which manipulations of x are included as contributions to realizing the given goal' (Houkes & Vermaas, 2004, 57).

Since sitting in the moonlight or putting a watermill on a river's path do not qualify as acts of use, the objects of these cases do not qualify as technological objects. If use takes use plans and manipulations of objects, an object is used when at least a minimum level of manipulation is applied to it. The moon and the river, in the previous examples, are not strictly used because they have not been manipulated. One might study under the moonlight and be unaware of the existence of the moon or have no concept of 'the moon' in the first place.

But is there a difference between the cases of the moon and the river on the one hand, and the case of the tree used as a meeting point on the other? It also does not appear that the tree is manipulated. And if that is true, the tree should not be considered a technological object either. Although the example of the tree seems similar to the examples of the moon and the river, there is a difference between these cases. The use plan which is executed in the case of the tree involves assigning a particular meaning to the tree which it does not naturally have; that is, the meaning of being a meeting point. This meaning ascription is a minimum form of 'manipulation', as it turns the tree into something which it naturally is not: a meeting point. But human intervention has not made the moon shed light or the river provide water pressure. The moon continues to reflect the Sun's light regardless of whether anyone sits in the moonlight to study, and the river maintains water pressure whether or not anyone places a turbine in its path.

Nevertheless, the fact that something does not qualify as a technological object does not mean that it has no instrumental value whatsoever. The moon and the river play roles in problem-solving activities as physical objects, and for this reason they have instrumental values. But since they are not physically manipulated and are not assigned any meaning to be able to play the role they play, they are not technologies. Not all problem-solving activities involve the use of technologies.

The second set of hard cases for the current definition of technology are structures built and simple tools used by animals. Anthills, beaver dams and bird nests are all physical structures which are created and used by animals and serve particular functions for them. In fact, there is an expanding body of literature on animal tool use and increasing evidence to support the claim that other animal species use objects in problem-solving activities. The crow that bends a wire and uses it as a hook to pull objects out of a narrow container, or the chimpanzees that strip leaves from tree branches and use them to fish or dig termites are relevant examples here (Beck, 1980; Shumaker et al., 2011; Weir et al., 2002). The question that might be asked is whether any of such animal constructs or the tools used by animals qualify as technologies.

As a response it should be said that whether any animal structures or tools qualify as technologies depends on the mental capacities of the animals and the extent to which they reflect on their acts of construction or use of tools to achieve goals. As discussed in the next chapter, engaging in problem-solving activities takes a reflective mind. Given the link between being a tool user and having a reflective mind, the question of whether animals are tool users or not informs our moral and regulatory decisions in relation to how we treat them. However, this question should be answered on the basis of the empirical question of whether or not these animals are reflective enough to consciously use material objects as a part of their devised solutions to what they perceive as problems. This empirical study is beyond the scope of this book. But if activities of other species can be meaningfully called problem-solving activities, then those species' constructions and the tools which they use would also be technological objects for members of those species.

SUMMARY

This chapter employed the activity realist approach introduced in the previous chapter to define the general category of technology. Technologies are generally defined as problem-solving physical instruments. Because what may be a problem for one person or group of people may not be a problem for others, the status of objects as technological objects is defined subjectively: what is a technology for a person or a group of people may not be a technology for others. Similar points can also be made about other general categories of objects, such as artistic, religious and entertainment objects. No object is an artistic, religious or an entertainment object in and of itself. Objects gain their artistic, religious or entertaining identities from the activities in which they are used. And the status of objects as artistic, religious and entertainment objects is determined subjectively.

In this activity realist definition, technologies can be understood as the material components of solutions to problems. Hence, being a technology becomes a matter of degree: some objects can be more technological than others. The degree to which an object is technological is determined by the complexity of the solution. Moreover, in this definition, there is a close connection between concepts of technology, use, control and autonomy. The more autonomy an entity has, the less meaningfully it is used, the less control others have over it and the less technological the entity would be. Finally, whether other animal species, or in fact, whether any other entity, qualifies as a technology user and problem solver depends on their mental capacities. Having certain mental capacities works as a condition of possibility for problem-solving activities and, accordingly, for technologies.

The next chapter will further explore this definition by examining the conditions of possibility of technologies and identifying worldly circumstances which motivate, and mental characteristics which enable, entities to engage in problem-solving activities.

Chapter 5

The Conditions for the Possibility of Technologies

Conditions for the possibility of any entity are the things which must be in place for that entity to become real. The conditions for the possibility of engagement rings, for example, are the presence of the culture of marriage and the presence of those entities who can get married. Without the culture of marriage or without any person who can get married, rings cannot acquire the identity of engagement rings. Conditions for the possibility of any entity, therefore, stipulate the type of world in which the entity can realise.

What are the conditions for the possibility of technologies? In what type of world can objects acquire technological identities? The activity realist definition of technologies developed and discussed in the previous chapters conceptualises technologies in the context of problem-solving activities. Objects acquire technological identities in worlds in which some of their inhabitants engage in solving practical problems. More specifically, for technologies to be a part of reality, there need to be (1) entities who can engage in problem-solving activities and (2) circumstances which motivate those entities to engage in such activities.

As such, the conditions for the possibility of problem-solving activities and, subsequently, the conditions for the possibility of technologies can be specified in two different domains. Firstly, there cannot be problem-solving activities or problem-solving instruments unless there are entities who have the capacity to engage in problem-solving activities. Thus, the first domain is the internal state of potential problem solvers: the characteristics which entities must possess in order to be able to engage in problem-solving activities and play the role of problem solvers.

Given that philosophy of technology has been exclusively about *human* technology users (as distinct from, say, *animal* technology users), this first domain has been historically investigated by advocates of 'humanist' conceptions of technology. Roughly, humanism is the claim that humans, and humans only, make technologies possible and create the conditions for the possibility of technologies. In this way, a theory which determines the conditions for the possibility of technologies by examining the characteristics of the (human) problem solvers would fall in the humanist camp.

The second domain where the conditions for the possibility of problem-solving activities and technologies can be found includes everything which is external to problem solvers. A problem solver's engagement in problem-solving activities is motivated by the worldly circumstances which surround the problem solver. When everything is 'in order', there is no need for an entity to engage in problem-solving activities and use material means to solve their practical problems. This second domain has been historically investigated by proponents of 'non-humanist' philosophies of technology. Roughly, non-humanism is the claim that the conditions for the possibility of technologies are constituted by factors external to humans.

This chapter first elaborates on different definitions of humanism and non-humanism. Then, it dissects the humanist and non-humanist conditions for the possibility for problem-solving activities and for technologies under an activity realist approach. Hence, this chapter will argue for a hybrid position in which both humanist and non-humanist conditions make technologies possible.

THE HUMANISM/NON-HUMANISM DEBATE

Humanism, as it is used in philosophical texts, has a narrow and a broad sense. The narrow sense of humanism is limited to moral values. In this narrow sense, moral values are derived from purely human needs and desires. Here, 'purely human' refers to that part of humanity which is not constructed by external factors. In this sense, humans' needs for food, water and sleep are purely human, and their desires to check their messages on an online platform or to lubricate their bikes' chains are not purely human. The latter cases are not purely human for the very reason that such desires and needs are partly externally constructed: the desires to check online messages and to lubricate a bike's chain are contingent on the presence of online platforms and bicycles.

The narrow sense of humanism is the claim that intrinsic moral values are those which are derived from purely human needs and desires. Other values are only instrumental for the achievement or protection of purely human needs and desires. In this sense, for example, a humanist would argue that farming is a valuable practice because it contributes to human nourishment.

The narrow sense of humanism stands against the narrow sense of non-humanism. The narrow sense of non-humanism is the claim that other entities can also have intrinsic moral values. Religious doctrines are classical examples of non-humanist ethics. Historically, as apparent in the Humanist Manifestos, I, II and III (American Humanist Association, 1973a, 1973b, 2003), humanism emerged and gained popularity as a rival to religion for explaining the roots of moral values. Religious doctrines, especially monotheistic religions, such as Christianity and Islam, are non-humanist because they contend that only the divine is intrinsically valuable. Environmentalism may be another form of non-humanist ethics. *Some* environmentalists may argue that the environment is valuable in itself, and for this reason we should protect the environment even if protecting the environment may not have clear benefits for humans.

The narrow sense of humanism can generalise from moral values to other social realms. In the broad sense of humanism, humans are designers of the social world, and their beliefs, intentions and attitudes determine what is the case. More technically, the broad sense of humanism is the claim that explanatorily sufficient factors in a given social field can be derived from purely human characteristics. Or in other words, it is the claim that all which is required to make sense of the social world is purely human factors; all other explanations can be reduced to and derived from purely human factors. This could be the derivation of ethical values from purely human needs and desires (as stated in the narrow sense of humanism), defining social institutions based on purely human actions and intentions or telling history solely on the basis of the humans who lived in each era. In any of these cases, the meanings of operative terms, descriptions of states of affairs and explanations of events are derived from human beliefs, intentions and attitudes, without any reference to other entities such as the environment, gods or material objects. Explanations and descriptions of material objects and modifications to the environment could also be derived from purely human characteristics. This broad sense of humanism can also be referred to as anthropocentrism.

Thus, in its broad sense, humanism can be seen as a rival thesis to any school of thought which relies on non-human entities in the meaning it gives to its operative terms, its description of states of affairs or its explanations of events.

HUMANISM AND NON-HUMANISM IN PHILOSOPHY OF TECHNOLOGY

Most discussions on the humanism/non-humanism debate in philosophy of technology have been related to the field of ethics of technology. In applied ethics, the debate manifests itself in questions such as these: Can technologies be held responsible for a morally wrong act? Can technologies be intrinsically good or bad? Non-humanists may give a positive and humanists would give a negative answer to these questions.

At the level of metaethics and normative ethics of technology, the humanism/non-humanism debate is on the possibility of technological moral agents. While humanists reject the idea of technological moral agency, non-humanists either see some technologies as moral agents, in a similar way that humans can qualify as moral agents (Johnson & Powers, 2008), or claim that in any action performed by means of technologies, neither humans nor technologies are exclusive moral agents. Moral agency, according to this group, is distributed over humans and technologies (Verbeek, 2009, 2011). Philip Brey divides those who believe in the moral agency of technologies into two groups. In what he refers to as the 'moral artefacts view', all technologies could be moral agents (Brey, 2014). And in the 'morally intelligent agents view', only highly evolved technologies, which are capable of autonomous behaviour and intelligent information processing, qualify as technological moral agents (ibid.).

In historiography and sociology of technology, the humanism/non-humanism debate is concerned with the forces which bring about social changes. Central questions to this dimension of the debate are as follows: which entities shape the course of history, humans or technologies? Should history be told in a humanist way, as a story of monarchs, philosophers, scientists, inventors, politicians and so on, or in other words, humans who lived at each time period? *Or* should it be told in a non-humanist way, as a story of sickles, wheels, steam engines, assembly lines, the internet and other material objects whose introduction affected the social order at their time and brought new possibilities for future social developments? Again, non-humanists would defend the thesis that non-human factors also shape the course of history, and their stories need to be included in writing history. One of the most influential socio-historical debates in philosophy and sociology of technology is that of the social construction of technology (Woolgar & Cooper, 1999) versus technological determinism (Ellul, 1964; Winner, 1980). Here, the question is whether it is the users and designers who decide which technologies should enter society *or* whether values and the social order are themselves shaped by technologies. Humanists (i.e. social constructivists) assert that humans autonomously decide the course of technological developments. Non-humanists (i.e. technological determinists) contend that technologies are an important force of social change. According to this group, technological developments follow their own course independently of the beliefs and intentions of individuals or groups of people, and the existing social order and social values are themselves products of past and present technological developments.

The Metaphysical Dimensions

At least three different dimensions of the humanism/non-humanism debate in metaphysics of technology can be identified. These three dimensions of the debate include (1) whether or not technologies have an agency similar to human agency; (2) whether or not human nature exists independently of technologies; and (3) whether, besides technologies' physical aspects – which they share with other material objects – purely human attributes are sufficient to conceptualise technologies.

Among these three dimensions, the first has received the most attention. This attention has further surged with the advent of modern algorithms and products which rely on Artificial Intelligence. Non-humanist defenders of technological agency either suggest that some technologies are agents in a similar, if not the same, way that humans are (Floridi & Sanders, 2004; Johnson & Powers, 2008; Jones & Cloke, 2008; Latour, 1992; Sutton, 2002), or claim that neither humans nor technologies could be agents *in themselves*. Agency, according to this latter group, is distributed over humans and technologies (Law & Mol, 2008; Malafouris, 2008; Sutton, 2008; Verbeek, 2011).

The second dimension of the humanism/non-humanism debate in metaphysics of technology is related to the interaction between (what can be assumed to be) human nature, on the one hand, and technologies, on the other. Bruno Latour, for instance, criticises humanist views and argues that technologies shape a part of what is human, and that human beings have never existed independently of technologies (Latour, 1993; Latour & Couze, 2002).

This dimension of the debate can also be studied in relation to the interaction between technologies and human intentions, actions, goals and values, since human intentions, actions, goals and values can be understood as constituents of human nature. Here, humanists would argue for the existence of purely human intentions, actions, goals and values, and non-humanists argue that human intentions, actions, goals and values do not exist in 'non-technological', purely human forms, and that technologies affect these and similar characteristics which are often assumed to be purely human.

Arguments for the extended mind thesis, too, support the non-humanist side of this second dimension. Proponents of the extended mind thesis (Clark & Chalmers, 1998) argue for the impact of environmental (including technological) resources on human cognition and action, and conclude that human cognition, which has traditionally been assumed to be purely human and confined to what goes on inside the skull, can be, and indeed is, extended by or distributed over technologies, which are called 'cognitive artefacts' or 'cognitive systems' (Heersmink, 2015). The extended mind thesis will be further examined later in this chapter. The significance of this thesis is that it challenges the assumption that cognition is an internal process and is confined within the boundaries of reflective beings' bodies.

The third dimension of the humanism/non-humanism debate in the field of metaphysics of technology is concerned with how technologies are conceptualised and whether human beliefs and intentions are sufficient for this conceptualisation. In a humanist view, the difference between technologies and other physical objects, or in other words, the metaphysical status of technologies, is reducible to the minds of humans (designers, policymakers, users etc.). Philosophers such as John Searle (2007) and Amie Thomasson (2007), for instance, conceptualise technologies in relation to the intentions of designers and users. In their conception of technology, what turns a physical object into a technology is the mental states of the designers and users. If humans assign a specific function to an object and by doing so, give a specific meaning to the object, that object becomes a technology. As an example, what turns, say, a piece of rock into a stepping stone is the fact that people intend to use it as a stepping stone. People might as well intend to use it as a paperweight, and this very fact would turn the rock into a paperweight. Nothing except what goes on in the minds of people is needed in order to understand this or any other technology.

On the other hand, some others have challenged the humanist understanding which approaches technologies purely as 'creations of the mind' (Latour, 1992; Law & Mol, 2008; Verbeek, 2005, 2009, 2011). In their view, often one cannot properly understand a given technology unless one takes into account the role that other technologies play in creating an environment in which the need to use the technology arises. To conceptualise antivirus software, for instance, one cannot ignore the role of other technologies such as computers, the internet or electricity which condition the invention and use of antivirus software.

Here it should be clarified that the three dimensions of the humanism/non-humanism debate in the metaphysics of technology are not all logically independent. In particular, the validity of the third humanist claim is contingent on the validity of the second humanist claim. The claim that human beliefs and intentions are sufficient to conceptualise technologies and distinguish them from other types of objects (which is the humanist position in relation to the third dimension of the debate) can be interpreted as a humanist claim only if human beliefs and intentions are themselves not shaped or influenced by technologies (which is the humanist position in relation to the second dimension of the debate). So, a non-humanist position in the second dimension of the debate logically entails a non-humanist position in the third dimension of the debate.

NON-HUMANIST CONDITIONS

What are the humanist and non-humanist conditions for the possibility of problem-solving activities and subsequently of technologies? As mentioned in the introduction, this chapter takes a hybrid position in relation to the humanism/non-humanism debate. This section explores the non-humanist conditions, and the remainder of this chapter identifies the humanist conditions for the possibility of technologies.

Non-humanist conditions for the possibility of problem-solving activities are factors external to, and outside the direct control of, problem solvers. These factors motivate engagement in problem-solving activities through shaping problem solvers' goals and values.

Problem-solving activities are conditioned by goals and values. This is because, as discussed in the introduction of the book, a state of affairs is problematic only when it contradicts the problem solver's expectations of what should be the case, and the problem solver's expectations of what should be the case is contingent on their goals and values. For instance, a piece of rock blocking a stream of water creates a problem if we wish the water to keep flowing without losing its pressure. If our goal is to create a pond or to have stepping stones to be used for crossing the river, the rock would be a part of the solution, and its absence would be problematic. Sexism, as a different type of example, is considered a problem only in relation to the social values of gender equality and human rights. If a society at some point does not perceive gender equality as a value, it would not regard sexist attitudes and behaviours as problematic. In such a society, problems can arise for individuals who *do not* manifest sexist attitudes and behaviours. Therefore, problems and, subsequently, problem-solving activities and technologies are conditioned by problem solvers' goals and values.

Human goals and values may appear to be purely human. For example, when a person decides to achieve a particular goal in their lives or respect a certain value, it may be argued that the person has decided to follow the goal and value *themselves*. It is *their* decision, and the decision is made in a seemingly purely human way: no other entity except for the person were involved in this decision. Similarly, it may be argued that when a person decides to use an object as a technology to solve a practical problem, the only factor which conditions the use of the object as a technology is the person's intention to solve their problem, and this intention to achieve a certain practical goal is formed by the person alone.

However, although human goals and values may first appear to be purely human, examination of human goals and values reveals that they can be influenced by external factors, such as technologies. In this way, a problem-solving context which requires us to use a particular technology can itself be conditioned by technologies. Technologies can create circumstances for moral and practical decision-making, and consequently, shape the problems that can arise in those circumstances.

As an example, as Jan Holvast (2009) has shown, there is a strong historical relationship between the development of monitoring technologies and the weight given to the value of privacy. As a result of the implementation of monitoring technologies, humans have become more sensitive to their privacy, and violating someone's privacy is perceived as a more serious crime. That is, the development of certain technologies in order to protect and uphold the value of privacy (e.g. security software) was conditioned by other technologies, namely, monitoring technologies. Monitoring technologies contributed to the development of security software because they contributed to our perception of privacy as a moral value. Similar connections have been shown between contraceptives and society's move towards more liberal sexual values (Keularts et al., 2004).

Moreover, technologies which increase human control over their surroundings can open dimensions for new moral decision-making. Consider ethics settings as an example. Ethics settings are technological features which can be added to autonomous systems, such as autonomous vehicles. These settings allow for morally significant decisions made by humans to be programmed into the systems. In the case of autonomous vehicles, for example, the absence of ethics settings means that all navigational decisions, including morally relevant ones, will be made by the algorithms which control the vehicle. But with the availability of ethics settings, manufacturers and/or users can go through the settings and adjust them so that the settings reflect their values. For example, they can adjust the settings on their autonomous vehicle so that their vehicle always slows down and allows upcoming vehicles to join the traffic on busy roads. Or users can customise their vehicle's settings so that it prioritises routes which result in the least amount of greenhouse gas emissions by the vehicle. So, ethics settings enable humans to exert control over the outcomes of morally relevant incidents.

But this control also creates moral responsibilities for manufacturers and users, as the manufacturers and users need to decide how to adjust the ethics settings, and they can be held responsible for their moral decisions (Soltanzadeh et al., 2020). As another example, as Verbeek (2011) has shown, the technology of obstetric ultrasound imaging has generated an atmosphere for moral decision-making for parents. Parents are now faced with the question of whether they want to undergo obstetric screening in the first place, and they need to make the decision of how to proceed with pregnancy if, for example, the foetus is diagnosed to have a likelihood of developing Down syndrome. These morally significant decisions have been made possible by the presence of obstetric technologies. What the example of ethics settings and ultrasound imaging have in common is that they both increase human control over the outcomes of everyday life incidents. In general, given the relationship between control and moral responsibility, any technology which increases the level of human control also creates a new environment for moral decision-making.

However, not only value-driven activities but all goal-oriented activities can be conditioned by external factors, including technologies. The need to develop cars or public transport systems arises in cities which are designed in a way that it is hard for citizens to walk from home to work and back. Designing and using cycling accessories only makes sense in societies where bicycles are used as means of transport or for leisurely or competitive purposes.

Thus, moral decisions that humans face, humans' perception of values and their goals do not exist in purely human forms, in a world unaffected by technologies and other factors external to problem solvers. External factors can motivate engagement in problem-solving activities and subsequently, the use of material objects as problem-solving physical instruments. These external factors constitute non-humanist conditions for the possibility of technologies.

HUMANIST CONDITIONS

In addition to the presence of goals and values which motivate engagement in problem-solving activities, other conditions also need to be met for reflective beings to be able to use material objects as problem-solving physical instruments, or in other words, as technologies. Unlike goals and values that can be shaped by external factors, these latter conditions highlight the intrinsic capacities which are required of entities to be able to engage in problem-solving activities. These conditions, which would be categorised as humanist conditions, can be identified through further examination of problem-solving activities.

Revisiting Problem-Solving Activities

What phases do problem solvers undergo to engage in problem-solving activities? Engagement in problem-solving activities can be broken down into four phases: *identification*, *planning*, *execution* and *evaluation*. The first phase of each problem-solving activity is identification of a state of affairs as a problem. After this phase, problem solvers need to creatively plan to devise a solution to the problem. Then they need to execute the plan. And finally, they need to be able to evaluate the success or failure of the plan.

As an example, imagine that on their way to their office, an individual may realise that the path which they usually take is closed. This makes them enter into a problem-solving activity which consists of the following phases. First, they become aware of the fact that the path is closed. In other words, they comprehend the reality of the problem. Second, they think to themselves that instead of taking the usual route, they should take another route which should also take them to the office. Here, they devise a solution to the problem which consists of finding an alternative route. Then they execute their plan and follow the alternative route to reach the office. Finally, they evaluate their solution based on whether the alternative route actually has taken them to the office, and based on other factors important to them, such as the (additional) distance that they needed to take, the number of traffic lights in the alternative route, and how safe and pleasant taking the alternative route was.

In reality, the phases of problem-solving activities can be iterative, and may not occur in the sequence presented earlier. A hypothetical evaluation of a plan, for instance, may often precede execution of the plan. If the result of this evaluation is unsatisfactory, the subject will go back to the phase of creative planning to devise a better plan. In the previous example, evaluating whether a route leads to the destination can be done by actually following the route. But it can also be done by looking up the route on a map. If a map is used, then the evaluation phase can be partly done prior to the execution of the plan. As the plan is being executed, modifications can also be made to the devised solution. This is often because problem solvers may become aware of other needs and desires that they wish to achieve by their solution. They may prefer the route that they take to the office to be safe and pleasant. So, problem solvers can adjust their plan if the route that they are taking does not satisfy those extra preferences. And so there can be, and often is, a dynamic feedback loop between the devised solution, the execution of the plan and the evaluation of the plan.

These four phases of problem-solving activities help us to identify the characteristics which problem solvers need to possess to be able to use objects as technologies in problem-solving activities.

Human Users

When something is used as a problem-solving instrument, it is used *by* and *for* a problem solver to reach their goals. The fact that technologies are used by humans and for humans constitutes a humanist condition on the possibility of technologies.

The relationship of use between problem solvers and technologies is central to what makes something a technology. As argued in the previous chapter, there is a close connection between the concepts of use, technology, control and autonomy. The more technological an object becomes, the more control users have over it. When there is no level of control over what an object does, no relationship of use is established with the object, and the object will not be a technology. This point can be further elucidated.

Making changes to the worldly states of affairs by virtue of its particular physical properties does not in itself turn an object into a technology. In the definition of technologies as problem-solving physical instruments, it is also necessary for objects to be *used* in order to be technologies. That is why two sets of consequentially similar phenomena can be seen as non-technological in one case and as technological in another, depending on whether they were used by humans or not. If sunlight goes through an icicle, concentrates on a point and burns that spot, the icicle will not be a technology. But if humans use an icicle for the purpose of starting a fire by concentrating sunlight on a point, it will be a technology. A forest fire which heats up its surroundings is not a heater because no one has intended for it to heat anything up. But if humans make a fire to keep themselves warm, that fire becomes a technology. A problem-solving physical instrument needs to be under some level of humans' control on the basis of which a relationship of *use* can be established between problem solvers and the object. It does not matter what humans want it to do. It could be the complex task of helping scientists carry out precise experiments in particle physics or the mundane task of providing a flat surface to sit on. For something to be a technology, therefore, it needs to be under the control of, and used by, a problem solver. This constitutes a humanist condition on the possibility of technologies.

But is it possible for a technological object to be controlled by other technologies? Can the relationship of use be formed between two technologies with one using the other? Imagine a robot which grabs a dustpan and a brush to clean a room. Cleaning the room can qualify as a problem-solving activity, even though the problem may not be a very hard one to solve. Now in this example, is the robot *using* the dustpan and the brush? Are the dustpan and the brush *technologies* for the robot?

The answer is no. The robot's actions do not qualify as acts of use. Even if we use the term 'use' to describe the relationship between the robot and the dustpan and the brush, this would be a thin sense of use. This is because use, in its thick sense, includes two distinctive phases of problem-solving activities which were explained in the previous section, namely, planning and execution. Robots are indeed able to execute some plans, but they do not yet have the capacity for creative planning. Moreover, their executions are not meaningful instances of 'actions'. Each of these points can be separately discussed.

A user needs to be able to make plans, which means users must have the required mental capacity to form goals and make plans to achieve their goals.

Although autonomous technologies may become reality, no robot with a creative 'mind' has been developed yet. Robots still operate based on their algorithms. Even when these algorithms allow robots to adapt to new environments, it is still the human programmers who write the algorithm for a robot to make it, for example, clean the floor with a dustpan and brush, and not, for instance, play football. Given that robots do not meaningfully engage in problem-solving activities for themselves, their relationships with other objects cannot be described as acts of use.

A similar argument, derived from theories of action, can be utilised to demonstrate why robots do not qualify as users. Let us consider the use of an object in a problem-solving activity as an action. We can then deduce that any necessary condition which applies to actions must apply to using an object in a problem-solving activity as well. Kenneth Himma (2009) notes that there are two general theories that explain the necessary conditions of actions:

> The difference between breathing and typing words is that the latter depends on my having a certain kind of mental state, while the former does not. Some theorists . . . regard the relevant mental state as a belief/desire pair; on this view, if I want X and believe y is a necessary means to achieving x, my belief and desire will cause my doing y – or will cause something that counts as an 'intention' to do y, which will cause the doing of y. Others, including myself, regard the relevant mental state as a 'volition' or a 'willing'. For example, if I introspect my inner mental states after I have made a decision to raise my right arm and then do so, I will notice that the movement is preceded by a somewhat mysterious mental state (perhaps itself a doing of some kind) that is traditionally characterized as a 'willing' or a 'volition'. Either way, it is a necessary condition for some event y to count as an action that y be causally related to some other mental state than simply a desire or simply a belief. (Himma, 2009, 20)

These two general theories of action that Himma refers to both rely on the actor's mental states, one on the capacity of forming beliefs and desires, the other on volition. Since we can presume that robots do not have such mental states, they do not qualify as actors. It is true that scientists still do not have a clear picture of the relationship between human mental states and brain states, but that only proves the point even further. If we still do not know how human mental states are produced, we would not know how to replicate artificial mental states for robots.

To be a user requires the ability to make plans and follow them accordingly, to have desires and beliefs or volition and, in a nutshell, to have a certain level of mental capacity. These abilities constitute a humanist condition on the possibility of technologies, as they highlight characteristics which entities need to possess in order to be able to play the role of problem solvers.

The Mind-Dependence of Problems

The second humanist condition for the possibility of technologies can be identified in the constitutions of a problem. Problems have a dual metaphysical status. Even though they often refer to states of affairs in the world, they are also partly subjectively constituted. In a sense, there is no such thing in the world as a problem. Problems are problems because they are perceived as problems.

A state of affairs which is problematic for one person may be helpful for another person. Consider the case of the piece of rock which is blocking a stream of water again. This state of affairs constitutes a problem for those who wish the water to keep flowing without losing its pressure. The same state of affairs would be desirable for those who wish to create a pond or use the rock as a stepping stone to cross the stream.

Nothing in the physicality of a worldly situation is or can meaningfully be problematic on its own. What makes it a problematic situation is that reflective beings find it problematic. If no reflective being existed, it would not make sense to refer to any state of affairs as a problem.

Perceiving a state of affairs as a problem and, subsequently, engaging in problem-solving activities require mental capacities. As such, the reality of problems and problem-solving activities is conditioned by the presence of beings who are endowed with the mental capacity to perceive certain states of affairs as problematic ones. Humans belong to the category of beings who are endowed with such mental capacities. Hence, the mind-dependence of problems works as the second humanist condition of possibility for technologies.

Human Evaluators

The third humanist condition on the possibility of technologies is that technologies are inherently open to evaluative and comparative judgements which are made by problem solvers. Technologies are inherently open to evaluative and comparative judgements on the basis of the degree to which their users feel their expectations are fulfilled. This humanist condition on the possibility of technologies is linked to the fourth phase of problem-solving activities discussed earlier, namely, evaluation. All problem-solving activities are open to evaluation as problem solvers need to know whether their plans are successful and whether the physical instruments which they use actually help them to overcome their problems.

A technology would be a good technology if what it does satisfy its user. It would be a better technology than another one if it leads to a higher level of satisfaction. However, it is problem solvers who make these evaluative judgements. The quality of technologies' performance is judged by humans.

If they fail to satisfy what humans want them to do, they will be judged as ineffective or malfunctioning technologies.

Here it might be argued that given a specific task and a specific physical instrument, evaluating whether the technology is suitable for that task and whether a technology is better than another one is reducible to mind-independent, objective facts. An objective evaluation of this sort can be made based on the degree to which the physical properties of a technology match the problem-solving properties that are required to function as the material part of the devised solution. As argued in the previous chapter, problem-solving properties are those physical properties which make objects suitable for the task at hand. To hit a nail into the wall, for instance, we need something light enough to be easily grabbed and carried, and we want it to have at least one hard end. For this task, a hammer could be more suitable than a piece of rock, a piece of rock would be more suitable than a screwdriver and a screwdriver would be more suitable than an airplane.

So, it may be argued that epistemically objective evaluations of the performance of technologies can be made, regardless of the mental states of the users or any other person. To make these evaluations, one does not need to know more than the nature of the task (i.e. the devised solution) and the physical properties of the technology at hand. Given the existence of an epistemically objective evaluation, technologies' being open to normative evaluations would not rely on anything mind-dependent or 'purely human'.

The above argument challenges the conclusion that the fact that technologies are inherently open to evaluative judgements indicates a humanist condition on the possibility of technologies. However, a distinction should be made between evaluation and rational evaluation. It is true that a form of rational evaluation of the degree to which the physicality of a technology is useful in performing a given task can be made based on objective facts. But humans constantly make judgements which deviate from norms of rationality. Users make an immediate evaluation of a technology based on the degree to which they feel satisfied. They do not have to be rational about these evaluations and perhaps in many cases they are not. After all, to make purely rational evaluations of how a technology performs a task, one needs to know the mechanism on the basis of which the technology is working. This is knowledge which, in most cases, users do not have. For instance, to rationally evaluate antivirus software that is running on our computers, we need to know what generation of viruses they can detect and how often they update themselves. But if we do not even know what a computer virus 'looks like', we cannot make a rational evaluation of the antivirus software that we are using. Still, this lack of knowledge does not prevent us from comparing software based on what we perceive to be the consequence of using the antivirus software installed on our computers. Our computer may be becoming slower over time because its memory is getting full, but we might (wrongfully) think that this speed difference means that the antivirus software which we used in earlier months of the purchase was better than the one that we later switched to. Based on this judgement, we even recommend the old software to our friends who may be as ignorant about antivirus software as we are. Users make judgements and based on these judgements prefer to use a given technology over others or stop using a technology in the future altogether. In any case, rational or otherwise, such judgements are made, and the fact that judgements are made by human users constitute a humanist condition on the possibility of technologies.

Hence, all three humanist conditions of possibility of technologies are rooted, in one way or another, in problem solvers' possession of a sophisticated mind. It is this mental capacity of humans which allows them to (1) identify a state of affairs as a problematic one, (2) creatively plan to solve the problem by means of physical instruments, and (3) evaluate the success and failure of their plans. However, if these seemingly intrinsic mental capacities are themselves influenced by technologies and other external factors, then these conditions of possibility of technologies cannot be categorised as humanist conditions. This issue is discussed in the next section.

COGNITIVE OBJECTS IN PROBLEM-SOLVING ACTIVITIES

The validity of the claim that human mental capacities can be influenced by technologies and environmental elements can be observed in people's everyday practices. Every time we write our ideas on a piece of paper or electronically save them, we extend our memories to material objects. Every time we use a compass, we appeal to an external object to perform the cognitive task of navigating from one point to another. What these cases highlight is that human cognition is not confined within the border of human skin, and certain human mental processes can be extended to surrounding objects (Clark & Chalmers, 1998). These claims are often referred to as the 'extended mind thesis' (ibid.). The core idea of the extended mind thesis is that human cognition can be and is extended to environmental objects or to 'cognitive artefacts', as Donald Norman (1991) refers to objects used to enhance human cognitive abilities. Cognitive artefacts, such as navigation systems, impact human mental capacities by influencing users' memory, perception, attention, intellectual autonomy and intellectual carefulness (Gillett & Heersmink, 2019).

Before proceeding with the arguments of this section, it should be noted based on the discussions of chapters 2 and 3 that the phrase 'cognitive artefact' is misleading and should be replaced with 'cognitive object'. The reason here being that the status of an object as an artefact (or a non-artefact) is irrelevant to the role it plays as a cognitive object. The category of cognitive objects and the distinction between cognitive objects and non-cognitive objects should be drawn from an activity realist perspective based on the roles which objects play in cognitive activities. Natural, non-artefactual objects, such as pebbles and sticks, can play a role in cognitive activities. Hence, the term 'artefact' in 'cognitive artefacts' may mislead us to think that non-artefacts cannot play cognitively significant roles. So, in the remainder of this chapter's discussions, the phrase 'cognitive objects' is used.

Now, the question is, to what extent do the claims of the extended mind thesis affect the three humanist conditions on the possibility of technologies discussed above? Could it be that the seemingly internal mental capacities which are used during problem-solving activities are themselves shaped by external factors, such as technologies? To answer this question, it is worthwhile to analyse the core concept of the extended mind thesis.

One of the key concepts used by extended mind theorists is that of 'epistemic action'. The claim is that during epistemic actions, the informational contents of cognitive objects work as a functional equivalent to the informational contents of some human mental states. But what are epistemic actions and what actions qualify as epistemic ones?

David Kirsh and Paul Maglio provided a definition of epistemic action in the paper that first gave a technical meaning to the term. 'Epistemic actions – physical actions that make mental computation easier, faster, or more reliable – are *external* actions that an agent performs to change his or her own computational status' (Kirsh & Maglio, 1994, 513–514, italic in the original). The function of epistemic actions, according to Kirsh and Maglio, can be threefold. They can reduce the memory load which is involved in mental computation, minimise the number of steps involved in mental computation or reduce the probability of error in mental computation (Kirsh & Maglio, 1994, 514).

Andy Clark and Davi Chalmers, as the first formal presenters of the extended mind thesis, also define epistemic actions as those which 'alter the world so as to aid and augment cognitive processes' (Clark & Chalmers, 1998, 9). Changing the direction of falling objects in a game of Tetris to figure out how to fit them, referring to a map to navigate to a place, and trying out different keys one by one to know which one opens a lock are some examples of epistemic actions.

In order to examine the possible ramifications of the extended mind thesis on how we understand the conditions of possibility for technologies, we need to analyse whether any phase of problem-solving activities fits into the category of epistemic actions. If phases of problem-solving activities *do* fall into the category of epistemic actions, then given the role of external objects in epistemic actions, those phases of problem-solving activities do not necessarily require purely mental capacities, and can be shaped by external, non-humanist factors. So the question is, does any phase of problem-solving activities fall under any of the three purposes of epistemic actions: namely, reducing memory load, reducing mental steps or reducing the likelihood of error? The short answer is 'no'. To explicate this answer, the three humanist conditions on the possibility of technologies (i.e. problem identification, technology evaluation and use) can be assessed against the three functions of epistemic actions.

Identification of a problem is the result of a conscious realisation that a state of affairs is not aligned with one's goals and values. It is true that to identify a complex problem, we might appeal to epistemic actions to break down the situation and to gather information in order to assess whether there is a problem. We might even use technologically generated graphs and charts for assessment purposes. Nevertheless, the final stage of realising that there is a problem to be dealt with is purely mental. This realisation does not pose any load on memory. Nor does it depend on taking significant computational steps. It only requires consciousness. Moreover, the concept of error does not even apply to the process of problem identification. One may find a situation problematic or not, and there is nothing correct or incorrect about this. Identification of a problem, therefore, necessarily requires intrinsic mental capacities from problem solvers: the perception that a state of affairs as problematic should come from the problem solvers. No technology or external factor can decide on someone else's behalf whether a state of affairs is problematic or not. This is because, as argued earlier, problems are metaphysically subjective: a problem is a problem because it is perceived as a problem.

Similarly, evaluation of a technology is the mental realisation obtained by the process of comparing the desired outcome with the outcome that has been brought about in practice. The comparison itself can be made easier by using cognitive artefacts. But the mental judgement of whether something is desirable or not does not require acting upon the world and taking epistemic actions. It does not pose a load on memory, nor does it depend on taking computational steps. Here, too, the concept of error does not apply, as what is important here, as discussed earlier, is the subjective evaluation of a technology and not the rationality of evaluation.

The third humanist condition of possibility for technologies is that technologies are necessarily used by problem solvers. The argument here is a bit more complex. To examine whether external factors influence this condition on the possibility of technologies, the act of use can be broken into its two constituents: namely, planning and executing the plan.

Planning can be improved, or made feasible altogether, by cognitive objects. Appealing to one's biological or external memory to remember what plans and technologies were successful in the past and what was not can help problem solvers in the planning phase of problem-solving activities. Moreover, the memory load and the computational steps required for planning a solution increase as the problem becomes more complex, and at some point, the feasibility of devising a plan would depend on the presence of external factors, such as cognitive objects. Technologies can also increase the accuracy of a plan and its execution. Therefore, although planning can be entirely performed by problem solvers, it may not rely solely on their intrinsic capacities.

External factors can enable problem solvers to fulfil the task of planning in at least two different ways. Problem solvers can use external resources, such as rulers, computers or pebbles, to improve the accuracy of their plan, enhance their working memory or draw or simulate the complex computational steps required by the plan. In such cases, problem solvers would still be at least partly involved in the act of planning, and use cognitive objects only to enhance their planning abilities. However, planning can also be entirely delegated to external entities. When a person follows a manual or others' verbal advice step by step on how to achieve a goal or how to use a particular tool or a machine, the act of planning has been completely delegated to others, and the problem solver only executes the plan which has been presented to them.

The other component of problem solving, namely, executing the plan can be delegated to external entities, such as technologies. But doing so does not mean that the problem solver is no longer the user; rather, the problem solver forms a new use relationship with the external entity delegated to perform their plan. For example, a person may plan to use a dustpan and a brush to have some shattered glasses cleaned. But instead of doing it themselves, they may get another person or a robot to use the dustpan and the brush to clean the glasses. When the task is delegated to another entity, the person ceases to be the user of the dustpan and the brush, but at the same time, they form a new use relationship with the other person or the robot: the problem solver uses the person or the robot to achieve their goal. As another example, as discussed in chapter 12, a person may delegate the performance of the task of driving a vehicle to go from their home to the office to an autonomous vehicle. When the task of driving is delegated to an autonomous vehicle, the person ceases to use the steering wheel, the pedals, the gear stick and the indicator. Instead, the person becomes the user of the autonomous vehicle as a whole. So even in cases where the performance of activities is delegated to external entities, the problem solver still remains the user. The only difference is that the object of use changes.

All in all, although problem solvers do not need to possess the mental capacities required for planning, the act of using a technology, as a necessary phase of practical problem solving, requires a form of engagement from problem solvers. Use is a relationship between a user, as a reflective being, and an entity that is being used. Maintaining this relationship, in one way or another, is necessary for the user to remain engaged in their activity. Unless one acquires supernatural powers to be able to make changes to the outside world by their sheer will, engaging in practical problem-solving activities logically requires the act of use. When a person does not use any entity, they cease to be engaged in the activity altogether. Their status changes from a problem solver to an observer. Therefore, the use, or execution, phase of problem-solving activities logically requires problem solvers' involvement. It cannot be entirely delegated to external entities.

What these arguments show is that problem-solving activities obtain their reality from active engagement of entities with certain intrinsic mental characteristics. Although external factors, such as cognitive objects, can expand an entity's cognitive abilities, to be able to engage in problem-solving activities and to use technologies as problem-solving instruments, entities do not rely only on external factors. Some conditions on the possibility of using technologies are satisfied by characteristics that problem solvers must possess intrinsically.

SUMMARY

This chapter examined the conditions on the possibility of problem-solving activities as the contexts in which objects acquire technological identities. These conditions of possibility were classified into two groups: factors external to problem solvers and characteristics intrinsic to entities who are able to engage in problem-solving activities and use technologies. If we focus on human problem solvers, the first set of conditions can be called 'non-humanist' and the second group can be called 'humanist' conditions. The humanism/non-humanism debate in philosophy of technology is about the extent to which humans have control over technologies and the extent to which technologies can be understood on the basis of purely human attributes.

External, non-humanist conditions include the worldly states of affairs that urge problem-solvers to engage in problem-solving activities. External factors can also condition problem-solving activities through shaping problem solvers' goals and their perception of values. Intrinsic, humanist conditions include the fact that problems are subjectively identified as problems and technologies are used and evaluated by problem solvers. Technologies are, therefore, conditioned by a combination of humanist and non-humanist factors. Objects can gain technological identities in a world in which all these conditions are satisfied.

This chapter marks the conclusion of the first part of this book. This part redefined the subject matter of philosophy of technology from an activity realist perspective, conceptualised technologies as problem-solving physical instruments, discussed the implications of this conceptualisation and clarified the conditions on the possibility of technologies. For the next three chapters, the focus of this book will be on the particular categorisation of technologies and developing an activity realist theory of function.

Part II

THE PARTICULAR CATEGORISATION

Chapter 6

A Taxonomy of Function Theories

The issues so far discussed in this book have been related to technologies as a general category of objects. However, as explained in the introduction of this book, metaphysical discussions of technology are not limited to the general categorisation of technology. Two other central debates in the metaphysics of technology include the particular categorisation of technologies and the ontology of technologies.

While in the general categorisation, objects are grouped into general categories, such as artistic, technological, religious and entertainment objects, in the particular categorisation, objects are classified into smaller and more specific groups. This latter way of grouping can be based on different criteria. For example, objects can be categorised based on their colour, shape, size, weight or the alphabetical letter by which their names begin. These categorisations may not be very useful. As discussed in chapter 2, useful categorisations are those which are impactful. Categorisations based on objects' colour, shape, size, weight or the alphabetical letter by which their names start may not be useful because usually people's decisions about which objects to use and their evaluations of the use of objects are not sensitive to such categorisations. People employ objects to achieve certain goals. Their colour, their shape, their size, their weight or the letter by which their name begins, if not totally irrelevant, are often at best secondary to the reason why people use them and the frameworks that people use to evaluate them. A more useful particular categorisation of objects can be achieved based on their 'function'. Here, each object belongs to the same category of objects as those with the same function.

Although at first glance, the concept of function seems to provide a philosophically justified way of grouping objects, function still needs to be defined in a practically useful way. If function itself is defined in a way that is insensitive to practical and contextual factors, the particular categorisation of objects based on the concept of function remains as useless as categorising objects based on their colour, shape, size, weight or the alphabetical letter by which their name begins.

The second part of this book, which includes this and the next two chapters, focuses on the functional categorisation of objects. This chapter provides a taxonomy of function theories by demonstrating different ways that the concept of function has been studied. The next chapter highlights the entity realist bias in the current literature and the practical irrelevance of entity realist theories of function. And chapter 8 proposes an alternative, activity realist theory of function.

WAYS OF STUDYING FUNCTION

Consider the case of the hammer described in the preface of this book that was used for a variety of purposes, including putting pressure on a puncture patch of a bike's inner tube, playing a game of croquet and cutting thick weeds growing in a garden. A few questions can be asked about the status of the hammer, which highlight different ways in which function can be studied.

The first set of questions are metaphysical questions: what actually is this object? When we consider its function, what category of objects does this hammer belong to? Is it an inner-tube-fixing weight, a croquet mallet, a gardening tool, a nail-pounding tool or perhaps none of these? Can it be an inner-tube-fixing weight, a croquet mallet and a weed-cutting tool at different points? Can it simultaneously be an inner-tube-fixing weight, a croquet mallet and a gardening tool? Can it be different things for different people?

The second set of questions are epistemological questions: regardless of what the hammer actually is, how can we know what it is? If we encounter the hammer, how can we form justifiable beliefs about what it is? If one person says it is a croquet mallet, and another person says it is a time machine, who should we believe?

The third set of questions are linguistic questions: regardless of what it actually is and the way we get to know what it is, what is the right way of referring to this object? If a person wants to ask another person to bring that object to them, how should they refer to it? Is it right to just call it a 'hammer'? Can there be a universal way of referring to the object? Or should it be named based on how it is used at each point in time?

Thus, function can be studied from different angles. The first angle is metaphysical. The role of metaphysical discussions of function is to define function and to explain the properties which constitute an object's function. The second angle is epistemological. This angle deals with beliefs and practices that can make reflective beings justified in their acts of function identification. The third angle is linguistic. The linguistic study of function is concerned with the way we categorise objects in our language, and with the right way of referring to them.

This chapter illuminates the study of function from each of these angles. Here the aim is not to introduce or defend any particular theory in relation to any of these dimensions of the study of function. Rather, it describes, classifies and unwraps the current status of the main metaphysical, epistemological and linguistic themes and theories in the study of function.

SOURCES OF FUNCTION

What gives a technology its function? From where do technological objects derive their functions? One of the important discussions in the field of the particular categorisation of technologies and the metaphysical theories of function is the sources of function.

Mark Perlman has introduced human intentions and objects' capacities (their physical and chemical properties) as two main sources of functions (Perlman, 2004, 40). These two proposed sources give rise to intentional theories and capacity-based and causal-role theories of function, respectively. Peter Kroes adds 'past or future events' as the third possible 'building block' for theories of functions (Kroes, 2012, 50), which gives rise to etiological or evolutionary theories of function. These proposed sources of functions are discussed in the next three sub-sections.

Intentional Theories

According to *intentional* theories, what gives technologies the functions which they have is human intention. Humans (often considered to be designers and sometimes users) make things for particular purposes and assign certain functions to them based on what they intend the products to do (McLaughlin, 2001, 2002). In intentional theories, function is something which is 'assigned' or 'ascribed' to objects. Objects derive their functional properties from the intentions of humans. Human intentions are external to technologies, and, as we see in the next chapter, this makes intentional theories 'externalist' theories of function.

Think about an anti-shoplifting gate and its beep for example. The shopkeepers and the customers can be indifferent to the beep, but the reason why they are not indifferent is that that beep has been assigned a particular meaning. The beep of the gate is not just a noise for the shopkeepers and the customers, rather it draws attention to possible cases of shoplifting. It is the human intention to interpret the beep in a particular way that gives meaning to the beep and becomes the source of the function of the anti-shoplifting gate. In fact, similar gates could be used in football matches as the goals, and with an RFID chip attached to the ball, the referees would be able to tell whether the ball has crossed the line. In such cases, the beep is interpreted as a goal, and the technology would have the function of a smart goal.

Note that in describing intentional theories, the word 'intentional' is used as an adjectival form of 'intention'. However, it is possible to use this term as an adjectival form of 'intentionality' to include all intentional mental states. This is the sense in which Wybo Houkes and Pieter Vermaas (2010) use the 'intentional', as they include other mental states, such as beliefs, as constitutive of intentional function theories. Focusing on beliefs is important for Houkes and Vermaas because, as discussed later here, their theory is an epistemological theory of function. However, here the word 'intentional' is reserved exclusively as an adjectival form of 'intention'. In the next two chapters, theories which define function based on users' beliefs will be referred to as 'belief-based theories'.

Because in intentional theories function is something which is assigned to physical objects, and in these theories there is segregation between the function and the physicality of objects, intentional theories can explain how different functions can be assigned to the same physical object. In the case of the hammer described earlier in this chapter and in the preface of the book, intentional theories would argue that the function of the object, the hammer, is what people intend it to be. It can be an inner-tube-fixing weight, a croquet mallet, a gardening tool, a nail-pounding tool or anything that it is intended to be.

Intentional theories can be categorised as humanist theories of function. As discussed in the previous chapter, a theory of X is a humanist theory if it defines X in terms of purely human characteristics. In intentional theories, function is defined solely in relation to users' intentions. Nothing external to users is considered important in how function is defined.

The purely humanist feature of intentional theories also works as one of their shortcomings. This point will be further discussed in the next chapter, but one point which can be made here about the problems of the intentional theories is that they allow unfeasible function ascriptions. In intentional theories, any object can have any function as long as someone intends to use it with that particular function in mind. Thus, if someone intends to use a personal computer as a plane or an air conditioner, the computer assumes the function of plane or air conditioner, because that is how function is defined in intentional theories. But this is unfeasible because the object is not able to function according to the user's intentions. It does not have the capacity for it; it cannot play such roles.

However, not all theories of function are purely humanist. Some theories define function entirely based on factors that are external to users. Two of such non-humanist theories are capacity-based and causal-role theories.

Capacity Based and Causal-Role Theories

Objects' physical and chemical capacities and the causal roles which they play in the environments where they are used are the other widely discussed sources of function. In *capacity-based* theories, the function of a technological object is rooted in its physical and chemical capacities, or in other words, in its material properties. For example, the hammer has the capacity to function as an inner-tube-fixing weight, a croquet mallet and a weed-cutting and a nail-pounding tool. But it does not have the capacity to function as an umbrella or a personal computer.

In *causal-role* theories, on the other hand, the function of a technological object is derived from the causal links that it has with its surroundings. Causal-role theories are often used as theories of biological functions. For example, a causal-role theorist would define the function of the heart as an organ to pump blood, and that of xylem to transport water and nutrients from a plant's root to its leaves, because these are the causal roles that the heart and xylem play.

Capacity-based theories and causal-role theories are different in that in the former, the focus is on the object itself. In other words, in capacity-based theories, the source of function lies within the material properties of the object. But in causal-role theories, the source of function is in environmental causal interactions.

Nevertheless, the distinction between these two ostensibly different proposed sources of function can be dissolved, especially if we limit functions to material functions, which are the physical consequences of objects' use. The reason here being that objects' causal interactions with their environments (their causal role) can be predicted from their properties (their capacity). In fact, scientific activities predominantly aim to identify the laws which govern objects' causal interactions with their environments *on the basis of* the physical and chemical properties of objects and those of their environments. Therefore, at least in theory, an object's properties reveal everything about the causal interactions that the object can have with its environments.

According to this joint version of causal-role and capacity-based theories, an organ's or an object's function can be described in terms of the causal roles that the biological organ or the object plays in connection to other parts of the system to which it belongs by virtue of its structural capacities (Cummins, 1975, 2002). For instance, a capacity-based theorist would say that a personal computer is a personal computer, and not an airplane or an air conditioner, because it has a monitor and a motherboard and a keyboard and all other physical features that make it function as a computer. The reason it is not an airplane or an air conditioner is that it does not have the capacities that planes and air conditioners must have. It does not have engines or wings to be able to fly, and it does not have any mechanism to cool its surroundings.

As Peter Kroes (2012, 31) notes, capacity-based theories provide a window to understanding the concept of function in a way that is similar to an engineer's approach. Engineers see any functioning technology as a system which, as long as it continues to receive its inputs, produces specific (and to a high degree, predictable) outputs. During the process of design, engineers think about how they want their products to interact with their surroundings, and on that basis, they design features into technologies to give them the capacities to partake in those interactions. Consider the case of personal computers again. The interactions that users have with personal computers through keyboards, mouses, monitors, speakers, cameras and microphones are explainable and predictable by its designers. This is because designers have engineered features into personal computers that enable users to have these interactions with computers. A system which is designed in such a way – to produce outputs via its monitor and speakers when it receives inputs from its keyboard, mouse, camera and microphone – cannot produce the type of outputs required of a plane or of an air conditioner. The input/output relationship is generated by the material properties of the technology.

Capacity-based theories define function based on objects' material properties. But describing all properties of each object can take a very long time. Moreover, some properties of an object may never be actually implemented for the object to perform what it is performing. For example, the colour of a baker's mixing bowl is irrelevant for what it is used for, so it is unclear why such properties should reveal anything about the mixing bowl's function.

To get around this problem of capacity-based theories, one needs to ignore a host of properties which, in theory, give an infinite number of functions to an object, and make function identification an endless practice. Instead, one can focus only on those functions which have been actualised. One way to do this would be to look into the history of the object, and in the case of artefacts, its production history, or in other words, the main reason for which it is produced. This is how etiological or evolutionary theories define function.

Evolutionary Theories

Past events can be seen as sources of objects' function. Theories which define function based on the history of objects' use and design are often referred to as *etiological* (Millikan, 1984; Neander, 1991) or *evolutionary* (Houkes & Vermaas, 2010) theories of function. Evolutionary theories are often introduced as theories of 'biological function' to explain the function of different organs in different species. This explanation is connected to evolutionary biologists' appeal to the evolutionary history of an organ or a species to explain its particular features and the way in which those features help the species to survive. In the case of technical functions, evolutionary theories link technologies' functions to their production history and to their long-term selection.

By drawing from arguments used in evolutionary biology, evolutionary theories of function can explain the changes and modifications that the design of technical *artefacts* undergoes over time. Principles of evolutionary biology explain that species undergo changes to fit into their environments and maximise their chances of survival. Similarly, changes in the design of artefacts can be explained in terms of a need to accommodate dynamic social forces into artefact design.

Various elements contribute to the social changes that affect artefact design. One such element is the user preference. Users' preferences may be shaped by their needs and personal desires or by trends and fashions. These preferences change over time and influence the features which users want an artefact to have. Mobile phone design, for instance, has changed from producing simple phones that only allow users to make and receive calls to smart phones which, among the old and many other new features, can be used to take pictures, connect to the internet, play music and monitor and organise users' daily activities. These design changes are partly made in order to accommodate users' desires and preferences.

Other environmental elements that affect the design of a particular artefact are economic factors. Each society goes through different economic phases of inflation and recession. Imports and exports are subject to the global political situations, tariffs and quotas, and sanctions and embargoes. Factories rely on the existence and production of raw materials, and any change at the lower levels of industry may also affect higher levels of industry. Overall, a multitude of economic factors can affect the design and the production methods of a given artefact in order to make it affordable for the customers and/or profitable for the producers.

Legal restrictions and regulations, too, can work as environmental elements which influence the evolution of artefacts. Governments and other regulatory bodies may place restrictions on the features that an artefact can have, and these restrictions may force designers to make modifications in order to comply with the laws. A good example of legal influences are the design of sports equipment and apparel for professional athletes. Any bicycle, motorbike or car used for professional racing, for instance, needs to fit into defined standards in relation to its weight and/or the size of its engine. These rules may change over time and the dynamic nature of the rules translates into the dynamic design of bikes and cars.

Evolutionary theories, therefore, are powerful in explaining how social changes contribute to the evolution of artefacts. However, despite changes to the design of an artefact, evolutionary theorists categorise each artefact in the same particular category as its 'ancestors'. Smart phones are still considered to be mobile phones, and not computers. Modern bicycles and cars are still grouped in the same category of objects as older models of bicycles and cars. So, for evolutionary theorists, an artefact's function is embedded in its production history.

Intentional, capacity-based, causal-role and evolutionary theories are the current dominant metaphysical theories of function. These theories, however, are not mutually exclusive, and can be amalgamated to generate combined theories of function. Amie Thomasson, for instance, merges capacity-based theories with intentional ones and regards both designers' intentions and objects' physical structures as the constituents of technologies' function: 'the particular natures of artifactual kinds are constituted by *makers' intentions* regarding *what particular features are relevant* to kind membership' (Thomasson, 2009, 206, emphasis added). Beth Preston, on the other hand, combines evolutionary theories with capacity-based theories to argue that an artefact's function is constituted by its production history and the physical properties which make it suitable for that particular use (Preston, 1998). Houkes and Vermaas (2010), as a final example, blend three common theories of function to propose their ICE theory. ICE in the 'ICE theory' stands for Intentional, Causal-role and Evolutionary. However, as explained in the next section, ICE theory is in fact an epistemological theory of function.

JUSTIFICATION OF FUNCTION ASCRIPTIONS

How can one be justified in ascribing a particular function to a technology? How can they know the function of a given technology? The second angle from which the particular categorisation of objects and the concept of function can be studied is the epistemological angle. The epistemological angle is concerned with the issue of justifying our beliefs about an object's function. In the example of the hammer given earlier, the epistemological question is how someone can know the function of the hammer. If they encounter the hammer out of the blue, how can they form a justified belief about what it is?

In the case of artefacts, designers have the epistemic privilege of knowing at least some of the purposes for which their products can be used for. They may not be able to predict all possible creative uses of their products, but based on what they had in mind in the process of design, they would at least know one way in which their products can function. Designers, therefore, can justify their beliefs in ascribing function to their products by knowing that their designed products have the physical capacities that they want them to have, and can be used in the ways that they intend them to be used.

Houkes and Vermaas's ICE theory spells out this point clearly. According to Houkes and Vermaas, two individually necessary and jointly sufficient conditions need to be met for a justified act of function ascription: (1) having justified beliefs that x has the capacity to ϕ, and (2) having justified beliefs that a particular use-plan leads to that use-plan's goal, at least partially, due to the fact that x has the capacity to ϕ (Houkes & Vermaas, 2010, 88–89). These conditions are met by designers due to having the epistemic privilege of being the product designers. They are justified in believing what their products are capable of doing. They are also justified in believing that by following particular use-plans, due to the physical capacities of their products, users can achieve particular goals.

Other members of society, however, do not have this epistemic privilege that designers do. Others may not have a clue about what a product can be good for, how it is manufactured, or why, by following a given use-plan, the physical capacities of a product leave certain impacts on the context of use. This means that many people cannot satisfy the two conditions required for a justifiable function ascription mentioned in the previous paragraph, namely, having justified beliefs that a particular object has the capacity to help them in achieving their goal, and that if they follow a particular plan of use, they can achieve their goal. So how can non-designers justify their acts of function ascription? Here, the evolutionary theories of function become useful.

Besides guiding users on how to refer to technologies, which is discussed towards the end of this chapter, evolutionary theories can play another role by helping users justify their beliefs about the function of products. Evolutionary theories can create an epistemic link between users and designers to communicate at least one particular way in which an artefact can be used. Houkes and Vermaas (2010) add the evolutionary theory to their ICE theory to explain how functional knowledge can be transferred from designers to other members of the society. The role that evolutionary theories play in the ICE theory is in the way in which use-plans are communicated from designers to users. Communication of use-plans can be in different forms such as manuals, TV ads or verbal instructions from a parent or instructor. This communication creates an epistemic bridge between designers' original beliefs and those of the users. In relation to justification of function ascription, the communicated use-plans provide *a* justification for the users. Users would know that using a given artefact in at least one particular way would help them achieve at least one given purpose. Users' justification is derived from the (implicit) testimony of designers. Users learn what designers believe a product can be good for and how they can use the product for that particular purpose.

LINGUISTIC CATEGORISATION OF OBJECTS

The particular categorisation of objects and the concept of function can also be studied from the linguistic perspective. The linguistic study of object categorisation is concerned with the issue of naming. It is about the ways in which different words are used to refer to different objects. In the example of the hammer given earlier, the question is whether a hammer that is used as inner-tube-fixing weight, a croquet mallet, a gardening tool or a nail-pounding tool should still be referred to as a 'hammer'.

The linguistic study of function has two important sub-components. First, this study has an empirical component, as the question of how a technology should be referred to can be answered by consulting existing linguistic conventions. The linguistically accurate way of categorising technologies is a topic that cannot be understood purely by a priori arguments and thought experiments. This dimension of studying function is rooted in everyday practices of language use and in child and adult language development. It is guided not only by dictionaries and other linguistic authorities that prescribe definitions of words but also by how speakers of language learn new words and apply the words that they have learned in different contexts. There is, therefore, an empirical component to this research. The empirical component collects data from speakers of language and makes generalisations based on observable patterns.

Second, the relationship between the linguistic and the metaphysical theories of function needs to be elaborated, as it is questionable whether these two studies of function should be treated separately. The empirical psychologists Barbara Malt and Steven Sloman, for instance, express doubts 'whether there really is a process constituting "categorization" that is distinct from the language-embedded process of naming' (Malt & Sloman, 2007, 656). This research suggests that in practice, speakers do not make two distinct types of categorisations. The way in which technologies are linguistically categorised and referred to is intertwined with non-linguistic categorisations of objects.

Paul Bloom's empirical studies, however, have led to a different conclusion. In response to Malt and Sloman, Bloom argues that the linguistically right way of referring to an object does not always correspond with that object's nature (Bloom, 1998, 2007a, 2007b). If we are justified in referring to an object as an 'A', for example, it does not follow that the object actually belongs to the category of As. So, according to Bloom, the grammar of word use and the linguistic categorisation of objects is separate from the actual categories to which objects belong.

Some philosophers of language have also argued that the metaphysical status of an object is distinct from its linguistic label, or the way it is referred to. Nathan Salmon (1979, 1982), for instance, contends that one can accept a theory of reference without committing oneself to any essentialist position in relation to the objects of reference. Similarly, Hilary Kornblith separates the metaphysics of function from linguistic studies:

> What makes an artificial kind the kind of thing it is has some essential connection to human intention, and this is an interesting point about the metaphysics of artifacts. But this point about the metaphysics of artifacts cannot be used to ground any theses about the semantics of artificial kind terms or about any sort of epistemological privilege. (Kornblith, 2007, 145)

The independence of linguistic categorisations of function from metaphysical ones can also be clarified with the example that we started this chapter with. A hammer may be used as an inner-tube-fixing weight, a croquet mallet or a gardening tool. By separating linguistic categorisations from metaphysical ones, referring to that object as a 'hammer' is justified, even if it is used for purposes other than most hammers. However, if linguistic categorisations are identical with metaphysical categorisations, then either that object would acquire a dynamic name, depending on what it is used for at each point in time, or its function should always be defined as that of a hammer, even if it is never used for pounding nails.

Nevertheless, as argued in the final discussions of chapter 10, linguistic categorisations are not *always* separate from metaphysical categorisations. While this separation is defensible in the case of the functional categorisation of technologies, in the case of non-technological objects, the distinction between language and reality is blurrier.

Creative Use

Cases in which someone uses an object in a different way from what it is often used for are known as cases of 'creative use' or 'innovative use'. Philosophers have appealed to different methods to solve problems that creative use can create for some theories of function. The problem is identifying the category of objects to which a creatively used object belongs. In the example of this chapter, the problem would be identifying the category to which the hammer belongs.

Here it should be noted that cases of creative use are particularly interesting for metaphysical theories of function. The problem is identifying the actual category of objects to which a creatively used item belongs to, not how to refer to the item. However, some philosophical explanations provided for the phenomenon of creative use have connotations for linguistic theories of function as well.

One of the most common ways to explain the phenomenon of creative use is to draw a distinction between *proper functions* and *accidental functions* (Millikan, 1989; Wright, 1973; Preston, 1998). Philosophers who adhere to this distinction argue that technologies maintain their proper functions in all contexts, independently of how they are used in practice. At the same time, people can use technologies in different ways and these innovative uses of technologies give objects their accidental functions. So, these philosophers would argue that the proper function of the technology in our example is to pound nails, but in this case, it has a few other accidental functions.

Among explanations given to the phenomenon of creative use, Peter Kroes's answer, which relies on the distinction that he makes between 'function ascriptions' and 'function kind ascriptions' is also worth mentioning (Kroes, 2012). Kroes makes a distinction between the category of objects which are used for ɸ-ing and those which are ɸ-ers. For example, the category of objects which are used for cutting weeds and the category of weed cutters. Saying that something is a ɸ-er, in his view, is a claim about the *function kind* to which the object belongs. Saying that it is for ɸ-ing, in contrast, is a claim about the function of that particular object (ibid.).

In this way, according to Kroes, we assign *function kinds* to objects like weed cutters, personal computers, planes or air conditioners, and by doing so, we categorise them as ɸ-ers. But if someone starts using a hammer to cut weeds or sits on a coffee table, the hammer and the coffee table would be used respectively for weed cutting and for sitting on (i.e. for ɸ-ing). So, Kroes would argue that the object which is used in our example is for fixing punctured inner tubes, playing a game of croquet and cutting weed out of a garden, but it belongs to the category of hammers.

Leaving aside some technicalities, the distinction which Kroes makes between objects which are ɸ-ers and those which are used for ɸ-ing can be mapped onto the distinction between proper and accidental functions that Millikan, Wright or Preston have made. ɸ-ers are objects which have the proper functions of doing ɸ, and objects which are used for ɸ-ing have the accidental function of doing ɸ.

The distinction made between objects which are ɸ-ers and those which are used for ɸ-ing is a valid distinction, and is indeed useful to deal with cases of creative use. However, while Kroes treats both projects as metaphysical ones, in an activity realist theory, the project to identify ɸ-ers and the project to identify objects which are used for ɸ-ing should be seen as two philosophically distinct projects.

As discussed in chapter 2, activity realism is concerned with practically useful categorisations. In this approach, objects are defined based on the roles that they play in the activities of reflective beings. Objects often play dynamic roles, and as such, they acquire dynamic identities. Cases of creative use do not create a problem for an activity realist theory of function, and do not receive a secondary treatment by being labelled as 'accidental'. In activity realism, objects' dynamic properties are not less 'proper' than their context-independent properties. On the contrary, in a user-friendly, activity realist theory, dynamic properties are more significant in identifying object functions. Therefore, in activity realism, identifying objects which are used for ϕ-ing is a metaphysical priority.

However, from an activity realist point of view, identifying objects which are ϕ-ers is not metaphysically relevant, as it results in a static and activity-independent identification of objects. Nevertheless, although identifying ϕ-ers would not result in user-friendly metaphysical categorisations, this project can be linguistically useful, as it can be linked to the practice of naming and the right way of referring to objects.

In the example of the hammer, if the hammer is used to fix a bike's inner tube, then it actually is an inner-tube-fixing tool; if it is used to play croquet, then it is an object of entertainment similar to croquet mallets; if it is used to cut thick garden weeds, then it is a weed-cutting tool. However, users can be justified in referring to the object as a 'hammer' by utilising the causal theory of reference.

Kornblith (2007) has argued that the way technologies are referred to can be explained by the causal theory of reference, developed by philosophers such as Saul Kripke (1980) and Hilary Putnam (1975). Kornblith believes that the causal theory of reference can be used to justify the practice of calling the hammer a 'hammer', even if, in practice, it is used for other purposes.

In Kripke's causal theory, a speaker is warranted to refer to an object as 'X' if there is a causal–historical link between the first person who named that object 'X' and the speaker who intends to use 'X' to refer to X. For instance, the reason why I can confidently refer to Broad Peak (which is the name of a mountain in the Himalayas) by uttering the phrase 'Broad Peak', without even having seen the mountain myself, is that there exists a causal–historical link between the moment at which that mountain was named 'Broad Peak' and the moments at which I utter this phrase to refer to the mountain. Some link similar to the following. At some point, a person or group of people started using the term 'Broad Peak' to refer to this mountain. Then the name was suggested to a committee, and, after being accepted, made its way onto maps and was used by others, including journalists, who appealed to maps or the committee's documents to refer to that summit by the phrase 'Broad Peak'. I learned the name in 2013 after reading and hearing about three Iranian climbers who successfully opened up a new route to the summit but got lost on their way back and lost their lives during their descent. Similarly, causal theories can describe the link between the moment at which the object in the example of this chapter was named a 'hammer' by some group of people and the moment at which the word 'hammer' is uttered by others to refer to that object. Because of this causal–historical link, regardless of what it is used for, the object can justifiably be called a 'hammer'.

Linguistic Values of Evolutionary Theories

In light of the previous discussions on the causal theory of reference, evolutionary theories can be revisited to highlight the role that they can play in the study of function. Although evolutionary theories are introduced as theories which metaphysically define function and explain how objects acquire their function, from an activity realist perspective, these theories are best suited to complement the *linguistic* categorisation of objects. The argument here is that evolutionary theories can complement the causal theories of reference to explain the way technologies are referred to.

Evolutionary theories attempt to define function on the basis of the production history of the artefact and the historical link that originates from initial designers and goes all the way to the users. Evolutionary theories are not successful in providing a user-friendly metaphysical theory of function because they cannot explain the phenomenon of creative use, unless they give it a secondary treatment by calling it 'accidental function'. These theories identify the source of function independently of the context of use. This of course should not be a big surprise because evolutionary theories are rooted in biology, and the idea of creative use does not straightforwardly apply to the evolution of biological organs.

Nevertheless, the historical link which evolutionary theories rely on is similar to the link which the causal theories of reference use to explain how speakers become warranted in using a particular name to refer to an object. Original designers give their products a name (an arbitrary name, or a name which in its face value says something about the object's intended function). Then, other designers apply that name to refer to the same product which might be modified over time. Designing companies sell the technology to distributors under that name. Users learn the name from the sellers and commercial ads and succeed in referring to the object by the name which was coined by the designers. The exact origin of the name may vary in each case, but the important point is the presence of a historical link. Evolutionary theories, therefore, are more successful as a part of the linguistic study of function, rather than as a metaphysical theory of function. They tell us how we succeed in referring to ϕ-ers, without claiming anything about what these ϕ-ers are actually used for.

SUMMARY

Function can be studied from different angles. The first angle is concerned with the metaphysics of function. It aims to provide a definition of function and discusses what constitutes an object's function. The main existing metaphysical theories of function include (1) intentional theories which define function in terms of human intentions; (2) capacity-based theories that define function based on the physical and chemical properties and the general material capacities of objects; (3) causal-role theories that define function in relation to the causal interactions that objects can have with their surroundings; and (4) evolutionary theories which explain function in relation to objects' past history, their reproduction history and how they have evolved over time.

The second angle from which function can be studied is epistemological. The concern here is the justification of beliefs concerning objects' functions. Designers can justify their function ascriptions by having the epistemic privilege of being the designers of their products. Others can justify their beliefs concerning objects' functions through the (implicit) testimonies of designers which are made available to them through manuals, TV ads, educational sessions and so on.

The third angle is linguistic and studies the ways in which objects' names are justifiably used among the speakers of language. This study has a normative as well as a descriptive, empirical component. While the normative component sets standards for right and wrong ways of referring to objects, the empirical component examines how, in practice, the speakers of a language use different terms to refer to different objects, and how objects are grouped by their names.

The distinction between the metaphysical and the linguistic studies of function, however, is not universally agreed upon. Some empirical studies have questioned this distinction, while others contend that the linguistically right way of referring to an object does not always correspond with that object's functional identity. From an activity realist point of view, the metaphysics of function is defined by studying the common characteristics of objects which are for ϕ-ing, and the linguistic study of function examines the set of ϕ-ers.

Evolutionary theories of function, while often suggested as theories which define function in the metaphysical sense, are more suited to enrich the linguistic and epistemological dimensions of the study of function. The production history of an artefact, which is an important element in evolutionary theories, complements the linguistic and epistemological studies of function in two ways: (1) it provides a causal–historical link on the basis of which speakers can justifiably use a particular term to refer to the artefact, and (2) through the communication of use-plans, it communicates (some) purposes for which, and (some) particular way(s) in which, artefacts can be used.

Chapter 7

Conservative Functions vs. Authentic Functions

Features of entity realist theories and, importantly, their lack of relevance for practical decision-making and normative evaluations were identified and discussed in chapter 2. Given the taxonomy of function theories in the previous chapter, the impact of the entity realist approach on the field of the particular categorisation of technologies can now be elucidated.

As explained in chapter 6, the particular categorisation of technologies is often pursued through theories of function. An entity realist theory of function implies that function is a property which objects keep in all contexts independently of how users relate to them. In this approach, the particular category to which an object belongs is defined based on its context-independent functional properties, and when an object is grouped with other objects with similar functions, it always remains in the same category of objects.

In the case of the hammer mentioned in the preface of the book, an entity realist position is that that particular hammer always belongs to the same category of objects as all other hammers. If it is used as a weight to keep pressure on the puncture patch glued to a bike's inner tube, the hammer is not grouped in the category of puncture-fixing kits; if it is used as a mallet in a game of croquet, it is not categorised as croquet equipment; if it is used to cut thick weed from a garden, it is not categorised as a gardening tool. The particular category to which the hammer belongs depends on properties which it keeps in all contexts, such as designers' intentions, its physical properties or hammers' history of production.

As noted in the previous chapter, intentions, objects' physical capacities and their history of production are used as the bases for the current dominant metaphysical theories of function. Theories which rely on human intentions, objects' physical capacities, and their history of production are respectively referred to as 'intentional theories', 'capacity-based theories' and 'evolutionary theories'. This chapter examines the entity realist approach behind intentional, capacity-based and evolutionary theories of function. Through this examination, it paves the road for the development of the activity realist theory of function in the next chapter.

ENTITY REALISM AND FUNCTION ESSENTIALISM

As explained in chapter 2, entity realism is a metaphysical approach which understands and categorises objects by investigating properties that they maintain in isolation. In this approach, the metaphysically significant part of reality is what is diachronically stable. Dynamic properties are not considered significant as they come and go. Entity realism is dubbed 'entity realism' precisely because it assumes that entities that can exist on their own, with unchanging properties, are the building blocks of reality. Because these entities and their properties are assumed to be independent of temporal and physical contexts, entity realism places the identification of universal properties at the centre of its conceptualisation of each object.

In the particular categorisation of objects, the entity realist idea that objects' functional properties are unchanging, universal properties is sometimes referred to as 'function essentialism'. In function essentialism, function is treated as an essential feature of technologies, something which technologies carry in all contexts as their essence. Function essentialism, as Houkes and Vermaas characterise it, 'would divorce an analysis of artefacts from the involvements that intentional agents have with them' (Houkes & Vermaas, 2010, 143).

Function essentialism in the particular categorisation of technologies, therefore, is the counterpart of the study of artefacts in the general categorisation of technology, which was discussed in chapter 2. In both cases, the definition of objects is severed from the practices in which they are used.

According to Houkes and Vermaas (2010), function essentialism is particularly linked to the theories which distinguish between proper and accidental functions. As discussed in the previous chapter, the distinction between proper and accidental functions is sometimes made in order to conceptualise cases of innovative or creative use, such as the use of a hammer to cut garden weeds, the use of a knife to tighten screws, the use of a lighter to open bottles or the use of a dishwasher to wash dirty clothes. Theories which make distinctions between proper and accidental functions treat proper function as the essential property of each technology.

Entity realist theories may associate proper function with the intention of designers and consider designers' intentions as a metaphysically necessary and definitionally inseparable constituent of a technology's function. In this form of entity realism, designers' intentions become (at least a part of) the essence of technical functions. These intentions are carried by technologies in all contexts, including contexts of use where designers are spatially and temporally absent.

Several authors, such as Ruth Garett Milikan (1989, 1999) and Lynne Baker (2004), have written on the topic of proper functions. Baker's theory in particular is an example of an essentialist theory of function where proper function is defined in relation to designers' intentions:

> a proper function is a purpose or use intended by a producer. . . . Thus, an artifact has its proper function essentially: the nature of an artifact lies in its proper function – what it was designed to do, the purpose for which it was produced. (Baker, 2004, 102)

In addition to theories which identify proper function by focusing on designers' intentions, such as that of Baker, another common form of entity realist theories of function are capacity-based theories. In fact, all capacity-based theories are entity realist theories. As explained in the previous chapter, capacity-based theories identify function based on the physical and chemical properties of objects. Since physical and chemical properties of objects are context-independent, in these theories, technologies' function remains the same in all contexts.

Although capacity-based theories and Baker's intentional theory are both entity realistic theories, they differ in that capacity-based theories are essentialist in the narrow sense of essentialism, but Baker's intentional theory is essentialist in the broad sense of the term. The narrow and broad senses of essentialism were explained in the introductory chapter of this book. Capacity-based theories are essentialist in the narrow sense of the term because the properties by which they define function are intrinsic to objects. Baker's intentional theory is essentialist in the broad sense of the term because the properties by which it defines function are extrinsic properties, derived from the relationship between an artefact and the designer. As explained in chapter 2, this is also the sense in which the definition of artefacts, as objects which are purposefully modified, is essentialist.

Preston's Theory

Entity realist theories of function are not restricted to intentional and capacity-based theories. Beth Preston's theory of function, for example, is a mixture of the evolutionary and capacity-based theories and is another example of an entity realist theory:

> Unlike naturally occurring objects, manufactured tools are designed for a specific use, and normally have a standardized form. More importantly,

they are identifiable as tools – indeed often as specific kinds of tools – apart from *any* actual occasions of use. A hammer is a hammer even if it never has and never will be used for hammering; and even if it has actually been used for something else entirely, e.g. as a paperweight or a wall decoration. But what grounds this individuation? The observable features of the object in front of you and its individual causal history are at best reminders of an independently known *normal* use history of objects relevantly like this one. Just as a stone may bear characteristic marks of actual usage as a hammer, so the Sears Craftsman implement in front of you looks like a hammer. It has a characteristic shape, for instance, and is made out of characteristic materials. There are clues to the specific use *for* which it was designed and made, and for which objects like this are normally used. It is this normal use, mediated by the design and manufacture process, which determines what the object is. But since the individual object does not have to have ever been *actually* used for this purpose in order to continue to count as a hammer, and indeed may actually have been used for something else, the individual *causal* history and the non-individual *normal use* history come apart in this case. What you need to know is what people normally do with things of this sort; not what has actually been done with this one. So some considerations essential to individuating a manufactured object cannot be read off the object itself, no matter how complete our description or how thorough our knowledge of its causal history. Without these non-individualistic considerations we cannot even say for sure *that* this is a tool, never mind what sort of tool it is. (Preston, 1998, 518, italics in original)

Preston, therefore, holds an entity realist position both in her general and particular categorisations of technologies. She holds an entity realist position in her *general* categorisation of technology as she believes that if there is no non-individual normal use history for an object, one cannot say that the object is a tool. She defines normal use by what people normally do with a particular item. According to Preston, a tool is a tool only if it belongs to a general category of objects which have been normally used as tools; a tool is not a tool because it is used to help users achieve practical goals. For her, a rock used to hit nails into a wall is not a tool even if it is always used for that reason, because it does not belong to a general category of objects that are normally used for this purpose; there is no non-individual normal use history for the rock. On the other hand, for Preston, the hammer mentioned in the preface of the book is always a tool, even if, as an artwork, it was hung on a wall in an aesthetically pleasing way: 'What you need to know is what people normally do with things of this sort; not what has actually been done with this one' (ibid.). This is an entity realist general categorisation.

Similarly, Preston takes an entity realist position in her *particular* categorisation of technologies with her non-individual identification of function. For her, even if a hammer is always used as a paperweight, its function is not that of a paperweight. Its identity as a paperweight is not recognised. What gives the hammer its functional identity are things that it keeps in all contexts as its essential properties: its physical features, its non-individual normal use history and the intention of its designers to reproduce more of the same object as other hammers. What *this* individual hammer is used for is irrelevant for its identification.

As such, Preston is interested in the collective identity of objects, not in their individual identity. Objects acquire their collective identity through a shared history of use and production, a shared genealogy. In this regard, Preston's identification of objects is similar to identification of an individual through their family name, something which an individual shares with those with the same ancestors. However, people of different genealogies may end up doing similar things, and those with shared ancestors may lead different lives. Likewise, objects with different histories may be used in the same activities and for the same purposes, and those with similar histories may be used in different activities and for different purposes. Entity realist theories struggle to recognise these kinds of dynamic, contextual variations.

Preston acknowledges that her theory of proper function does not say much about individual instances of use. Hence, she later appeals to the notion of 'system function' to explain instances where actual uses of objects deviate from their proper function (Preston, 2013). System function is a notion developed by Cummins (1975, 2002) and is the phrase that causal-role theories of function often use to explain biological functions. For example, causal-role theories describe the system function of the heart as a blood pumping organ in the system of the body: the heart plays the role of pumping blood; it causes blood to circulate in the body.

Preston argues that in the case of material objects which are used for purposes other than their proper functions, we can focus on the causal roles which objects play in the systems in which they are used. A hammer which is used, say, as a paperweight or as a gardening tool to cut thick weeds plays a causal role with its environment, respectively, to exert pressure on a pile of papers or to cut thick weeds. Preston refers to these roles, or functions, of the hammer as the system functions of the hammer. For Preston, system functions describe the causal roles that objects play in practice, and unlike proper functions, they do not say anything about how objects should be identified. Preston's notion of system function, therefore, is similar to the notion of accidental function. As mentioned in the previous chapter, accidental function is often proposed to make sense of the phenomenon of creative use.

In this way, Preston argues that proper functions disclose something about the production history of objects, and as such, they are culturally and historically significant. This is something that system functions do not do. System functions only tell us about specific uses of objects by specific individuals. They do not disclose anything about why the artefact has been reproduced.

ASSESSING ENTITY REALIST THEORIES OF FUNCTION

In addition to making distinctions between proper functions and system (or accidental) functions, another common way in which entity realist function theories can be expressed is through a distinction between the concept of function and that of *functioning-as*. Those who adhere to the distinction between functioning and functioning-as would say, for example, that the function of a hammer is pounding objects; but a hammer can also function, for example, as a paperweight. The function of an anti-shoplifting gate is to draw attention to possible cases of shoplifting. But it can also function as smart goals in football matches. The distinction between function and functioning-as, therefore, can be mapped onto the distinction between proper functions and system (or accidental) functions. Functioning-as, similar to system function, is supposed to refer to what the object is used for in practice, and function, similar to proper function, is supposed to reveal something context-independent about the object.

Regardless of the way entity realist function theories are expressed, arguments similar to those used in chapter 2 to show the practical irrelevance of the artefact/non-artefact distinction can be used here to show the practical irrelevance of the distinction between proper functions and system (or accidental) functions, or between function and functioning-as.

From an activity realist point of view, all that matters for functional identification of objects is functioning-as. What matters is the ways in which objects are used in practice. Factors which are irrelevant to the context of use should not affect the identification of objects. Identifying an object based on its proper function may be completely irrelevant for the context of use: it may be irrelevant to the role that the object plays in practice.

An activity realist, therefore, can also question Preston's distinction between proper and system functions. Why are proper functions privileged over system functions in identifying objects? What makes them *proper*? And what makes *them* proper, as opposed to fluid functional identities? Is something more significant achieved when an object's 'proper function' is identified compared to when its 'system function' is identified? And if the answer is yes, then the question is, more significant in the context of what values? The significance of anything is assessed against a set of values. What makes proper functions more significant than system functions?

It is true that if we value the cultural significance of the reproduction history of objects, then proper functions become culturally significant. However, if this argument is used to justify why proper functions are *overall* more significant than system functions, then there are two problems with this line of reasoning. First, this is a circular argument. The significance of proper function is justified by its very own definition. One still needs to argue why it is important to consider the cultural history of objects in the first place. Second, even if we accept that understanding the reproduction history of objects is valuable, there is no reason to limit our values to this particular value and give it more weight than other values. If we value creativity and artistic expression more than following customs and traditions, for example, we would privilege system functions over proper functions. When we do so, we could even change our vocabulary and describe these two functions differently in order to highlight where our values lie. For instance, we could refer to 'proper function' as 'conservative function' and 'system function' as 'authentic function'. So, although there may be motivations to privilege proper functions over system functions, there are equally reasonable motivations to privilege system functions over proper functions.

The entity realist believe that while technologies can function as other technologies, they have some universal identities which are more significant than the actual roles which they play. This claim is expressed *as if*, among all potential identities, material objects find one particular functional identity more appealing than others and choose it as their proper function to maintain wherever they go. But why should a hammer always be identified as a tool to pound nails even if it is used as a paperweight, to fix a bike's inner tube, play a game of croquet or cut thick garden weeds? Why should aspirin always be identified as a painkiller even if it is used by some people only to prevent heart problems? And in general, why should we privilege one function over the others and decide to see it as *the identifying* function of the technology? Such entity realist identifications only distort the identities that objects acquire in practice.

The second activity realist criticism of the distinction between proper and system functions is that such a distinction is not practically useful. As argued in chapter 2, usefulness requires impact. Something is useful when it can have desired impacts in the activities in which it is used. A border is useful if we are expected to behave differently on either side of it. A metaphysical distinction is practically useful if we need to use different decision-making and evaluative frameworks for objects that belong to different sides of the distinction. In other words, a practically useful distinction is one that can play a role in decision-making and normative frameworks. However, the distinction between proper and system functions does not require the use of different decision-making frameworks or different normative standards to evaluate objects' use. The decision to use an object to tighten a screw, for example, and the evaluation of the act of using an object for this purpose are indifferent to the distinction between proper and system functions. A knife used in the capacity of its system function to tighten a screw may be even more suitable for performing this task than a screwdriver which is identified with the proper function of tightening or loosening screws. In fact, Preston acknowledges that 'having a proper function is not contingent on exercising that function, or even on having the capacity to exercise it' (Preston, 2013, 196). This means that using an object based on its proper function may even lead to irrational practices, as it would be irrational to use an object for a particular purpose when it does not have the capacity to be used for that purpose.

Thus, the distinction between proper and system (or accidental) functions, or between function and functioning-as, has no impact on decision-making and normative frameworks. This renders the distinction not impactful and of little to no practical use. If we want to make normative assessments of objects, we need to examine how they are actually used and what their intended impacts are. Identifying objects according to some essence which may be unrelated to the impacts that users aim to achieve by interacting with them does not help with practical decisions and evaluations.

Thus, the main reason to reject the entity realist theories of function is that they lead to context-independent identification of objects. On the one hand, this context-independent identification distorts how objects should actually be identified in practice, and on the other hand, it is irrelevant for decision-making and normative evaluations.

ENTITY REALISM, THE CAUSAL THEORY OF REFERENCE AND THE STUDY OF KINDS

So then, what are the entity realist theories of function useful for? Entity realist theories are not user-friendly metaphysical theories of function because they lack context sensitivity and categorise and identify objects based on their essential properties. But this does not mean that these theories have no place in the general study of functions. In fact, entity realist theories of function can supplement the linguistic study of function. In other words, from the activity realist point of view, while entity realist theories cannot be used to metaphysically *identify* objects, they can be used to explain how objects are *referred to*.

In the previous chapter, it was argued that the linguistic and metaphysical studies of function are independent from each other: the terms used to refer to objects do not necessarily say anything about their functional identity. It was also argued that the evolutionary theories of function complement the causal theory of reference to explain how speakers of language can successfully refer to objects of different kinds by using their names. The causal theory of reference draws a socio-historical link between the instance of using a term to refer to an object and the instance at which the object was initially named. In the case of artefacts, evolutionary theories of function highlight this link which connects users to the history of artefact production.

Now, if we use the causal theory of reference in the linguistic study of function, how can entity realist theories of function complement this linguistic theory? Before this question can be addressed, a few words need to be said about the causal theory of reference, and its conceptual and historical relationship with the study of natural kinds.

It has been argued that the causal theory of reference makes metaphysical assumptions, and in particular, it requires accepting an essentialist position in metaphysics. This is particularly argued in the case of natural kind terms, such as terms used to refer to elementary particles, chemical compounds or biological species (e.g. 'positron', 'water' or 'kangaroo'). The reason for attributing this essentialist assumption to the causal theory of reference is that in this theory, terms which refer to natural kinds *necessarily* do so: the reference of the term is necessarily identical with what it refers to. In other words, in these theories, it is impossible for a natural kind term to *not* refer to the natural kind that it names. For example, according to the causal theory of reference, it is impossible for the term 'water' to not refer to the chemical compound which is made of two Hydrogen and one Oxygen atoms; water is necessarily H_2O. This is because in the causal theory of reference, the reference of a term is *fixed* at the instance of naming, making it impossible for the term not to refer to what it was named to refer to.

One interpretation of the necessity of the identity between the reference of a term and the natural kind to which it refers in the causal theory of reference has been an essentialist interpretation. In this interpretation, the reference of the term is fixed by an essence which remains the same in all possible circumstances where the object may appear. For example, in the case of water, it has been argued that water is essentially H_2O; or in other words, H_2O is the essence of water, and this is why the term 'water' necessarily refers to H_2O.

This is where entity realist theories of function come into play. The essentialist reading of the causal theory of reference and the entity realist theories of function both assume the existence of an essence which defines, respectively, the reference of a term and the function of an object. This common essentialist approach deprives users from assigning their personal identity to terms or objects. In the causal theory of reference, what fixes the reference of a term is external to the speakers; that is, speakers cannot willingly decide for the term to refer to something else. Similarly, in entity realist theories of function, the user of an object has no authority to determine the function of the object. The object's proper function is set, say, by the intentions of the designers or the production history of the object. In this way, entity realist theories of function are similar to the causal theory of reference.

More specifically, entity realist theories of function can explain why terms which refer to artefact kinds have fixed referents. What fixes the reference of the term for the causal theory of reference is what is purported to be the essential properties of artefacts by entity realist theories. So, for example, it can be argued in this view that the reason why the word 'hammer' always refers to hammers (and not to other objects) is that all hammers have their functional properties in common; these properties constitute the essence of hammerness; and this essence fixes the reference of the term 'hammer' to hammers and only hammers. So, this is what entity realist theories of function can be useful for: they complement the linguistic study of function by identifying the essential property of objects which is required to fix the reference of terms.

Nevertheless, we need to be careful of the conclusions that we draw here. The conclusion is *not* that because entity realist theories are essentialist theories, then by endorsing their usefulness for the linguistic study of function, we should also endorse essentialism in relation to the metaphysical study of function. The essence which is used to fix the reference of a term does not play any role in identifying an object's function. It merely fixes the reference of the term. What fixes the term's reference does not say anything about the functional identity of objects – at least not in the user-friendly, activity realist way of identifying objects.

It should be noted here that essentialist theories of function can also contribute to a different project in metaphysics of technology, which is also governed by the entity realist approach. This broader project, which will be discussed in the third section of the book, aims to examine the ontological status of artefact kinds (Meijers, 2009; Franssen et al., 2014). Essentialist theories of function contribute to the study of artefact kinds in that examining function as an essential property can be helpful with the task of defining artefact kinds. It can, then, be argued that accepting the entity realist notion of proper function commits one to accepting the existence of artefact kinds. While this chapter examines the limitations of entity realist theories of function, chapter 9 will examine entity realist ontological theories.

As noted earlier, the causal theory of reference is historically and conceptually connected to a project similar to the project of studying artefact kinds in philosophy of technology, which is that of studying natural kinds in philosophy of science. Before concluding this section, it is worth mentioning a few words about this historical connection and about whether it is warranted for philosophy of technology to follow in the footsteps of philosophy of science in this regard.

In classical philosophy of science, it made sense to talk about kinds because scientifically postulated entities are believed to be mind-independent. But the post-empirical turn, analytic metaphysics of technology uncritically followed the footsteps of analytic philosophy of science and sought to conceptualise technologies through the same methods and questions that were used to study scientific theories. However, there is no reason to define the research agenda of the metaphysics of technology on the basis of the same questions that governed the metaphysics of science in the twentieth century. Technologies are useful objects. Unlike scientific knowledge which can be valued intrinsically, technologies, first and foremost, help us to achieve practical goals. The categorisation of technologies, therefore, should not necessarily be guided by a search for essential properties, which reveal some form of universal truth about the world. Given that the usefulness of each technology is determined in relation to contextual elements, context-independent properties cannot lead to a satisfactory categorisation of technologies.

Moreover, one of the reasons why the study of kinds is scientifically valuable is that science aims for simpler conceptualisations of reality. Simplicity is considered a virtue of scientific theories by philosophers such as Willard van Orman Quine and Joseph Silbert Ullian (1978) and Thomas Kuhn (1962). One effective way to simplify the scientific explanation of reality is through using generalisations and appealing to fewer theoretical terms. This is why the study of natural kinds is valuable, because it strives to provide a simple and coherent picture of the natural world. But the motivation to provide a simpler and more universal explanation of reality does not apply to philosophy of technology simply because most technologies do not have the epistemic role of explaining and predicting events. Even though, as discussed in chapters 5 and 11, some technologies can be used in epistemic activities, such as scientific experiments, technologies are characterised by their practical problem-solving roles.

Given that technologies can be used differently and can have different consequences in different contexts, the function of a technology should be defined based on what we believe it actually does. This is an individualistic task and should be dealt with on a case-by-case basis.

FROM INTERNALIST TO EXTERNALIST THEORIES

Given the practical irrelevance of entity realist theories, we now know what a user-friendly theory of function should *not* look like. But what *should* a theory of function look like?

To guide the task of developing a satisfactory theory of function, let us contemplate the following question: what are we saying when we make claims like 'this object is for ɸ-ing'? The answer to this question is illuminating because a practically useful theory of function should be sensitive to the *reasons* for which objects are used. This theory should group all objects which are used for the same purpose, say for ɸ-ing, into the same category. This should be a dynamic categorisation; it does not fix the function of objects. Rather, it gives a fluid functional property to objects, allowing them to be placed in different categories at different times.

In response to the above question, capacity-based theories would argue that we need to look at the physical structure of objects to determine their function; by saying that an object is for ɸ-ing, and we are making claims about the object's physical structure.

Of course, if an object does not possess the right physical structure, it will not be able to ɸ. For instance, if an object does not have any wheels, it cannot function as a bike. But this does not mean that by saying that something is for cycling, we are making claims about its wheels. We may *imply* that it has wheels, but that is not the central claim. In general, by saying that something is for ɸ-ing, we are *not* making claims about that object's physical structure. The claim about the object's physical structure might be *implied*, but it is not the main claim.

When we say something is for ɸ-ing, we are, more than anything else, expressing our beliefs about the changes occurring in the world during and after the object is used and about what we can achieve in the process of using it. For instance, when we identify the function of what we call 'an airplane' as a flying vehicle, we do not make any claims about how it looks or its physical structure. Rather, we refer to the fact that when we use that object in a certain way, people can travel with it in the air from one place to another. In fact, a plane's physical structure suits the function of a flying hostel too. But we identify its function as a flying vehicle because it is used as a flying vehicle and not as a flying hostel. Of course, if a person or a group of people use an airplane as a hostel, it will have the function of a flying hostel. This is in the same way that ships which can be used for navigation between different locations on water can also be used as holiday getaways, as is the case with cruise ships. As another example, when we identify the function of an object as an anti-shoplifting gate, we do not make claims about its physical capacities; rather, we refer to the fact that the object, when used in a particular way in a certain context, will create outputs that we interpret as the object alerting us to possible cases of shoplifting. However, the same object can also be used in football games as a smart goal. In that context, we identify its function differently because we believe that the consequences of its use as a smart goal are to help us decide whether the football has crossed the line.

It should not be surprising, however, that capacity-based theories cannot explain cases in which a single object can receive different functional ascriptions when being used for different purposes in different contexts. After all, these theories identify technologies' function with their intrinsic physical characteristics and therefore hold an entity realist position. These theories only consider what is internal to technologies to determine their function, and what is internal to technologies remains the same in all contexts. Any other theory which looks inside technologies to define their function would also be pragmatically unsatisfactory as it would separate the study of function from the purposes for which technologies are actually used and the impacts that they have in their context of use.

Rather than focusing on what is internal to technologies, in order to define their function, we can change our perspective. We can focus on what is external to technologies. This may help to avoid the problems associated with entity realist views. Intentional theories are examples of externalist theories of function. Intentional theories suggest that the source of function is human intention, which, unlike technologies' physical characteristics, is external to technologies.

FROM INTENTIONAL TO BELIEF-BASED THEORIES

Can intentional theories avoid entity realism? Not necessarily. When in intentional theories intention is interpreted as the intention of *designers*, we will end up with another entity realist definition of function. Although in such theories, technologies acquire their function from an external source (i.e. designers' intentions), after this moment of function ascription, the function stays with the technological object in all contexts as its universally identifiable feature. Once a designer assigns a given function to a technological object, that function becomes a necessary and inseparable identifying feature of the object.

As explained earlier, Baker's theory of function falls into this category of intentional, entity realist theories. She defines proper function based on designers' intentions, as an essential property of technologies (Baker, 2004). In her view, what we call an 'anti-shoplifting gate' retains its function as an anti-shoplifting gate, even if it has always been and will always be used in soccer matches as a smart goal.

But how about identifying the source of technologies' functions in users' intentions instead of those of designers? In this way, the source of function remains something external, and function would be defined in a context-sensitive and fluid way. For instance, if someone decides to use an anti-shoplifting gate as smart goals in football matches, the function of that object does become that of smart goals, and it remains so until it is used in a different context and for different purpose.

User-oriented intentional theories of function take a step in the right direction, by avoiding entity realism. However, they are still not satisfactory from a pragmatic point of view. The problem with theories which reduce technologies' function to users' intentions is that they result in counter-intuitive conclusions. According to user-oriented intentional theories, for instance, one can intend to use an airplane, a computer or a football, respectively, as a cup, a boat or a voltmeter, and the fact that these objects are intended to be used as cups, boats and voltmeters provides good reasons to understand their functions as being cups, boats and voltmeters. This is not an acceptable conclusion because there is no way for airplanes, computers and footballs to function as cups, boats and voltmeters. User-oriented intentional theories, therefore, are too permissive in how they assign functions to physical objects. Kroes (2012) has discussed this problem of permissiveness of the intentional theories of function. Criticising mainly McLaughlin's intentional theory, Kroes discusses how in intentional theories 'whether or not the object is actually able to perform the function is not important for the function attribution' (Kroes, 2012, 37).

One might try to defend user-oriented theories against the above examples by relying on the distinction between functioning and malfunctioning technologies and argue that the objects in those examples would be malfunctioning technologies. In making this argument, one can insist that we can assign the function of a cup to an airplane if it is intended to function as a cup, but if it does not in reality function as a cup, we can just define it as a *bad* cup. Bad cups are, nevertheless, cups. We might even say the same about computers used as boats or footballs used as voltmeters. Computers and footballs will not be good boats or good voltmeters, but they would still be boats and voltmeters if someone intends to use them for those reasons.

In response to the above argument we can make yet another distinction, a distinction between malfunctioning technologies and non-technologies. There are objects in the world which can function as a specific type of technology, for example, as an object from which to drink liquids. Among these objects, some do the job better than others: a cup is more suitable for enabling us to drink liquids than a jam jar. A jam jar is a more suitable vessel for drinking liquids than the lid of a jam jar. And perhaps the lid of a jam jar is more suitable than a cup which has a small hole in it. The lid of a jam jar or a cup with a small hole in it could, therefore, be seen as malfunctioning cups. A malfunctioning technology is not a technology which has stopped working. Rather, it is a technology which still more or less does the job required of it, but it does not do the job very well. The lid of a jam jar can be used to keep liquids, but not much liquid can be contained in it. A cup with a small hole in it, too, can be used for drinking liquids, but the liquids may slowly drip out of it. Neither object would function very well for this purpose: they would *mal*function.

In addition to objects such as the lid of a jam jar or a cup with holes in it, there are also objects in the world which cannot be used to drink liquids at all. A sieve, a branch of a tree and an airplane are among these objects. The point about these objects is that one cannot even say that they are not very suitable for enabling us to drink liquids. They simply must be ruled out as objects which can be used for holding liquids that we wish to drink. The reason for this is that we cannot justifiably believe that a sieve, a tree branch or an airplane can help a user to solve the problem of drinking liquids from an open, waterproof and portable container. Cups can have this function because we can use them to keep hot beverages on our desk or in our hands in a way that we would also be able to drink them without burning our hands. Sieves, tree branches and airplanes are useless in solving this problem. In dealing with the problem of drinking liquids, they would not be malfunctioning technologies; they would be non-technologies. Similarly, a broken TV does not qualify as a malfunctioning TV. It would be a non-TV, even though we are still justified in *calling* it a 'TV' for reasons explained in the previous chapter.

So, intention is not sufficient to define an object's function. But now the question is, is intention even necessary? Do people need to intend to use an object to be able to define its function? The answer is still no. One can relate to an object through pure observation, without any form of intention to use the object. Despite lacking intention to use the object, they can still justifiably identify the function of the object by observing others using it. As an example, imagine an anthropologist who has never heard of the game cricket and who, while visiting Australia, watches some games of cricket on free-to-air TV. The anthropologist can sit back and observe what cricket bats do in a game of cricket. They probably never form any intention to play cricket, let alone of being a cricket player. Their relationship to cricket bats would be only ever as an observer. But does this lack of intention to use cricket bats prevent them from identifying the function of cricket bats? No. Despite their lack of intention, the anthropologist can still identify the function of cricket bats as objects used to hit cricket balls in a game of cricket. This act of function ascription by observing others intentionally use an object can be called 'observational function ascription'. Observational function ascriptions show that intention to use an object is not necessary for function identification.

Here someone might argue that intentional theories can be modified by making provision for observational function ascriptions. In this modified version of intentional theories, one does not need to personally form the intention to use an object. But nevertheless, it is necessary for 'someone' to intend to use the objects for the person to be able to identify the object's function. In the cricket example above, the observer may not intend to use the cricket bat, but for them to be able to identify the bat's function, someone (i.e. a cricket player) needs to use the cricket bat.

There are two points which should be mentioned in response to this modified version of intentional theories. First, in this version of intentional theories, one assigns a function to an object by observing others using it. This means that for this modified version to have explanatory value, there must always be at least one person who is using the object or there will be no act of use to be observed. However, the existence of at least one user is not always necessary for identifying the function of an object. A person might, for example, successfully design a time machine which can only take them forward to a minute before they die. For obvious reasons, that person may never even intend to use this time machine. Moreover, because the person may not show the machine to anyone else, even if some strangers might hypothetically be interested in using the machine, the person would also be unable to observe others use the machine. But the person's lack of intention to use the machine and their inability to observe others use the machine does not prevent them from identifying its function as that of a time machine. Therefore, observational function ascriptions do not require the presence of intention to use the object by anyone.

Second, observational function ascriptions can be generalised to all cases in which a person identifies an object's function without intending to use it themselves. This generalisation is to acknowledge that function identification can be achieved without the presence of any intention to use the object. In this general sense, observational function ascriptions do not strictly qualify as intentional theories. This is because in observational function ascriptions, function identification primarily relies on the observer's *beliefs* about what is intended to happen in the world, and not on the *user's intentions*. It is, thus, more appropriate to refer to observational function ascriptions as 'belief-based' rather than 'intentional'.

Two sets of cases can explain why observational function ascriptions, in their general sense, rely on what observers believe to be the case. The first set of cases occur when the intention to use is lacking altogether. This was described in the previous example of the time machine which no one intends to use, but whose function can be identified as a time machine. In the second set of cases, there may be a user, but the user may not intend to achieve any particular goal by using an object, and instead only aimlessly 'play' with the object. Despite the user's lack of intention to achieve any goal, an observer may still interpret the user's interactions with the objects as intentional, goal-oriented behaviours and assign a function to the object based on their beliefs. Therefore, what constitutes function identification is the subject's beliefs about an object's potential role; the presence of an intention to actually use the object for a particular goal is not necessary.

SUMMARY

Entity realist theories used for the particular categorisation of objects through defining their function are also known as essentialist theories of function.

Given the contextual-insensitivity of entity realist theories of function, here it was argued that these theories face two problems: they distort how objects should actually be identified in practice and they are irrelevant for decision-making purposes and normative evaluations.

Entity realist theories can complement the causal theory of reference and the linguistic study of function. The causal theory of reference is historically and conceptually linked to the study of natural kinds in the analytic metaphysics of science in the twentieth century. However, technologies and scientific theories play different roles, and there is no justification for philosophy of technology to implement approaches of philosophy of science and look for essential properties of objects.

Theories of function in philosophy of technology should recognise and conceptualise dynamic interactions between users and objects. In this analysis, no particular function should be regarded as more essential or proper than others because theories of function are not meant to disclose something context-independent about objects; they are meant to conceptualise different functional identities which objects acquire in different contexts.

All of the three dominant types of the metaphysical theories of function which were introduced in the previous chapter, namely, intentional theories, capacity-based theories and evolutionary theories, lead to function essentialism. Intentional theories can avoid function essentialism if, instead of designers' intentions, they identify function in relation to users' intentions. However, on the one hand, such user-oriented intentional theories are too permissive and, on the other hand, the presence of an intention to use an object is not necessary to identify the object's function. This point was clarified with the example of observational function ascriptions where a person identifies an object's function without intending to use it.

The example of observational function ascriptions shows that a user-friendly theory of function needs to define function in relation to the beliefs of the person who identifies an object's function. Belief-based theories can provide a starting point to build a user-friendly, activity realist theory of function. Such a theory would avoid the problems associated with entity realist theories and those with user-oriented intentional theories. The next chapter, as the final chapter of this part of the book, develops and explores a belief-based theory of function.

Chapter 8

A User-Friendly Theory of Function

Belief-based theories of function can be defined as those which identify objects' function in relation to the beliefs of reflective beings. Beliefs, however, can be about different things, such as the object which is being used, its users and the environment in which the act of use is happening. So, unless the object of belief is clarified, belief-based theories are not specific enough to define function.

If a belief-based theory identifies an object's function in relation to a person's beliefs about the physical structure and characteristics of an object, then the theory can be called a 'belief-based structural theory' of function. Belief-based structural theories would define function based on what reflective beings believe the physical structure of each object is capable of. However, the physical structures of objects usually remain the same in all contexts, and most people's beliefs about the physical structure of objects do not change either. This means that in belief-based structural theories, for most people, the function of an object remains the same in all contexts. Due to this context-insensitivity, belief-based structural theories resemble entity realist theories, particularly capacity-based theories. Capacity-based theories, as defined in chapter 6, define function in relation to the physical properties of each object. Because belief-based structural theories are context-insensitive, they would suffer from the same practical inadequacies of entity realist theories of function which were discussed in the previous chapter.

However, the difference between belief-based structural theories and capacity-based theories is that belief-based structural theories are relative to the individual. Since individuals can have different epistemic access to, and different beliefs about, the physical structure of an object, a single object might have different functions for different individuals. Capacity-based theories prevent this relativity because the actual physical capacities of objects are independent of individuals' beliefs, and in capacity-based theories, function is defined in relation to actual physical capacities of objects, not what people know about those capacities. In general, all belief-based theories are relative theories because different individuals can have different beliefs about the same object.

To avoid the practical shortcomings that belief-based structural theories and entity realist theories of function face, the particular categorisation of technologies can follow an activity realist approach. The activity realist approach was used in the first part of the book to produce a practically useful definition of technology, as a general category of objects. This general definition of technology was developed by examining the notion of usefulness. A similar approach can be adopted here to develop a practically useful theory of function.

As discussed in chapter 2, usefulness is a relational property and is characterised by desired impact: something is useful for a particular purpose if it can have desired impacts in the activities in which it is used. For a particular categorisation of technology to be useful, it needs to define function in relation to the impacts of using objects.

A form of belief-based theories of function which can be built upon this analysis of usefulness would be the *belief-based consequentialist theory* of function. In the belief-based consequentialist theory, identifying the function of an object amounts to having particular beliefs about what that object could bring to its surroundings, or what the intended impacts of its potential use would be.

The belief-based consequentialist theory avoids entity realism as people's beliefs about the impacts of using an object are context-sensitive. Depending on how an object is used, it can have different consequences, and as such, the function by which it is identified can change. Consider the case of the hammer. When the hammer is used as a puncture-repair kit, its intended consequence of use would be to put pressure on a puncture patch on a bike's tube; when it is used as a croquet mallet, its intended impact would be to hit croquet balls; when it is used as a gardening tool, its intended impact would be to cut garden weeds.

Now, how exactly is the function of an object identified in the belief-based consequentialist theory of function? And what are the conceptual and practical ramifications of this method of function identification? According to the belief-based consequentialist theory of function,

the function of an object is identified by justified beliefs about the intended impacts of its use.

The remainder of this chapter explores this definition and investigates some of its conceptual and practical consequences.

THE BELIEF-BASED CONSEQUENTIALIST THEORY

One of the key terms used in the belief-based consequentialist theory of function is the word 'use'. In identifying an object's function, this theory does *not* take into account the impacts which the object automatically leaves on its surroundings by virtue of its properties. Rather, it focuses only on the impacts of its *use*. If all impacts were considered, each object would automatically acquire the function of being a space-filling object.

Additionally, in this definition, not *all* impacts of using an object contribute to the identification of its function. Only those impacts which are believed to be *intended* constitute the functional identity of the object. Otherwise, one of the functions of a bike helmet becomes spoiling cyclists' hairstyles; one of the functions of internal combustion engines becomes polluting the environment; and one of the functions of asbestos becomes causing cancer. The reason why the objects in these examples do not have those functional identities is that we do not believe that anyone uses bike helmets with the intention of spoiling their hairstyle, cars with the intention of polluting the environment or asbestos with the intention of causing cancer. Of course, if we believe that some people do use some bike helmets to spoil their hair, cars to pollute the environment and asbestos to cause cancer, then these intended consequences would be used to identify the functions of the helmets, cars and asbestos used in those cases. But in general, although any act of use can have unintended consequences, only the intended consequences are constitutive of the functional identity of objects. The emphasis on intended consequences rather than all consequences differentiates between functional effects and side effects.

Nevertheless, the fact that the focus of this definition is on the intended impacts of use does not make this theory an *intentional* theory of function. As discussed in chapters 6 and 7, intentional theories define function in relation to human intentions. In the belief-based consequentialist theory, however, function is defined in relation to human *beliefs about the intended impacts of use*. Having beliefs about the intended impacts of use does not require the presence of an intention to use. Technologies need not be used or even intended to be used to be identified with a given function. Even non-users can identify objects' functions based on what they believe the intended impacts of objects' possible use would be. The example of the time machine given towards the end of the previous chapter highlights this point. A person may never intend to use a time machine which can take the user to a minute before their death. But the person is still able to identify the function of that machine as a time machine if they believe that that is the consequence of using the machine. Therefore, intended impacts of use need to be believed to constitute the functional identity of objects, but this does not mean that the object needs to be intended to be used.

Another feature of the belief-based consequentialist theory of function is that depending on the purpose of the activity in which an object is used, different consequences can be intended. Accordingly, a single physical object can have more than one function. This makes this theory of function a pluralist theory as it gives a fluid functional identity to objects. For instance, for a physician, an aspirin can be a pain-reliever, a blood thinner and a cancer-preventing drug. The hammer mentioned in the preface of the book can be an inner-tube-repair weight, a croquet mallet and a weed-cutting tool.

Houkes and Meijers refer to this feature of objects – the feature which allows them to be identified with multiple functions – as the 'underdetermination' of function. They argue that any satisfactory metaphysical theory of artefacts should be able to explain that each material structure can realise a variety of functions (Houkes & Meijers, 2006, 120). Kroes, on the other hand, refers to this characteristic of technologies as 'multi-functionality' (Kroes, 2001), and Preston as 'multiple utilisability': 'Artifacts are *multiply utilizable*. Some artifacts are designed to serve only one function, but more typically they are designed to serve several, often simultaneously' (Preston, 2009, 215, italic in original).

Of course, as shown in chapter 2 and in the previous chapter, limiting the scope of a theory of function to artefacts arises from a misplaced, entity realist position. A satisfactory theory of function should be able to explain the functional properties of all objects, not just those of artefacts. Nevertheless, in the belief-based consequentialist theory each object can be multi-utilised. Multiple utilisability makes the belief-based consequentialist theory a pluralistic theory, as in this theory objects can acquire various functional identities.

The counterpart of multiple utilisability is 'multiple realisability'. Multiple realisability, as Preston defines, is the idea that functions can be realised 'in a variety of materials and/or forms, provided some general constraints are satisfied' (Preston, 2009, 215). So, while multiple utilisability connects one physical object to multiple functional identities, multiple realisability connects one function to multiple objects. The belief-based consequentialist theory of function also accounts for multiple realisability of function. Two or more objects, with different physical structures, can have similar functions if it is believed that the intended consequences of their use are the same. For instance, a person who needs to tighten a screw can reasonably believe that they could achieve their goal by using a knife, a screwdriver or a credit card. For that person, in that situation, the knife, the screwdriver and the credit card all acquire the identity of screw tighteners; the function of tightening screws is realised in different objects.

In addition to being pluralistic, the belief-based consequentialist theory is also relative. In this theory, one and the same object can be categorised differently by different people based on perceptions that each person may have of the consequences of using the object. Mark Perlman has also discussed the relativity of function identification:

> When they [i.e. users] do provide explanations of their behavior and use of objects, an 'objective' outsider might ascribe different functions to behaviors than the practitioners do. . . . Thus some religious ritual might be seen by those who practice it . . . as involving tribute to a deity, and the artificial objects used in the ritual might be said by the adherents of that religion to have various supernatural functions. But an anthropologist might analyse the situation as one in which the behaviors serve to reinforce kinship relations, and the object functions as status indicator and economic vehicle, even if no one in the group has the intention, and even if no one in the past ever had that intention. (Perlman, 2004, 28)

The relativity of function identification is derived from the fact that function identification is a subjective matter, and can vary depending on the subject's interpretations. The belief-based consequentialist theory is able to explain this relativity because it is a belief-based theory and different individuals can form different beliefs about the intended impacts of using the same object.

Another example which can demonstrate the relativity of function identification is the ways in which the functions of the internet and social media are identified. Totalitarian governments often find the internet and social media as dangerous means, and for this reason, they increase online surveillance and restrict or completely block the citizens' internet access. For these governments, the internet and social media are politically destabilising tools which are used to leak government secrets or organise protests. This is one way they identify the function of the internet and social media. On the other hand, many people use email services and social network websites to connect with their friends, relatives and acquaintances. For these people, the internet is a tool for communication. Some others use the internet as a means in order to connect with others who work in the same profession as them, join online workshops and seminars, and have online team meetings and discussions. This is something that many people have been doing during the restrictions imposed due to the Covid-19 pandemic on social gatherings. In the belief-based consequentialist theory, different people can have different beliefs about the impacts of using an object. A single object can have different functional identities for different people.

This also means that totalitarian governments are not necessarily making any philosophical mistake in identifying a free internet as a tool which threatens their existence. If they justifiably believe that their citizens intend to use the internet to leak their secrets or organise protests, they are right in identifying the function of the internet as a destabilising tool. If there is any problem with the totalitarian governments' acts of increasing online surveillance and filtering and blocking online websites, it is a moral problem. However, this moral problem is itself conditioned by the way in which they identify the function of the internet. Depending on how the function of a technology is identified, different possibilities of moral decision making can arise. The presence of a technology, in other words, as discussed in chapter 5, can condition one's perception of moral values.

Here it is worth mentioning that the relativity of function identification in the belief-based consequentialist theory does not render this theory too permissive. Although in this theory a single object can be seen as having different functions for different people or for one person, this does not imply that any function identification is acceptable. In the belief-based consequentialist theory, beliefs that are used to identify an object's function need to be *justified*. And this takes us to a significant point to be explicated in this theory of function.

JUSTIFIED BELIEFS VS. TRUTH

The belief-based consequentialist theory defines function based on *justified* beliefs regarding the intended consequences of using an object, not based on *true* beliefs. Each object can have multiple functional identities, and no particular function is 'truer' than others. In fact, truth is a notion which is more suitable for entity realist theories. In entity realist theories, objects retain their functional properties across all contexts. As discussed in the previous chapter, entity realist theories appeal to concepts such as 'proper function' or 'normal use history' in order to define essential functional properties of objects independently of how users interact with them. So even though entity realist theories may accept multiple utilisability of objects, for them there is still a universal truth which defines what objects are supposed to do, regardless of people's interactions with them: 'Because of the multiple realisability of structure, knowing what something now does will not tell you for sure what it *is supposed to do*' (Preston, 2013, 145, italic added). In entity realist theories, the truth and falsity of acts of function identification are assessed against what is purported to be the essential functional identity of an object. A function identification is a true function identification if it matches the purported essential functional identity.

However, in an activity realist theory of function, given that an object can be used in different activities, and depending on the purpose of each activity, the object can acquire different functional identities, truth becomes an irrelevant notion. There is nothing truer in the hammer used as a weight on the puncture patch of an inner tube than the one used for cutting garden weed. There is nothing truer about a knife used to peel an orange than the one used to tighten a screw. In this activity realist theory, function is defined in relation to the intended impact. Because it does not make sense to claim that one particular intended impact is truer than others, it is equally meaningless to claim one functional identification is truer than others. Objects' functional identity is exhausted by individuals' justified beliefs about them. There is nothing more into objects' functional identity than these beliefs.

The fact that the belief-based consequentialist account relies on justified, rather than true, beliefs can be further clarified with an example. Imagine that at the time when the theory of phlogiston was accepted in the seventeenth and the eighteenth centuries, scientists used certain instruments to measure the amount of phlogiston flow from one object to another. Let us call those objects 'phlogiston-meters'. According to the belief-based consequentialist theory, for those who believed in the phlogiston theory, the function of phlogiston-meters was to measure the amount of phlogiston flow. Since the beliefs of those phlogiston-meter users were justified by the theory which they upheld, phlogiston-meters had the function of measuring phlogiston flow for them. For anyone who did not or does not believe in the theory of phlogiston, or more specifically, for anyone who did not or does not justifiably believe that the changes in the gauges of phlogiston-meters indicate the amount of phlogiston flow, the function of those instruments is not to measure phlogiston flow.

The emphasis of the activity realist theory on justified beliefs also differentiates the belief-based consequentialist theory from pure consequentialist theories, such as that of Larry Wright's classic theory of function. Wright's 1973 article is one of the early pieces written on the topic after what is referred to by a few authors as 'the recent philosophical resurrection of theories of function' (Perlman, 2004; Hughes, 2009). According to Wright (1973, 161), saying that the function of X is Z means:

a. X is there because it does Z,

b. Z is a consequence (or result) of X's being there.

In order to define an object's function, similar to the belief-based consequentialist theory, Wright's theory gives a significant definitional weight to consequences. But this emphasis on consequences also highlights the differences between these two theories. Consider the question: which consequences? And consequences of what? Wright's answer is, the consequences of the technology's *being there*. But as several authors have pointed out, this statement is ambiguous (Boorse, 1976; Godfrey-Smith, 1994; Hughes, 2009). The ambiguity is partly due to the fact that Wright's aim was to give a general theory of function which can be used for both technological and biological functions. However, there are some relevant distinctions between technological and biological functions. In the case of technological functions, there is necessarily a form of intentionality involved: only the consequences which are believed to be intended and result from acts of use should contribute to the definition of function. But in the case of biological functions this intentionality is absent, and there is no meaningful act of use. The heart does not pump blood because someone intends it or uses it to pump blood. So, 'being there' for biological organs has a different meaning from 'being there' for technologies. Unlike biological organs, technologies are intentionally used. (The relationship between use and technological-ness was discussed in chapter 4.)

The main difference between the belief-based consequentialist theory and Wright's theory is that the former theory relies on justified beliefs whereas Wright's theory relies on objective facts. This allows the belief-based consequentialist theory to be pluralist in the ways discussed earlier. Wright's theory, however, is more rigid: X does Z; an object's function is the same for everyone. In the example of the phlogiston-meter, Wright's theory would defer deciding the functional status of phlogiston-meters to the truth or falsity of the phlogiston theory. X either does Z or it does not. Phlogiston-meters either measure the flow of phlogiston or they do not. In this way, he would either say that phlogiston-meters never had the function of measuring phlogiston flow, or that they have always had, and will always have this function. In the belief-based consequentialist theory, phlogiston-meters had the function of measuring the flow of phlogiston for those who believed in the phlogiston theory in the eighteenth century, but these objects do not have that function for us because we do not justifiably believe that they measure the flow of phlogiston.

Note that the fact that an object can have a specific function for a group of people and not for others has nothing to do with the truth or falsity of the beliefs of either group. Rather, the difference in function identification shows that the two groups rely on different justification frameworks. Acceptance of a scientific theory provides a method for justifying one's beliefs. This method of justification is unavailable for those who do not accept the theory. Those who accept the phlogiston theory rely on different justification frameworks compared to those who do not accept the phlogiston theory. Accordingly, the former group can justifiably identify the function of phlogiston-meters as measuring phlogiston flow, while the latter group justifiably believe that phlogiston-meters do not measure phlogiston flow. Neither of these function identifications is truer than the other.

Note also that given the distinction between linguistic categorisations and metaphysical categorisations discussed in chapter 6, everyone can justifiably *refer* to those instruments as 'phlogiston-meters'. However, the linguistic phrases used to refer to an object do not necessarily reveal its function.

The conclusion of the example of the phlogiston-meter can also be generalised to the instruments which are currently used to measure scientifically postulated entities or phenomena. Since there is no guarantee that the current scientific theories will not be abandoned in favour of future theories, the function of the instruments which are currently used in scientific experiments can change over time. A machine which is currently used in scientific experiments may lose its function if at some point scientists do not believe that what the machine measures is real or has such and such measurable effects. The interaction between scientific reality and technologies will be examined in further detail in chapter 11.

Cases like that of the phlogiston-meter, where the object is later believed not to have the function it was once identified to have, involve the phenomenon of function change. Function changes create problems for entity realist theories of function as these theories cannot explain how an object can be a phlogiston-meter in one era but not a phlogiston-meter in a different era. This is because entity realist theories define function based on static, universal properties as some form of truth about objects. This feature of entity realist theories of function reveals at least two other explanatory weaknesses.

First, entity realist theories of function are unable to differentiate between justified and unjustified cases of function identifications. Those who did not believe in the theory of phlogiston, for example, considered the identification of the so-called phlogiston-meters as machines which measured the amount of phlogiston flow to be a mistake. Nevertheless, this function identification was justified for those who had accepted the phlogiston theory. At the same time, there can be cases where it is simply not plausible to justify a particular function identification. For example, there is no imaginable justification framework which can be used to identify the function of a football as a voltmeter. Entity realist theories, however, cannot distinguish between cases in which people justifiably, but, according to some, mistakenly, identify an object's function (the phlogiston-meter) and cases in which an object cannot be justifiably said to have a given function altogether (the football as a voltmeter). These theories treat both cases equally by labelling them as improper function identifications.

Second, entity realist theories of function, and more specifically, the evolutionary theories which define function in relation to the reproduction history of objects, are unable to explain the function of novel prototypes. Novel prototypes are artefacts which are recently designed and tested, but have not been introduced into society yet. If someone designs a robot for brushing people's hair, that technology will be a novel prototype until it is widely used and produced in society. In evolutionary theories, such as Preston's, novel prototypes do not have proper functions because they lack a history of use and reproduction (Preston, 2013). According to Preston, novel prototypes can only have system functions (defined in the previous chapter) which for her do not have the same status as proper functions in identifying objects.

However, for a practically useful theory of function there is no reason to discriminate between the way the function of novel prototypes are identified and the way the function of repeatedly reproduced technologies are identified. Due to the role which the patterns of use and reproduction histories play in Preston's theory of function, her theory is fruitful for cultural and anthropological studies. However, there is no reason to metaphysically or practically differentiate between objects which have a reproduction history and those which do not. What we need to consider, from a practical point of view, is the reason for which objects are used and the impacts which their use can have on their surroundings.

Additionally, a practically useful theory of function should enable us to identify the function of objects whose reproduction history is unknown to us. Any evolutionary theory which relies on an awareness of the reproduction history of objects to determine their function is unable to meet this requirement. This is because sometimes we may not have any epistemic access to the reproduction history of an object, and sometimes an object may not have any reproduction history at all. However, we still want to be able to identify the function of those objects and use this identified function to evaluate their use. The example provided in chapter 2 can further clarify this point.

Imagine (1) a mass-produced hammer, (2) a rock and (3) a small object lying on a river bank. The third object, which we believe is a piece of sandstone, was in fact purposefully carved and regularly produced and used by members of a past civilisation. Both the first and the third objects have histories of use and reproduction, but we believe that only the first object has such a history. Now, consider these objects are being used to (1) hit tent pegs into the ground, (2) break a window to escape from a building which is on fire or (3) threaten someone in order to take their money. Do the hammer, the rock and the small object have different functional identities in each one of these scenarios? Does the reproduction history of the hammer and the small object give them a different function compared to the rock? And does our lack of awareness of the reproduction history of the small object give it a different functional identity in those activities than the hammer? Not really. In general, neither the reproduction history of an object nor our beliefs about this reproduction history affect the practically relevant functional identity of objects.

The belief-based consequentialist theory of function does not discriminate between novel prototypes and commonly used technologies. Nor does it rely on our knowledge about the history of objects. It allows us to identify the function of different objects, including objects which do not have a reproduction history and those whose reproduction histories are unknown.

BLACK BOXES AND NON-MATERIAL CONSEQUENCES

A black box is an object or system for which there is not enough, or any, knowledge of its internal components. Everything which can be known about a black box is through its interactions with its surroundings. Many modern electronic devices, for example, are black boxes for most people. Most people do not have any knowledge of the internal components of these devices. People can only observe the interaction of electronic devices with their surroundings through their inputs and outputs. So, how can the function of a black box be identified?

Identifying the function of a black box creates problems particularly for theories which require the knowledge of the physical properties of objects for function identification. Belief-based structural theories, mentioned in the beginning of this chapter, are an example of such theories. These theories define function in relation to one's beliefs about the physical capacities of objects. When no knowledge of the physical capacities of an object is available, function identification becomes problematic for belief-based structural theories. More specifically, the lack of knowledge about an object's physical capacities can create a particular and a general problem for belief-based structural theories.

The particular problem arises in cases such as electronic devices mentioned earlier. When some users do not have any knowledge of the physical capacities of objects, there is at least one particular group of people who, according to the belief-based structural theories, are not able to identify the function of the object, even though they regularly use the object. The general problem is that in some cases, the knowledge of the physical capacities of objects may be unknown to everyone and/or this knowledge may be irrelevant altogether. A good example here would be objects which play cultural or religious roles. As mentioned in the introduction of this book, technologies can be seen as class markers for some people and function as the material expressions of social identity. Such cultural functions of objects are not causally brought about by their physical structures. As an example, consider the Black Stone, located in Kaa'ba, which plays a significant role in Muslims' pilgrimages. Not only are the Black Stone's physical properties unknown to worshippers, the scientific study and description of the Black Stone can be considered to be sacrilege. So, can belief-based structural theories respond to these objections?

One theory of function that has elements of the belief-based structural theories is the ICE theory of Houkes and Vermaas (2010). As mentioned in chapter 6, the ICE theory also has elements of intentional and evolutionary theories. ICE is a theory about the justification of function ascriptions: it is concerned with how one's beliefs about the function of an object are justified. How are function ascriptions justified in the ICE theory? What role do beliefs about the capacities of objects play in this theory? These two questions receive a joint answer in the ICE theory. In this theory, function ascriptions are justified through beliefs about objects' physical capacities. According to the ICE theory, saying that the function of an object x is to ϕ amounts to justifiably ascribing the physicochemical capacity to ϕ to x, relative to a particular plan of use (Houkes & Vermaas, 2010). In other words, in the ICE theory, assigning a particular function to an object means justifiably believing that the object's physical capacities, when used in a particular way, can assist the user to achieve particular goals. Thus, this is how beliefs about the physical capacities of objects are incorporated into the ICE theory: they play justificatory roles.

Houkes and Vermaas are aware of the particular problem that the lack of knowledge about an object's physical capacities can create for their theory. If such knowledge is required for the justification of function ascription, then most users are not able to justifiably ascribe functions to complex artefacts, such as modern electronic devices. In response, Houkes and Vermaas discriminate between designers and users in the way each group can justify their beliefs about objects' function. Designers have a knowledge of the physical capacities of their products, and they can directly justify their beliefs by reference to those capacities. Users, on the other hand, have the option of justifying their beliefs through the testimony of designers. This can happen, for example, through manuals and promotional videos. Even though users may not understand how the physical capacities of an object contribute to its function, they rely on the testimony of the designers to justifiably draw the link between the properties of the object and its function.

Although Houkes and Vermaas's ICE theory sufficiently addresses the particular problem that the lack of knowledge about an object's physical capacities can create for belief-based structural theories, the general problem derived from this lack of knowledge remains unanswered. As explained earlier, this general problem arises particularly in cases, such as culturally or religiously significant objects, where objects' physical capacities are not only unknown, but also potentially irrelevant in the role which objects play. These cases create an intractable problem for any theory which draws some link between function identification and the physical capacities of objects.

So, how would the belief-based consequentialist theory of function identify the function of black boxes and objects whose functions are not linked to their physical capacities? Neither of these two types of cases create problems for the belief-based consequentialist theory because this theory does not define the functional identity of objects in relation to their physical properties or beliefs about those properties.

In belief-based consequentialist theory, the knowledge of the physical properties of objects can provide *one* route to justifiably believe that the object would have such and such impact. As mentioned in the previous section, justification is an important feature of the belief-based consequentialist theory. Indeed, in some cases of function identification, one way to justify one's beliefs would be through a reference to the physical properties of objects. For example, someone who knows Archimedes' principle of buoyancy can explain why a metal barrel can float on water and acquire the functional identity of a boat. This person would justify their belief regarding the impacts of using the barrel as a boat by reference to the physical properties of the barrel and the causal link between those properties and the surrounding water.

However, this is only one out of many possible ways of justifying one's belief that a barrel can function as a boat. One can simply appeal to inductive reasoning to justify this belief without any reference to, or awareness of, Archimedes' principle of buoyancy. In this way, one can simply tell oneself that all previous barrels floated on water, so this particular barrel would also float on water. In fact, historically, Archimedes' principle came long after humans were building and using boats, and were assigning the function of objects which stay afloat and can be used for carrying people and goods on water to their boats. Therefore, awareness of the causal links between the physical properties of an object and its environment is not necessary for identifying the object's function.

Similarly, the belief-based consequentialist theory can be used to determine the functional identity of a black box without any reference to the designers of the black box. This is because in this theory, function identification does not require the knowledge of, or imply anything about, objects' physical capacities. The black box's function can be identified merely by observing its inputs and outputs and making inferences about its impacts on its surroundings.

Here it is worth mentioning that the practice of function identification of a black box based on observing the black box's interaction with its environment is also used in a branch of control engineering called 'System Identification'. In this branch of control engineering, black box models are sometimes used in order to identify a system's function. This method of function identification is achieved solely through observing and measuring the interactions of a system with its environments through the system's inputs and outputs.

In belief-based consequentialist theory, thus, function identification requires observing what happens *outside* an object as a consequence of its use; it is an externalist theory of function, in the sense defined in the previous chapter. Although in this theory, understanding objects' physical capacities can be helpful to justify individuals' beliefs about objects' functions, such understanding is not required to identify objects' functions.

Because the belief-based consequentialist theory does not make any links to objects' physical capacities in identifying their function, this theory can also explain non-material consequences of objects' use and incorporate them in the functional identity of objects. Non-material consequences are often contingent on the social contexts in which an object is used and manifest themselves particularly in culturally or religiously significant objects, such as the Black Stone. The function of the Black Stone is identified via its intended impact in the practice of pilgrimage. This function can of course be identified subjectively. Worshippers may believe it helps them to connect to their prophet; anthropologists and sociologists may believe it impacts the social behaviour of groups of worshippers. But in either case, there is no obvious link between the Black Stone's functional identity and its unknown physical properties. These functions are identified by non-material consequences. Some other examples of function identifications that consider non-material consequences of objects' use might include showcasing a symbolic object to strengthen community ties, listening to a piece of music to promote mental health and using prayer beads for their spiritual significance. The functions of objects in these examples are not explainable by studying their physical properties.

SUMMARY

This chapter marked the conclusion of the second part of this book. It provided and explored a theory of function which particularly categorises objects based on their usefulness, which, as defined in chapter 2, is determined by their impact. In this activity realist theory of function, an object's function is identified based on what is justifiably believed to be the intended impact of its use. This particular categorisation gives a fluid and relative identity to objects. It is fluid because at each point in time, each object is categorised with other objects which are believed to have similar intended impacts. A hammer, a rock and a chair are all ascribed similar functions when they are used as weights in the context of repairing a punctured inner tube to exert pressure on the puncture patch. A hammer, a weed killer and a whipper snipper are all ascribed similar functions when they are used to get rid of garden weeds. A hammer, a croquet mallet and a golf club are all ascribed similar functional identities when they are used to hit a ball in a homemade game of croquet.

This particular categorisation is relative because different people can identify an object's function differently. A rock used in religious ceremonies can play a holy role for the worshippers, yet be identified with its impact on the community of worshippers by an anthropologist. Social media can be identified as platforms to connect with friends by some people, yet be identified as a tool to destabilise a nation and organise protests by totalitarian governments. A phlogiston-meter can be identified with the function of measuring the phlogiston flow by those who believe in the theory of phlogiston and be identified as a piece of junk by those who do not believe in the theory. There is nothing true or false about functional identities of objects. Objects' functional identities are derived from their usefulness.

The linguistic categorisation of objects, on the other hand, as discussed in the previous two chapters, is static and universal. A hammer can always be called 'a hammer' by everyone regardless of what roles it plays, and a piece of rock can always be called 'a rock' by everyone regardless of its impact on individuals or groups.

The next part of this book will deal with the third branch of the metaphysics of technology, namely, ontology.

Part III

ONTOLOGY

Chapter 9

Existence of Artefacts

Ontology is a subfield of metaphysics that deals with questions on being, on what is and what is not. The claims 'unicorns do not exist' and 'electrons are real' are examples of ontological claims. In the metaphysics of technology, ontological discussions have revolved around questions such as these: 'Are technologies real in the same manner that lakes, rocks, and trees are?' 'Can technologies' existence be reduced to the existence of the material objects that they are made of?' 'Does the creation of new technologies add anything to reality?'

The reason why technologies are ontologically particularly interesting is that it seems that technologies have something extra which entities like lakes, rocks and trees do not have. The existence of lakes, rocks and trees can be defined through their material descriptions. Lakes are environments that are made up of interactions between an extremely large number of molecules which cover a given area on earth. Rocks are formed as a result of strong chemical bonds between a large number of atoms. And trees are biological systems made up of different types of cells which in turn can be broken up into smaller molecules. Even though such descriptions do not explain their social and cultural *significance*, it is possible to describe the *existence* of lakes, rocks and trees by describing their material constituents. However, it is questionable whether the same thing can be said about technologies such as hammers, tables and dishwashers when used as technological objects. These objects seem to be more than mere physical objects. As argued in chapter 5, a full description of technologies needs to also take into account the necessity of the presence of reflective beings with certain mental capacities who condition the reality of technologies. Technologies are not merely lumps of matter; they are what they are partly because reflective beings want them to be what they are. Without the presence of reflective beings, in other words, there cannot be any technologies. This ontological dependence of technologies on reflective beings is often referred to as 'the mind-dependence of technologies'. The mind-dependence of technologies cannot be explained by their material constituents.

Similar to other subfields of the metaphysics of technology, research into the ontology of technologies has also been largely pursued through an entity realist approach. The entity realist approach in this subfield of the metaphysics of technology can be diagnosed in two prominent features of the current literature. The first feature is the focus on artefacts and their ontological status. As explained in chapter 2, artefacts are defined in an entity realist fashion. Hence, any metaphysical study of artefacts would have its subject matter defined in an entity realist way. The second prominent feature of the current literature is that its notion of being, or in other words, its understanding of ontology, is also shaped by the entity realist approach. This chapter focuses on this second feature, as the first feature was extensively discussed in the second chapter of the book. After unwrapping the entity realist notion of being, this chapter provides a brief summary of the arguments presented against and in support of the existence of artefacts and artefact kinds.

AN ENTITY REALIST NOTION OF BEING

What does it mean for an ontological exploration to be conducted through the entity realist approach? What does it mean for a notion of 'being' to be an entity realist notion?

Entity realism is a metaphysical approach that characterises objects based on their universal properties. In other words, identifying universal properties which accompany objects in all contexts is the approach of entity realism. Pursuing ontology through this approach requires characterising being as a meta-property of objects; a meta-property which is inseparable from its bearer. In this notion, being is an absolute matter. Anything which is, is. And anything which is not, is simply not. For example, according to the entity realist notion of being, the claim 'electrons exist', if true, would be true regardless of worldly states of affairs. Whether it is morning or evening, whether there is war or peace, whether or not Joseph Thomson had conducted his cathode ray tube experiments, whether any atomic theory is developed, or whether humans or other animal species live on the planet Earth or not, the existential status of electrons does not change. Similarly, in the entity realist approach, the claim 'unicorns do not exist', if true, would indicate the absence of unicorns, and regardless of all stories, songs, animations or toys which are produced about unicorns, unicorns would not come into being.

So, entity realism approaches and characterises being from its signature universal perspective. In addition to its universality, the entity realist notion of being is a binary notion. This notion is similar to what we ordinarily mean by the term 'existence' and its verbal form 'to exist'. Things either exist or do not exist. Nothing exists to a lesser degree than other existing things, and the existential status of objects is independent from their role in the activities of reflective beings. This entity realist notion of being is the same notion which is meant in questions, such as 'do numbers exist?', 'is there a God?' or 'does dark matter exist?' When we ask these questions, we are expecting yes-or-no answers. We are also not asking where they exist, how we can know they exist or whether it is possible for us to perceive numbers, God or dark matter. These latter questions would be the subject of an epistemological inquiry, concerning the ways in which we can gain knowledge of numbers', God's or dark matter's existence. The ontological question simply is whether such things as numbers, God and dark matter exist, regardless of our perceptions, beliefs and practices.

Similarly, in the case of technologies, the entity realist question is whether technologies exist or do not exist. For example, do hammers exist or do not exist? Note that here the question is not whether the bits and pieces which constitute a hammer exist or do not exist. The answer to this latter question is almost uncontroversially positive. Rather, the question is whether in addition to the bits and pieces which constitute a hammer there is also a hammer, as a whole. In other words, the question is whether the existence of a hammer can be reduced to its bits and pieces *or* whether there is something more to hammerhood which exists besides a hammer's constituents.

All entity realist theories share this absolute notion of being as a universal and binary meta-property of objects. But different metaphysical theories differ in their criteria for existence. Consequently, different theories make different ontological commitments and include divergent objects in the realm of being.

ENTITY REALISM AND THE ONTOLOGY OF ARTEFACTS

Artefacts, as defined in chapter 2, are (1) intentionally (2) modified (3) material objects. Moreover, most artefacts that enter society (at least, currently) are also (4) mass-produced. Each of these four features of artefacts (i.e. being mass-produced, being material, being modified and being the products of intentional acts of design) makes the existence of artefacts, as distinct from the existence of their constituents, questionable. A few words can be said about problems that these features raise for the ontology of artefacts.

The first problem concerns only mass-produced artefacts. Do all mass-produced replications of an original object independently exist? Mass-produced objects are copies of original prototypes. Even if the existence of the original is accepted, there are reasons to be sceptical of the ontological status of individual tokens of mass-produced objects. Each copy is meant to represent the original. The copy is not meant to be something different. In fact, if a copy were different from its original, it would not be regarded as another original, but as a bad copy. So, on the one hand, copies take their existence from the original, and if the original did not exist, copies would not either. And on the other hand, it is questionable whether copies add anything new to the world which has not already been added to the world by the original. Their constituents are different from the constituents of the original, but the existence of artefacts is supposed to be different from the existence of their constituents. As wholes, copies do not seem to add anything new to the world. Consider artworks as an example. Copied artworks do not seem to add anything new to the art world. There is only one original, and the rest are merely copies. There is only one *Starry Night*, and its copies do not have the same status. Copies of *Starry Night* do not have anything novel which Vincent van Gogh's *Starry Night* does not have.

The second feature of artefacts which makes them ontologically problematic is their materiality. It can be argued that the causal powers of artefacts can be reduced to those of the physical structures of which they are constituted, and that, if artefacts really existed as distinct from their constituents, an artefact and the lump of matter constituting it would have had to occupy the same spatial point at the same time (Merricks, 2001; van Inwagen, 1990).

Third, the fact that artefacts are by definition modified objects also makes one wonder whether they add anything to the realm of being which is not already added by their constituents. Artefacts are products of modifications made to existing objects; they do not naturally exist in the world. But does the process of modification create new beings, as distinct from the things which were modified? It is hard to maintain the absolute, entity realist notion of being, yet assert that the process of modification adds something new to the realm of being. Such an assertion would have counter-intuitive ramifications.

For example, if modification adds new items to the group of things which exist, does destruction also take something away from the totality of existing things? Consider the process of creating or decoupling a hammer. When the head and the handle of a hammer are put together, an artefact is constructed. But it is counter-intuitive to claim that suddenly, as the head of the hammer is put together with the handle, something new has been added to the realm of being, and as soon as the head is detached from the handle, something has vanished. Moreover, what happens when an artefact is reconstructed? For example, what happens when the handle of the hammer is replaced by a different handle? Does the previous hammer suddenly cease to exist and a new object comes to exist? As Franssen et al. (2014) have shown, deconstruction and reconstruction create challenges for generating plausible existence conditions for artefacts. Similarly, Peter van Inwagen (1990) has argued that composite material objects including artefacts do not exist. According to him, the only way in which the process of composition leads to new existing entities is when living organisms are generated. For example, van Inwagen would argue that animal species and humans exist in addition to cells which they are composed of. This is because, as wholes, animal species and humans are also *alive*. But artefacts are not alive and in their case, the process of composition does not lead to the creation of new existing entities.

Fourth, the fact that artefacts are products of intentional design processes also has implications on their existential status. Designers' intentions, as one of the essential features of artefacts, render artefacts mind-dependent. But how can something created by the mind actually exist? Fictional characters are also created by the mind. Do fictional characters also exist? It is self-contradictory to acknowledge the existence of fictional characters. Thus, unless further stipulations are made to the conditions of existence, entities either do not exist or, if they do exist, their existence is mind-independent. In other words, it is contradictory for something to exist and be mind-dependent. Accepting the mind-dependence of artefacts implies that artefacts do not exist. Only their mind-independent material constituents exist.

These objections show that it is difficult, if not contradictory, to ascribe ontological status to artefacts. As a result, some philosophers have changed their focus from assigning existence to individual artefacts to assigning existence to artefact *kinds*. As explained in chapter 7, artefact kinds are often defined based on the notion of proper function. Artefact kinds are also meant to play a role in philosophy of technology similar to the role that natural kinds play in philosophy of science. Natural kinds are what we discover through empirical sciences, although some elementary particles and other unstable instances of natural kinds can exist only in controlled environments, such as laboratory conditions. Nevertheless, by discovering natural kinds, we identify things which exist in the world, including entities whose existence is fleeting. Similarly, one may argue that by identifying artefact kinds, we reveal something about what exists in the world. In this way, one may claim that hammers, tables and dishwashers exist out there in the world, in the same way that electrons, water molecules and animal species exist.

But are natural kinds and artefact kinds metaphysically similar? After all, a commonly accepted metaphysical characteristic of natural kinds is their mind-independent nature (Kripke, 1980; Searle, 1995, 2007). Natural kinds are *discovered*. But artefact kinds are not really discovered; they are *constructed*. And anything which is constructed would be mind-dependent. And, again, anything which is mind-dependent does not exist in the same sense that mind-independent things exist.

It can be argued that natural kinds are also partly constructed, and to an extent, membership in natural kinds is arbitrarily decided. Philosophers such as John Weckert, for example, believe that even in the field of philosophy of science, talking about kinds does not say as much about the essential features of the entities as it says about our linguistic categorisations (Weckert, 1986). As an example, consider the categorisation of whales and bats as mammals rather than as fish or birds. Because the general category of mammals is defined as all species that give birth to their live offspring and breastfeed them, whales and bats belong to the category of mammals. But if the general categories of fishes and birds were defined as species which, respectively, only swim under the water and are capable of flying in the air, then whales would be fish and bats would be birds.

Nevertheless, the arbitrariness in the *categorisation* of natural kinds does not render the *existence* of natural kinds mind-dependent. Although linguistic categorisations are arbitrary and mind-dependent, they still need to match what exists in the world; otherwise, they would be fictional categorisations, such as vampires, unicorns and mermaids. In other words, even though linguistic categorisations are, to an extent, arbitrary, being a category in language does not in itself commit one to accept the existence of the category in the world. So, the way natural kinds are defined may be an arbitrary matter. But this arbitrariness does not affect the ontological status of the members of natural kinds. What is arbitrary is where the lines are drawn, not whether members of different sides of the lines exist or not.

The above argument, however, cannot be generalised to artefact kinds. Linguistic categorisations of artefact kinds only refer to socially constructed objects. In other words, in the case of artefact kinds, not only the linguistic categorisations but also things that these categorisations are meant to refer to are socially constructed. Artefact kinds are themselves constructed, and hence, mind-dependent. To repeat, they are not discovered. Their ontological status, from an entity realist point of view, is closer to that of vampires, unicorns and mermaids, rather than that of water, whales or bats.

HOW TO ASSIGN EXISTENCE TO ARTEFACTS

Some philosophers disagree with the claims that artefacts do not exist and that there is an ontological distinction between artefacts and natural objects. Of these philosophers, some question the natural/artefactual distinction in at least some types of artefact kinds (Elder, 2007), some claim that even if there is any distinction, maintaining the distinction is unhelpful (Baker, 2004), and some provide novel existence criteria which can be used to commit to the existence of mind-dependent entities, such as artefacts (Thomasson, 2009). These positions can be elaborated separately.

If it is contradictory for mind-dependent objects to exist, then one way to argue for the existence of artefact kinds would be through denying their mind-dependence. By denying the mind-dependence of artefacts and artefact kinds, one can treat instances of artefact kinds in the same way as instances of natural kinds. In this view, in the same manner that the existence of water, carbon dioxide, kangaroos and other physical and chemical elements and compositions is independent of a perceiving subject, the existence of hammers, tables, dishwashers and other artefacts would also be mind-independent. Accordingly, the ontological status of artefacts could be treated in isolation; their existence would not depend on their surrounding contexts, and their relation to humans would become a metaphysically peripheral issue. This position is often referred to as the 'realist' view towards artefact kinds.

One philosopher who defends a realist view towards artefact kinds is Crawford Elder. While Elder considers mind-dependence to be contradictory to existence (1989), he defends the mind-independent existence of some artefact kinds (Elder, 2007). Elder argues that 'copied kinds' (as a subgroup of artefact kinds) have a mind-independent nature (Elder, 2007). By copied kinds he means artefacts which are mass-produced and are mere copies of their original prototypes. His argument to show that copied kinds should be treated as natural kinds relies on the premise that members of copied kinds, similar to members of natural kinds, preserve the same essential properties in all their instances. As members of natural kinds share their essential properties, so too do members of copied kinds share their essential properties. Essential properties of members of copied kinds are their kind's function history. Each copied kind's function history, according to Elder, is its essential property:

> In the case of natural kinds usually discussed, the characteristic properties accompany one another in instance after instance, sample after sample, because of a common physical composition or microstructure. In the case of copied kinds, the properties essential to the kind accompany one another in instance after instance because of a common history of function. (Elder, 2007, 34)

Introducing a common history of function as an essential property of artefact kinds renders Elder's theory an evolutionary theory of function. As explained in chapters 6 and 7, evolutionary theories are entity realist theories of function that define an artefact's function in relation to the history of its kind's production. When function is defined as an essential property, it is often characterised as 'proper function'. Elder's position is significant because it draws a bridge between the particular categorisation of artefacts and the ontology of artefacts. It argues that accepting the entity realist notion of proper function in the particular categorisation commits one to accepting the existence of copied kinds.

Lynne Baker, on the other hand, questions the relevance of the distinction between artefacts and ordinary objects. Baker accepts that human intentions are partly constitutive of artefacts: 'An artifact's being the kind of thing that it is depends on human intentions' (Baker, 2004, 106). But she believes that neither this nor the fact that artefacts are made up of nothing but material elements provides a good reason to metaphysically downgrade artefacts in comparison to natural objects: 'there is no reasonable basis for distinguishing between artifacts and natural objects in a way that renders natural objects as genuine substances and artifacts as ontologically deficient' (Baker, 2004, 105). She argues that humans are also a part of nature and for this reason, human products should not be seen as different from other natural phenomena (Baker, 2004, 2008). Baker, therefore, puts artefacts and natural objects into one and the same ontological category.

A third path to defend the existence of artefacts and artefact kinds is to propose new conditions of existence based on which artefacts would exist. Existence conditions are criteria that determine what objects exist and what objects do not exist. They play an explanatory as well as a prescriptive role. On the one hand, existence conditions explain why those things that are intuitively accepted to exist do exist. And on the other hand, in the case of entities whose existence cannot be intuitively accepted, they prescribe whether they exist or not. For example, lakes, rocks and trees are entities whose existence can be intuitively accepted. And one way to explain this intuition is to look at what lakes, rocks and trees have in common. Lakes, rocks and trees have different features in common, including being found on the planet Earth. Being found on the planet Earth can explain the existence of lakes, rocks and trees, but it would not result in a defensible condition of existence for all entities. This is because it would not give the same ontological status to anything outside the planet Earth as it does to those which are on the planet. However, since Copernicus, it has been accepted that the existence of other planets and what lies on them is on a par with the existence of the Earth and what lies on it. Thus, we need to search for another common feature of lakes, rocks, and trees to explain their existence and generate a defensible condition of existence for all existing entities. One such common feature is being mind-independent. Mind-independence can explain the existence of anything which can be intuitively accepted to exist. As such, it may be generalised to generate an existence condition for all entities. After being accepted as a defensible condition of existence, mind-independence can be used as a condition of existence in its prescriptive role. In this way, the ontological status of any entity whose existence is questionable can be assessed against the criterion of mind-independence. The existence of mermaids, vampires and emotions is questionable; so the existence condition of mind-independence can be utilised to assess their existence. Because mermaids, vampires, and emotions are mind-dependent, they can be ruled out as existing entities. In this way, by changing existence conditions, objects which are accepted as existing entities may no longer be considered as existing, and objects which are determined to be non-existent may be included in the realm of being.

One philosopher who has questioned the legitimacy of the existence conditions which are used to assess the existential status of artefacts is Amie Thomasson. Thomasson abandons the idea that being mind-independent is the central criterion for existence and suggests that different existence conditions should be adopted for things of different kinds (Thomasson, 2009). She believes that the criteria of existence adopted by those who reject the existence of artefacts have been derived from a narrow set of objects and have been illegitimately generalised to all sorts of objects. The problem here is that the existential status of mind-dependent entities is assessed by criteria that are developed to explain the existence of mind-independent entities. And, in Thomasson's view, there is no convincing reason to generalise an existence condition which is derived from mind-independent objects to all entities. So, according to Thomasson, those who deny the existence of artefacts fail to provide a non-circular reason for their denial. It is unsurprising to conclude that artefacts do not exist, if the existence criteria assume that only mind-independent entities exist.

Thomasson proposes an alternative existence condition which can accommodate artefacts in the realm of being. She calls this existence condition 'the formal condition of existence'. According to her formal condition of existence, 'for any term "K", things of kind K exist just in case the application conditions critically associated with proper use of the term are met' (Thomasson, 2009, 208). Thomasson believes the formal condition of existence provides a neutral approach to existence.

Central to Thomasson's definition of the formal condition of existence is the proper use of terms. To distinguish between proper and improper uses of terms, application conditions of terms are needed. These conditions would determine whether a particular use of a term has been proper or not. If the application conditions of a term which denotes an entity are met, then the entity exists. In other words, in the formal condition of existence, as long as the term that refers to a particular entity satisfies its conditions of proper use, the entity exists.

But what are the application conditions of terms? For Thomasson, the application conditions differ for different terms. For some terms human intentionality (mind-dependence) is necessary, for some it is not:

Those conditions appeal to human intentionality in some cases, but not in others: so human intentionality of certain forms may be necessary and sufficient for the existence of a story or an imaginary object, merely necessary for the existence of an artifact, and completely irrelevant to the existence of a rabbit. But in each case, provided the relevant criteria *are* met, we have no reason to deny the existence of the relevant objects. In the case of artifacts, the application conditions for terms like 'table' are apparently are [*sic*] satisfied by the circumstances in my dining room and millions of others around the world. So if we combine the basic facts about meaning with obvious empirical facts, we can conclude that there *are* tables. (Thomasson, 2009, 197, italic in original)

Instead of providing one concrete condition of existence, Thomasson gives a generic criterion that leads to different conditions for entities of different kinds. This allows Thomasson to argue for the existence of artefacts, as their existence is assessed through a different condition than natural objects. Nevertheless, Thomasson's formal condition of existence is linguistically bound, in the sense that for any entity to exist, there needs to be a term in language which stands for it. As it will be argued in the next chapter, this creates limitations for what is included in the realm of being, especially if being is to be understood in a practically relevant way.

SUMMARY

This chapter focused on the third dimension of the metaphysics of technology, namely, ontology, which is the study of being. Most of the current works on the ontological status of technologies take an entity realist approach. On the one hand, they focus on artefacts, which as discussed in chapter 2, are defined in an entity realist way. On the other hand, and more importantly, these works understand being in an entity realist fashion, as the universal and binary notion of existence. Existence is defined as a meta-property which is shared by all existing objects regardless of their surroundings.

In the case of artefacts, several philosophers have argued that artefacts, *qua* artefacts, do not exist; only their constituents exist. Some others, however, have provided arguments to support the claim that artefacts, *qua* artefacts, do exist. These arguments are presented by revising the conditions of existence or the way we conceptualise artefacts.

The entity realist distinction between what does and what does not exist shares the character of practical irrelevance with other entity realist distinctions. The existential status of objects such as planets outside the Milky Way, mermaids and Hobbits does not say anything about people's attitudes towards them. Nor does the existential status of objects such as hammers, tables and dishwashers affect the practical decisions made to use these objects or the normative frameworks employed to evaluate their use. Hence, to create a practically relevant ontology, the notion of being needs to be reconceptualised. The next chapter proposes and explores an alternative, activity realist notion of being.

Chapter 10

Reality of Technologies

As mentioned in the previous chapter, the entity realist approach towards being generates conditions of existence for entities of different kinds. These existence conditions are binary and universal, and similar to other entity realist categorisations, their practical usefulness can be questioned. What can be gained by drawing a line between existing and non-existing entities? What is the practical impact of such a distinction? As discussed in chapter 2, a categorisation is useful when someone's practical decisions discriminate between what belongs and what does not belong to the category. The distinction between existing and non-existing entities is useful if it impacts practical decisions. And there are activities in which the existence of an entity and people's beliefs in the existence of the entity may seem to make a difference. The religious activity of worshiping a deity is a good example here. The activity of worshiping a deity presumes the existence of the deity, and it is meaningless for a person to worship a deity if, at the same time, they believe that the deity does not exist.

But in a number of other activities, including problem-solving activities, the *existential* status of objects is irrelevant. Consider someone who denies the existence of hammers, *qua* hammers, while believing that only the subatomic particles which constitute a hammer exist. How would this denial affect their use of hammers? Regardless of their denial, they can still use a hammer as a weight on the puncture patch of their bike's inner tube, a mallet in a homemade game of croquet, a tool to cut weeds out of a garden or a tool to smash electronic pieces out of an old washing machine. Neither the existential status of the hammer nor one's beliefs about its existential status would impact the practical decisions to use the hammer for different purposes. The same can also be said about the normative evaluations of using a hammer. The normative evaluations of using a hammer are independent of its existential status or people's beliefs in its existential status. Regardless of hammers' existential status and people's beliefs about their existential status, the act of stealing someone else's hammer remains morally impermissible. The entity realist notion of existence is practically irrelevant for such normative evaluations.

But there is another way to understand the notion of being. If being is understood as the presence of something significant, something which one relates to, then it would not be practically irrelevant for things to be or not to be. Compare a cup which may be sitting in a shed for years without anyone touching it or caring about it to another cup which is placed on someone's desk as a precious gift from their late grandfather. The existential status of both cups is the same: they both exist. But it can be argued that stealing the second cup is morally more wrong than stealing the first cup. This may be for the simple reason that stealing the second cup causes more harm. The first cup is not really there or anywhere, even though it actually is there. But the second cup is very well present at least for the person who is keeping it. There are many memories attached to it; many stories can be told about it. It is *significant*. Or consider the hammer mentioned in the preface of the book. There is a sense in which the hammer was more present for the housemate who engaged with the hammer by appreciating the beauty of the way it is hanging on the wall, talking about it and using it for different purposes, compared to the flight captain who never used it and probably never even noticed it.

What is this sense of being and how can it be captured? This sense of being is similar to what William James refers to as 'practical reality' which he contrasts with 'divine reality' (James, 1981). Divine reality for James is similar to the entity realist notion of existence: it is binary and universal. According to James, divine reality should be of interest only to God. Practical reality, on the other hand, is defined based on what is 'interesting and important to us' (James, 1981, 924). But how do we determine what is interesting and important? The activity realist approach can be used to capture this practically relevant notion of being: things become interesting and important through the activities in which they are used.

As the final chapter of the third part of the book, this chapter first proposes and explores the activity realist notion of being. After defending the problem-based reality of technologies, it argues that the activity realist notion of being is largely independent of the entity realist notion of existence.

AN ACTIVITY REALIST NOTION OF BEING

The activity realist notion of being can be referred to as 'reality', as distinct from 'existence', which is the entity realist notion of being. The reality of objects is activity-dependent: objects derive their reality from entering into the activities of reflective beings. For instance, the reality of engagement rings depends on activities which involve romantic relationships and marriages, the reality of mermaids and Hobbits is dependent on the activities that involve fantasy storytelling, and the reality of electrons depends on theoretical descriptions of electrons, scientific experiments that are used to detect electrons and devices which function on the basis of manipulating electrons.

John Dewey (1905) also discusses a similar notion of reality, which he refers to as the 'experienced reality'. The experienced reality of anything, according to Dewey, is defined in relation to the immediate experience of that thing: 'things are what they are experienced as' (Dewey, 1905). Experience for Dewey has a broad meaning: there can be different experiences of things, and each experience creates a new reality. For example, things can be experienced aesthetically, technologically, religiously or economically. These experiences are all real, and here, it can be said that each of them shapes the reality of things.

Hence, because objects can be used in various activities (or be experienced in various ways, as Dewey would put it), it is possible to talk about different dimensions of their reality, depending on the type of activity from which they derive their reality. For example, we can talk about the technological reality of something as distinct from its artistic or religious reality. A bicycle wheel, for example, is technologically real for the function that it has in a pushbike. But it could also be artistically real if someone uses it in a work of art, as Marcel Duchamp presented it in his *Bicycle Wheel* (Duchamp, 1913). Similarly, a Qibla Finder is an object that is epistemically as well as religiously real. As an epistemic object, it shows the geographical direction to a particular point on the planet. As a religious object, it enters Muslims' religious activities of praying to God.

The reality of objects is subjectively determined. Something that is real for one person may not be real for another person. Phlogiston was scientifically real for those who accepted the theory of phlogiston and perhaps built instruments and designed experiments that manipulated it. James Watt, for example, conducted experiments in which he believed he manipulated phlogiston to make water. For the twenty-first-century scientists, phlogiston is not scientifically real. This is *not* simply because the twenty-first-century scientists believe that phlogiston does not *exist*. Rather, it is because it has no place in the scientific activities of the twenty-first-century scientists. The hammer of the shared house mentioned in the preface of the book is real for the housemate who appreciates its beauty when it is hanging on the wall, talks about it and uses it for different purposes. But it is not real for the housemate who is indifferent about it.

This also means that the reality of objects is dynamic. An object which may be real for a person at a point can lose its reality for them later in their lives, or the other way around. Phlogiston was real for those who had accepted the phlogiston theory and conducted experiments involving phlogiston. But when they abandoned the phlogiston theory and reinterpreted their experiments, then phlogiston lost its reality for them. Similarly, the housemate who never paid attention to the hammer of the shared house can start using it or talking about it. And as the hammer enters their activities, it gradually becomes more real for them. This point brings us to the next important feature of reality.

Being real, unlike existing, can be a matter of degree. The degree to which an object is real depends on the number, variety and importance of the activities in which it plays a role. The reality of the dwarf planet Pluto, for instance, is shaped by few activities. These include the activity of using telescopes to observe Pluto and that of using scientific theories to describe Pluto's properties and its gravitational interactions with the planets of the solar system and other dwarf planets. The reality of water, on the other hand, is shaped by all activities that involve using water. These include, among many other things, drinking water to meet the biological need to stay hydrated, scientifically describing the structure of water molecules, writing poetry about water, using water to clean dirty items and generating hydroelectric power through watermills or turbines. Therefore, water is much more real than Pluto because there are many more significant activities in which water is used. The difference between the degree to which Pluto and water are real is despite the fact that the existential status of water and Pluto is equal from an entity realist view.

The independence of the reality of an object from its existential status also implies that a fictional entity can be more real than an existing one. Santa Claus and Hobbits do not actually exist. But, for most people, they are more real than planets which exist outside the Milky Way, to which there is no direct epistemic access. This is because, compared to planets outside the Milky Way, there are more varied activities in which Santa Claus and Hobbits play a role. Nevertheless, it is also possible for planets which exist outside the Milky Way to be more real for an astrophysicist than Santa Claus or Hobbits because detecting and theorising about those planets may be much more significant for the astrophysicist than the stories told, the games played and the cultural events organised about Santa Claus or Hobbits.

Note that Thomasson's approach towards existence can also be used to argue that Santa Claus and Hobbits exist also in the entity realist sense. As mentioned earlier, according to Thomasson's formal condition of existence, it is sufficient to say an entity exists if the application conditions associated with the use of its term are met. For the existence of fictional objects such as Santa Claus or Hobbits, the application conditions are derived from the linguistic conventions that regulate proper use of the terms in traditions and stories told about Santa Claus or Hobbits.

Nevertheless, there are some stark differences between Thomasson's notion of existence and the activity realist notion of reality. Some of these differences have already been mentioned: being real, unlike existing, is subjective, dynamic and a matter of degree. But there is another important feature of the notion of reality which can be highlighted in contrast to Thomasson's conception of existence. Thomasson's conception of existence is confined by language in a way that reality is not. Things can be said to satisfy the formal condition of existence, as Thomasson describes, only if there is a distinct linguistic term for them and that term's use conditions are satisfied. But not all real objects and events are captured by language. If there is no word for something, there would not be any conditions of proper usage for that word either, and for this reason, that thing cannot be said to exist in Thomasson's sense. But as long as that thing enters human activities, it would be real.

Think about feelings for examples. There are several linguistic terms for feelings, such as 'happiness', 'anger', 'hopefulness' and 'jealousy'. But there are also many situations in which a person may not be able to express their feelings with any of the existing words or may get confused by them. Consider the feelings which one may get by looking at an abstract art or listening to a piece of music. These feelings can be pre-conceptual: no linguistic term may stand for them. But such feelings are still real, as they would shape the person's attitudes and guide them to decide whether or not to purchase the abstract art or to recommend the piece of music. As another example, a person may not know whether their feelings for someone should be called 'love', 'lust', 'affection' or perhaps none of these words. In these situations, since the person is not equipped with any particular word, there is no term for which they can consider conditions of its proper usage, and hence, they cannot assess their existential status. But such feelings are real for the person as much as they are interesting and important. The person can make life decisions on the basis of those feelings. For things to enter the realm of being in the activity realist sense, therefore, they do not have to be accompanied by linguistic terms.

The point that entities can be real despite not being captured by language can also be noted in the case of technologies, such as those used in scientific experiments. As Davis Baird writes on the significance of Michael Faraday's electric motor:

> When Faraday made the device [i.e. the electric motor], there was considerable disagreement over how it worked. Today, many people still do not know the physics that explains how it works. Both then and now, however, no one denies *that* it works. . . . Whatever explanations would be offered to the device . . .

would have to recognize the motions Faraday produced. . . . Or to put it another way, we learn by interacting with bits of the world even when our words for how these bits work are inadequate. (Baird, 2004, 3, italic in original)

During scientific experiments conducted by means of technological instruments, real phenomena can be observed for which there may not be any corresponding linguistic terms. However, linguistic inadequacies do not necessarily stop scientists from accepting those phenomena as parts of scientific reality. The influence of technologies on scientific reality will be further explored in the next chapter. It will be argued that although theoretical, linguistic descriptions provide one pathway for entities to enter scientific reality, other activities such as experimental observations and practical applications can also shape the reality of scientific entities.

THE PROBLEM-BASED REALITY OF TECHNOLOGIES

As discussed in the first part of this book, in an activity realist philosophy, technologies are characterised by their problem-solving instrumentality. Think about objects used to stay dry in the rain or those used to clean the floor. Technologies can be as simple as basic tools or as complex as a particle accelerator. Whether simple or complex, they are used for problem-solving purposes. Accordingly, the reality of technological objects can be said to be derived from the reality of the problems they are used to assist in solving. If it never rained or snowed, and the sunlight was always moderate, people would have never used things like umbrellas or big leaves to keep themselves dry in the rain or protect themselves from ultraviolet rays. If there was no need to clean dust and the rubbish on a floor, either because cleanliness was not valued or because dust did not exist, it would have been senseless to invent and use vacuum cleaners. Technological objects, therefore, have *problem-based* realities. If there were no problems, objects would not acquire technological identities.

The problem-based reality of technologies implies that technologies are mind-dependent. This is because, as discussed in the introductory chapter of this book and in chapter 5, problems are always mind-dependent. In fact, there is no problem *simpliciter* in the world; rather, people's reports of problematic situations refer to their perceptions of those situations. A problem is a problem because it is perceived as a problem. Thus, because a situation can be a problem for one person but not for another, as discussed in chapter 4, the problem-based reality of technologies renders technological-ness a subjective matter. Something can be technologically real for one person but not for another.

The problem-based reality of technologies can be used to question an entity realist assumption in the field of metaphysics of technology. The assumption is that the property of being technological is abstracted from existing things which happen to have this property in common, just in the same way that the property of being blue can be abstracted from existing blue objects. The assumption is that technology is more fundamental than technological-ness; that there are things which are technologies, and the property of technological-ness is abstracted from them.

In the activity realist philosophy the order is reversed. Things become technologies by virtue of acquiring technological identities, by virtue of being used in technological activities. A technological activity is a problem-solving activity. A technological object is a problem-solving physical instrument. Saying that an object is a technology does not say anything about its intrinsic properties; rather, it is a report about the type of activities in which it is used. Problem-solving activities add a new dimension to the reality of objects. They create an environment in which objects can become technologically real. Objects derive their technological reality from these environments and as a result become technologies. The property of being technological is, therefore, metaphysically more fundamental than being a technology.

Pablo Schyfter has reached similar conclusions regarding the primacy of human activities over the objects that we consider as technological objects. In his view, 'physical entities cannot in and of themselves be said to possess any form of technological ontology: technology is ultimately and necessarily bound up in social practice' (Schyfter, 2009, 108). However, while in Schyfter's view, the being of technologies is bound to social institutions and collective actions, and while Schyfter explicitly distances his account from those based on individual intentionality (ibid., 110), in the activity realist approach, the reality of technologies can be based on individual as well as collective problem-solving practices. Here an object becomes a technological object for any individual or group engaging in problem-solving activities and using material objects in their devised solutions. Accordingly, objects used creatively by individuals to solve their private problems would also qualify as technologies for those individuals.

What here has been said about the reality of technologies can be generalised to other types of objects, such as objects of entertainment or religious or artistic objects. Entertaining, religious and artistic activities create environments for objects to become entertainingly, religiously and artistically real. A hammer which is used as a weight to put pressure on the puncture patch on a bike's inner tube is technologically real. The same hammer can be artistically real when it is hung on the wall in an aesthetically pleasing way, with a spotlight shining on it. The hammer can become entertainingly real when it is used as a mallet in a homemade game of croquet. And for those who may use it to perform some religious rituals, the hammer can become religiously real. As another example consider a knife. When a knife is used to cut objects, it acquires a technological reality. When it is used in an artwork, say, to carry out an anti-violence message, it becomes artistically real. And when it is carried by Sikhs, it becomes the kirpan, which is a religious object.

EXISTING REALITIES

Do we need to first presume the *existence* of an entity to be able to discuss different dimensions of its *reality*? Many entities, including institutions, fictional characters and abstract objects can be real without existing 'out there' in the world. However, in the case of physical objects which can be perceived and used in practical activities, some may argue that the activity realist notion of reality presumes an entity realist notion of existence. The argument is that objects need to first *exist* in order to have the capacity to acquire different practical realities. So, in the example of the hammer discussed earlier, some may argue that a hammer after all needs to exist; otherwise, what is this 'thing' which has been used in different activities and has become technologically, religiously, artistically or entertainingly real? If there is not already a hammer 'out there', how can it acquire different realities?

However, one does not need to first commit to the existence of any particular entity in order to be able to acknowledge its reality. A hammer is made up of its constituents, which at the very subatomic level would be the elementary particles that purportedly constitute the entire universe. As discussed in the previous chapter, it is questionable whether the hammer exists independently of its constituents, and many philosophers have argued that only the constituents of hammers exist; hammers *qua* hammers do not exist. Nevertheless, regardless of the position taken in relation to the existential status of the hammer, this particular assembly of constituents as a whole *is real*. It is real because people form beliefs about it, perceive it and use it for different purposes. Whether the hammer, *qua* hammer, exists in the divine sense is irrelevant. This is similar to the irrelevance of the existential status of a sports team. A sports team is real, regardless of its existential status as a whole, as distinct from the existential status of its players.

But the entity realist argument can be pushed further. An entity realist may concede that it is irrelevant whether the hammer, as a whole, exists or not. And for the same reason they may concede that it is also irrelevant whether the handle and the head of the hammer and indeed whether any observable parts of the hammer, as wholes, exist or not. But what about the elementary particles which have constituted the hammer? Regardless of our position in relation to the existential status of the hammer as a whole or its macroscopic parts, is it not necessary to commit to the existence of elementary particles in order to be able to acknowledge the reality of the hammer? Is it not necessary for these particles to exist in order to be some 'thing' which can be used in different activities?

In the next chapter, the reality of scientifically postulated entities, such as elementary particles, will be discussed. It will be argued that the reality of these entities is shaped by different activities, including theoretical descriptions, experimental observations conducted by means of laboratory instruments and practical applications achieved by manipulating these particles. So, in the activity realist approach, elementary particles are themselves conceptualised in terms of their reality rather than existence.

Moreover, the history of physics is full of examples of particles which were once considered to be elementary, but were later known to be composed of other particles. So, there is no guarantee that the currently accepted set of elementary particles will not turn out to be composite particles. And if they turn out to be composite particles, then on the one hand, their existential status as composite particles can be debated, in the same manner that the existential status of hammers *qua* hammers can be debated. On the other hand, this existential status remains irrelevant to acknowledging their reality or the reality of the hammer that is constituted of these particles. This would be in the same way that the existential status of the hammer, as a whole, is irrelevant for acknowledging its reality.

Nevertheless, it is true that in the case of the hammer, there should be something that is used in different activities. There must be something to play different roles and acquire different realities. The reality of imaginary objects, such as mermaids and Hobbits, is derived only from stories; there is nothing about them which can be perceived by sensory organs, and they do not causally interact with the rest of the world. So, it is not necessary to commit to the existence of anything to be able to acknowledge the reality of mermaids and Hobbits. Their reality is confined within language and the imagination. However, a hammer can be perceived by sensory organs, and it does causally interact with its surroundings. So, in the case of the hammer, unless the existence of the material world is questioned altogether, it is necessary to acknowledge the existence of some *thing* or *things* which are used in different activities. This acknowledgment is the extent of the required existential commitments. It is only necessary to acknowledge that something material needs to exist for a hammer to be used in different activities. Existentially, there is nothing which needs to be acknowledged about the hammer or any of its constituents except for the fact that something exists. Whatever that may be. Because as soon as we describe what that thing is which exists, we run the risk of that thing being a composite object whose existential status would be questionable. Of course, one *can* acknowledge the existence of the elementary particles which constitute a hammer. One can also acknowledge the existence of the hammer, as a whole. But one can equally reject the existence of both. The existential status of the hammer or that of its constituents is irrelevant for conceptualising their reality.

LANGUAGE AND REALITY

Earlier in this chapter it was argued that reality cannot be fully captured by language and that entities can be real despite the fact that there may be no linguistic term for them. However, the relationship between language and reality, and in particular, the extent to which linguistic activities can shape reality, can be further explored.

It needs to be first acknowledged that linguistic activities *are* one type of activity that can enrich objects' reality. Consider the linguistic practice of naming. Naming an entity makes it harder to ignore the entity and creates possibilities for that entity of playing different roles in new activities. For example, naming social issues can impact the way we address them. Social issues become more real when they are named. Since racism and sexism were given names, for example, they have been taken more seriously; demonstrating racist and sexist behaviours are perceived as more wrong. These terms help speakers of language to be more eloquent and avoid verbosity as well as inarticulacy when they wish to describe certain discriminatory attitudes and behaviours. And because these discriminatory attitudes and behaviours can be described by simple terms, it has become much easier to build social institutions whose objective is to address them. Each of these activities make sexism and racism more real compared to when they were not named and compared to other forms of discrimination that are not given names yet.

As a second example consider mathematical pronumerals (x, y, z, n, ...) which are central to algebra. Pronumerals which are used in algebraic expressions and equations are in fact names which are given to knowns and unknowns. These names enable mathematicians to engage in a variety of mathematical activities, such as expressing, creating and solving problems. Without pronumerals and algebraic expressions, mathematical problems would all be word problems which need to be solved by trial and error. Without pronumerals and algebraic expressions, not only would it be infeasible to solve mathematical problems but also it would be impossible to even comprehend or express most problems. Indeed, elementary algebra has become a condition of possibility for all modern branches of mathematics.

One final point can be made here about the relationship between language and reality. In chapters 6 and 7, it was argued that the linguistic categorisation of technologies' function is independent of the metaphysical categorisation of function. For example, a hammer may acquire different functional identities, depending on how it is actually used; and this is despite the fact that the object is always called a 'hammer' regardless of how it is actually used.

Here it should be argued that while the separation between the linguistic and metaphysical categorisations is valid in the case of the functional identification of technologies, in the case of non-technological objects, this distinction becomes blurry. This claim can be substantiated with some examples.

One aspect of the linguistic categorisations of objects is that they rely on available linguistic terms. Given that different languages have different sets of words, the linguistic categorisation to which an object belongs depends on the language which is used. As a result, two or more objects that are categorised differently in one language may have the same term in a different language. For example, the English words 'door' and 'lid' have the same translation in Farsi, which can be transliterated into English as '*dar*'. This means that in Farsi, linguistically, doors and lids belong to the same category.

If linguistic categorisations said something about metaphysical categorisations, then because there is no one-on-one relationship between the terms of different languages, then the reality of entities would depend on the language used to refer to them, and by changing our language, we would change the reality of entities. This conclusion cannot be defended in the case of technological objects, but it is defensible in the case of non-technological objects.

The above conclusion is not defensible in the case of technologies because technologies are problem-solving physical instruments. Their reality is restricted to the changes which they make to the outside world. In the case of most technologies, this change is simply a change in the worldly states of affairs. Changes made to the worldly states of affairs are independent of the language used to describe them. They are objective. Because objects derive their technological reality primarily from objective changes made to the outside world, and not from linguistic activities which describe them, it can be argued that in their case, linguistic categorisations do not translate into metaphysical categorisations. In other words, linguistic activities do not shape the technological reality as much as practical problem-solving activities do, and hence, linguistic changes do not significantly change technological reality. For example, doors and lids are objects which are primarily used as technological objects. Most doors and lids do not have significant non-technological realities. In reality, whether one speaks Farsi or English, the main activities from which doors and lids acquire their reality remain the practical applications of these objects to enclose spaces. Assuming that these activities are independent of the language spoken, we can conclude that linguistic categorisations do not necessarily say anything about the reality of doors and lids as technological objects. In other words, the reality of doors and lids, used as technological objects, remains the same regardless of the language used to refer to them. In general, in the case of technologies, linguistic categorisations do not necessarily reveal anything about the functional identification of objects.

However, the above argument does not hold for non-technological objects. Non-technological objects can play roles in activities which are significant in some cultures but not in others. Non-technological activities cannot be reduced to changes made to the worldly states of affairs; they are not necessarily objective. Hence, linguistic terms used to refer to non-technological objects can reveal the significance of the objects in their respective cultures. And this significance may not be translatable into other languages because activities which give meaning to the term may be absent in other cultures. Therefore, linguistic activities can play a significant role in how non-technological objects acquire their reality. Hence, in the case of non-technological objects, linguistic categorisations can impact metaphysical categorisations. Consider the kirpan as an example. Even though technologically, the kirpan can be categorised as a knife, referring to an object as a 'kirpan' imparts something about the object's reality that the word 'knife' does not impart. The reality of the kirpan transcends that of a knife. The kirpan is a religious object. It has symbolic meanings in Sikhism.

There is another conclusion which can be drawn from the connection between linguistic and metaphysical categorisations of non-technological objects. Given that one object can be used in different non-technological activities, it makes sense for the object to have multiple names, and hence, multiple realities in one culture but not in another. A comparison between Farsi and English can illuminate this point. In Farsi there are at least seven words and phrases for the English word 'wine', transliterated as *Sharaab, Mey, Mol, Nabeez, Baadeh, Dokhtar-e-raz* and *Dokhtar-e-golchehr-e-raz*. This is because wine and wine-making and wine-drinking practices are significant in Persian culture. Persian literature is replete with references to wine. There are different wine-drinking activities in Persian culture which vary depending on the occasion or even on the time of the day at which wine is consumed, and there are different linguistic phrases used to describe those activities. Different linguistic terms used to refer to wine in Farsi, therefore, reflect different realities that wine can acquire in Persian culture. Wine is not often used as a technological object, and the linguistic terms used to refer to it can impact its reality.

SUMMARY

The practically relevant, activity realist notion of being is reality. This notion captures the presence of significant things. Similar to other activity realist notions, reality is defined in relation to the activities of reflective beings. The reality of an object is determined by the activities in which it is used. This determination is subjective, dynamic and is a matter of degree. The degree to which an object is real is established by the number, variety and importance of the activities in which the object is used.

Technologies derive their reality from problem-solving activities. In other words, problem-solving activities provide possibilities for objects to become technologically real. Other activities can also enrich the reality of objects. Objects can become entertainingly, artistically or religiously real if they are used in entertaining, artistic or religious activities.

Acknowledging the reality of objects does not require committing to their existential status. Nevertheless, in the case of objects which causally interact with their surroundings, as long as the existential status of the external world is accepted, it is necessary to acknowledge the existence of 'something' to be able to acknowledge their reality. But nothing more is required to be said about that 'thing'.

Reality is extensible beyond the boundaries of language. Objects can be real without having any linguistic term standing for them. But linguistic activities are one type of activities which can shape and enrich the reality of entities. The linguistic terms which stand for technologies do not significantly contribute to the reality of technologies, and hence, the linguistic categorisation of technologies' functions is independent of the metaphysical categorisation of function. However, linguistic activities contribute to the reality of non-technological objects. Hence, in the case of non-technological objects, linguistic categorisations can influence metaphysical categorisations: the way in which an object is linguistically referred to can impact its reality. Chapter 12 examines another difference between technological and non-technological objects to argue that systems can be automated when used in technological activities, but not in non-technological activities.

This chapter marks the end of the book's third part. The next two chapters, as the final part of the book, use the activity realist approach to address specific philosophical problems. They serve as examples of topics which can be explored with this user-friendly philosophy. The next chapter applies the activity realist notion of reality to conceptualise the reality of scientifically postulated entities and to argue the extent to which this reality is shaped by technologies that are used in scientific experiments. The final chapter investigates the structure of different human activities to argue that autonomous systems can only be employed as technological systems, characterised by solving practical problems and making objective changes to the outside world.

Part IV

ACTIVITY REALISM IN PRACTICE

Chapter 11

Scientific Reality

Which activities constitute the reality of scientifically postulated entities? And to what extent do technologies shape scientific reality?

Sciences can be technology-dependent in different senses. Technologies facilitate scientific experiments, and it is practically difficult and sometimes impossible for scientists to collect data without using technologies. The role of telescopes in our understanding of other planets and galaxies is a good example of this sense of the technology-dependence of sciences. The data collected by means of technological instruments is also epistemically valuable. In the absence of instruments, scientists need to rely on personal, subjective observations which create more possibility for disagreement. What helps scientists to form a consensus is the evidential value and reliability of data gathered by technologies (Bogen & Woodward, 1992).

Moreover, the experiments carried out by means of technologies may be argued to provide good reasons to believe in the existence of scientifically postulated entities. Ian Hacking, for example, believes that successful experiments that involve manipulation of postulated entities justify our beliefs in the existence of the manipulated entities (Hacking, 1983, 1984, 1988). If, for example, we manipulate electrons in order to study other phenomena, then we have good reasons to believe that electrons exist.

Finally, technologically mediated data is phenomenologically different from the data gathered through direct perception of objects. According to Don Ihde (1979, 1991), this implies that the science that is developed about an object through the use of technological instruments would be different from a non-technological understanding of that object.

This chapter examines the role of technologies in shaping the reality of scientifically postulated entities. This form of the technology-dependence of sciences does not concern the *truth* conditions of scientific theories, nor does it say anything about the justification of our beliefs about the *existence* of scientifically postulated entities. Rather, it concerns itself with the *reality* of those entities, in the sense defined in the previous chapter. Hence, to study *this* sense of the technology-dependence of sciences, we need to scrutinise the activities from which scientific entities acquire their reality.

CLARIFYING TERMINOLOGY

A few terms and phrases need to be clarified before formulating this chapter's arguments. The first phrase to clarify is 'scientific entity'. A scientific entity is an entity whose properties are used to explain the properties of other entities. Scientific entities are believed to be responsible for causal relations in the material world. 'Scientific terms' which are meant to stand for scientific entities are used in providing scientific explanations of the material world. Electrons, genes and gravitational waves are examples of scientific entities. Frying pans, Sherlock Holmes and Romain Bardet, however, are not scientific entities. This is because, unlike the former group, the latter group are not used in scientific explanations of the world. Although all material objects *enter* causal relations with other material objects, non-scientific entities are not believed to *trigger* causal relations with other scientific entities. The material properties of non-scientific material entities are explained by those of scientific entities.

The status of an entity as a scientific entity is relative to social and temporal contexts. New entities are constantly introduced by scientists; and although some of them keep their scientific status, others are abandoned. Phlogiston and entelechy are examples of scientific entities which are now abandoned from scientific reality. Gravitational waves have only recently acquired this status.

Note that, similar to the rest of this book, here the term 'entity' is used in its broad philosophical sense. It is not restricted to physical objects or to legal entities. An entity is anything of any kind. Animal species, robots, humans, planets, waves and particles are all examples of entities.

The second term to clarify is 'objectivity' and its adjectival form 'objective'. Here, the term 'objective' is used in the same sense that trees, rivers and mountains are objective. Here something is objective if it can be referred to and perceived by human sensory organs. This sense of objectivity is what Heather Douglas (2004) identifies as the first mode of objectivity. This mode of objectivity, as Douglas explains, 'focuses on processes where humans attempt to interact with the world, such as scientific experimentation or interactions in daily life; in particular, these processes attempt to directly "get at objects" in the world' (Douglas, 2004, 455). But as Douglas has argued, it needs to be stressed here that this sense of objectivity is agnostic about the *existence* of objective entities: 'Additional (realist) arguments are needed to move from the bare bones objectivity$_1$ [the sense of objectivity used here] arising from examination of process to the ontological claims about the product, e.g., that the objects described are "really there"' (ibid., 456–457, brackets added).

This notion of objectivity can be used to clarify the third important phrase of this chapter, namely 'objectifying technologies'. If we consider various technological instruments that are used in scientific experiments, we note that there is one group of technologies that make extreme cases in their contribution to the perception of and the reference to scientific entities. These technologies *objectify* scientifically postulated unobservable entities. They enable an observation of unobservable entities. These technologies can be referred to as *objectifying technologies*. Objectifying technologies provide objective indications of scientifically postulated unobservable entities. In other words, objectification of scientifically postulated unobservable entities is a function with which these technologies are identified. We can also be specific in our reference to an objectifying technology and speak of electron-objectifying technologies, positron-objectifying technologies or kaon-objectifying technologies to be more clear about the functional identity of the instrument in question.

Cloud Chambers are examples of objectifying technologies. During successful experiments conducted by means of Cloud Chambers, scientists observe the trajectory of postulated particles such as the positron. The objectifying mechanism happens inside a chamber which is supersaturated by water vapour or alcohol vapour. The vapour is kept at an unstable thermodynamic state so that any minor disturbance could condense it into its liquid form. The particles travelling inside the chamber ionize their neighbouring vapour molecules and cause them to condense. The path of this condensation, as the trajectory of the particle, can be seen and made more visible by a light source. Scientific theories tell us that the trajectory of each particle depends on its mass and its electric charge. So, by examining the curves of condensations, scientists can calculate the mass and the electric charge of the particle which has formed the trajectory, and ultimately, identify the type of particle that is objectified. As Xavier Roque (1997) has shown, historically, Cloud Chambers played a crucial role in the acceptance of the positron.

The fourth term is 'unobservability'. An unobservable entity is one that cannot be directly perceived by humans or by any other subject whose sensory perceptions have similar temporal and spatial limitations. Unobservability, therefore, does not amount to immeasurability. Nor does it entail non-ostensibility. Scientists use objectifying technologies to make postulated unobservable entities ostensible or to measure their properties.

But obviously these measurements do not turn the particles into observable entities. Electrons remain unobservable despite the fact that scientists can measure their properties and point at their effects on the detectors.

And the final term to be explained is 'observation'. Observation has a narrow and a broad meaning. In its narrow sense, observation is synonymous with seeing; it refers to visual sensation. But here observation is used in its broad sense, which is the commonly used sense of the term in the field of the philosophy of science. In its broad sense, observation can refer to any sensory perception, be it visual, auditory, olfactory, tactile or gustatory. Nevertheless, it should be acknowledged that most scientific observations in the broad sense are instances of observations in the narrow sense of the word.

THE REALITY OF SCIENTIFIC ENTITIES

As argued in the previous chapter, entities acquire their reality by entering into the activities of reflective beings. Unlike their existential status which is universal, entities cannot have independent, universal realities. Being real, unlike existing, is also a matter of degree. The degree to which entities are real depends on the number, variety and the significance of activities in which they are used.

Here, the distinction between existence and reality can be highlighted in the context of scientific entities. For an entity to become scientifically real, it needs to be accepted by a scientific authority, based on some theoretical or empirical evidence; whereas entities that *exist* in the actual world do not need to be accepted by anyone in order to exist. Entities that are considered scientifically real also vary over time, depending on the scientific theories that are accepted in each era. However, making a similar claim about the entities that exist in the actual world would be counter-intuitive. Phlogiston, ether, entelechy, atoms and gravitational waves were accepted in scientific reality for certain periods and some of them still are. But it is counter-intuitive to claim that these entities *existed* in the actual world only for certain periods.

To study the *reality* of scientific entities, we need to examine the activities from which scientific entities derive their reality. The three generic activities that shape the reality of scientific entities are *theoretical descriptions*, *experimental observations* and *practical applications*.

Theoretical descriptions are in the form of linguistic phrases or mathematical equations used to describe the intrinsic or relational properties of an entity. The claims that the electron is negatively charged and that it orbits around the nucleus are examples of theoretical descriptions about the electron. Descriptions make entities real or more real. The more we can talk about an entity, the more real the entity becomes. One of the reasons why the electron is more real than the positron for most of us is that we can talk more about the electron. We know that the number of electrons in each stable atom corresponds to its atomic number. We can even draw a basic picture of electrons orbiting the nucleus of an atom. But apart from knowing that the positron is the antiparticle of the electron, most of us may not be able to say much more about the positron. Theoretical descriptions, therefore, are one of the main activities from which scientific entities derive their realities.

The second generic activity from which scientific entities derive their reality is experimental observations. Experimental observations result in the detection or the measurement of a scientific entity or its effects. Observations can be in the form of technologically mediated experimentation or direct perception of an entity or its effects. Entities which are observed are more real than those which are not observed. Every new experiment that helps scientists to detect an entity or its effects enriches the reality of that entity. The cathode ray experiment, for example, made electrons more real, because their effects could be observed and their properties could be measured. The experiments conducted in CERN with the Large Hadron Collider (LHC) in 2012, as another example, made the Higgs boson more real.

And the final generic activity which enriches the reality of scientific entities is application. Application refers to doing things with an entity and achieving goals by practically using the entity. Manipulating an entity during a scientific experimentation is a common form of application of scientific entities. The discovery of the Higgs boson, for example, was made possible through manipulating protons. Protons were accelerated and made to collide to generate the Higgs boson. This application of protons to achieve other goals makes protons more real. The X-ray, as another example, is produced by manipulating electrons. Using electrons to produce X-rays enriches the reality of the electron.

Note that of these generic activities, application cannot bring any entity into reality. Entities need to first become scientifically real through one of the other two generic activities before they can be practically used. This is because, as discussed in chapter 4, use is an intentional relationship that a user forms with what is used. One cannot form an intentional relationship with something which is not real. So, application can only *enrich* the reality of already real entities. Theoretical descriptions and experimental observations, on the other hand, can bring entities into reality *or* enrich their reality.

An entity becomes more scientifically real than another if it is used in more significant and more varied activities. Later it will be argued that experimental observations play a more crucial role than the other activities in shaping the reality of scientific entities. Nevertheless, what it means for an entity to be more real than another is that the former is more significant for us, it is more 'present', in the activity realist notion of being. Consequently, when sciences of more real entities undergo revolutions, the revolutions would be more significant than when sciences of less real entities undergo revolutions. Water is more real than the electron, and the electron is more real than the positron. Revolutions in the scientific understanding of water will be more significant than revolutions in the scientific understanding of the electron, and revolutions in the scientific understanding of the electron will be more significant than revolutions in the scientific understanding of the positron. As discussed later in this chapter, this also means that scientists can be less conservative in proposing new theories of less real entities, such as the positron, compared to more real entities, such as water.

THE TECHNOLOGY-DEPENDENT REALITY OF UNOBSERVABLE ENTITIES

How do technologies shape the reality of scientific entities? Technologies play significant roles in experimental observations. And this is particularly the case for sciences of unobservable entities. The perceptual identification of unobservable entities *requires* the use of objectifying technologies, because by definition, there is no direct perception of unobservable entities available. By enabling perceptual access to unobservable entities or to their effects, objectifying technologies shape the reality of these entities.

Unobservable entities sometimes acquire their initial scientific reality through experiments conducted by objectifying technologies which produce accidental and unexplainable results. Such cases can be called 'accidental discoveries'. For example, statistical abnormalities in the data gathered by the detectors of the Large Hadron Collider in CERN may lead to the discovery of a new particle whose properties cannot be explained by any accepted theory. X-rays and radioactivity, too, were accidentally discovered before any theoretical description of them was available: they acquired their initial scientific reality through experimental observations.

The case of accidental discoveries can be used to argue for the technology-dependence of the scientific reality of unobservable entities. When entities acquire their initial reality through experimental observations, theoretical descriptions need to follow and be consistent with this observed reality. Theories cannot construct a new reality about those entities. Otherwise, if theoretical descriptions do not match observations, they would describe something else instead of the observed entities. From the moment at which new entities are observed, therefore, it would be up to the proposed theories to match experimental observations. Hence, considering the indispensable role which objectifying technologies play in experimental observations, the scientific reality of accidentally discovered entities would always be technology-dependent. Accidental discoveries urge scientists to develop theories whose purpose is to explain the new technologically conditioned scientific reality. Subsequent theoretical descriptions can further consolidate the place of accidentally discovered entities in scientific reality.

However, not all postulated unobservable entities are first detected by technological instruments before being theoretically described. Unobservable entities sometimes acquire their initial scientific reality from sheer conjectures. When theoretical descriptions precede experimental observations, the place of the postulated entity in scientific reality can be consolidated if the experimental observations conform to what is described by the theory. The positron, for example, was theoretically postulated to have the same weight as the electron with the opposite charge. To enrich the reality of this postulated entity, experiments had to reveal an entity with these particular characteristics in order for them to consolidate the place of the positron in scientific reality. Experiments which resulted in observations which did not match the theoretical descriptions of the positron could not enrich the reality of the positron, because they were not about *that* postulated entity. So, in the case of entities which acquire their initial scientific reality from theoretical descriptions, prior to the discovery of the entity, it is up to the experimental observations to detect an entity whose properties match theoretical descriptions.

Nevertheless, after the successful detection of a postulated entity through experimental observations, theoretical descriptions switch roles with experimental observations in relation to their contribution to the reality of postulated entities. At first, the postulated entities primarily derived their reality from the available theoretical descriptions. But after their detection, they derive their reality primarily from experimental observations. It is now a requirement of theoretical descriptions to explain what is being observed. If current theories are replaced by new theories, the new theories must still explain and acknowledge the reality of what is observed. Think about Cloud Chambers and their role in objectifying the positron again. Scientists might, for any reason, abandon current theories that explain the interaction of the positron with other subatomic particles and replace them with new theories. They may decide that the positron is constituted of other, yet to be known, elementary particles. But even if they do so, they cannot deny the reality of what appears on the screen of the Cloud Chambers anymore. There is now something (a curve, a dot, a pattern) on the screen of the objectifying technology that demands theory match its reality. There is an 'instrumental objectivity', as Baird (2004) would phrase it, that is independent of any theory that scientists may use to describe their observation.

It is in this strong sense that the scientific reality of unobservable entities is shaped by technologies. The reality which is presented to scientists by technologies overshadows theoretical descriptions. Thanks to experimental observations, some entity has gained a status in scientific reality which is more secure than the theory which initially predicted it or any subsequent theory used to explain it. As long as scientists believe in the function of their objectifying technologies, they cannot abandon this reality.

COMPARING THE THREE ACTIVITIES

The conclusion of the previous section can be used to show that experimental observations play a more significant role in shaping and securing the reality of scientific entities than theoretical descriptions or practical applications of those entities. Two examples from the history of science can illustrate this point.

James Watt's experiments to produce water by manipulating phlogiston and pure air show why practical applications (often in the form of manipulations) may not provide a secure place for an entity in scientific reality. Watt believed in the theory of phlogiston and was able to manipulate phlogiston to create water with it (Baird, 2004, 137). Phlogiston was real to Watt, and its reality was richer than the reality of a purely theoretical entity because he had also found a way to practically use phlogiston. But after about a century, phlogiston was abandoned as a scientific entity, and today it has no place in scientific reality. But the fact that phlogiston has no place in scientific reality anymore is *not* because if scientists follow Watt's instructions today, they will not be able to produce water. They may use a different language to describe those experiments, but if anyone follows Watt's procedures, they would be able to produce water. Those procedures remain reliable in a similar fashion that the procedures to make electronic and mobile devices will remain reliable even if one day scientists abandon Maxwell's theory of electromagnetics and replace it with a novel and revolutionary theory. Our mobile devices will not stop working if that happens. So, there was nothing *practically* wrong with how Watt was able to manipulate phlogiston and produce water with it. But now the question is: if there was a theory of phlogiston, and if there were ways to practically use it, why has phlogiston lost its status in scientific reality? To answer this question, it is worth scrutinising the history of another scientific entity, namely, the electron.

Since Joseph Thomson's cathode ray experiments, which is known to be the first instance of the objectification of the electron, different atomic theories have been suggested and upheld by scientists: the blueberry muffin atomic model of Thomson, Ernest Rutherford's planetary model, Niels Bohr's modified planetary model and the electron cloud model of quantum physics. Each of these models provides a different theoretical description of the movements of electrons and their position in relation to the nucleus. Now if theoretical descriptions were the primary activities which shaped the reality of scientific entities, then we should believe that each of the above theories dealt with different types of entities given that each theory was considered revolutionary compared to its predecessors. However, although each atomic theory provides a different description of electrons, these theories are considered to provide descriptions of the same entities, namely, those which were detected through Thomson's cathode ray experiments.

In the case of phlogiston, after the abandonment of its theory, scientists stopped accepting phlogiston as a part of scientific reality. This was despite the reliable practical applications of phlogiston. This implies that the reality of phlogiston was mostly derived from theory. In the case of the electron, even though its respective scientific theories have changed, the electron has not lost its place in scientific reality. In fact, scientists believe that different theoretical descriptions of the electron are theories of the same entity. These mean that the reality of the electron is to a large extent independent of theoretical descriptions. But what is the difference between the case of phlogiston and that of the electron? Phlogiston and the electron are both unobservable entities. So why is it that the reality of phlogiston was mostly shaped by theory, but the electron has a rather secure scientific reality outside theory?

The difference can be explained by the fact that the electron was objectified, but phlogiston was never objectified. Objectification plays a significant role in securing the place of scientific entities in scientific reality. This is because objectification changes the way in which the meaning of scientific terms is understood.

Prior to the objectification of a scientifically postulated entity, the entity's reality is mostly derived from theoretical descriptions. These descriptions determine the meaning of the scientific term which is meant to stand for the entity. Phlogiston, for example, was defined as a substance that flammable materials release during the process of burning. This was what the term 'phlogiston' meant, and there was no other way to define the term.

However, when scientific entities are objectified, their reality is no longer primarily determined by theoretical descriptions, and the terms which stand for them no longer derive their meanings from theory. This is because objectification creates the possibility of naming by 'ostension'. When entities are named by ostension, a robust link is created between what is objectified and the scientific term used to refer to it. After the establishment of this link, the meaning of the term is no longer purely determined by theory.

Naming by ostension is an important step in causal theories of reference. As discussed in chapter 7, in the causal theory of reference, a term necessarily refers to its referent. In other words, in these theories, after the instance of naming, the reference of terms is fixed. Naming, itself, happens when someone points at something and gives it a name. Objectification of entities creates the possibility of naming by ostension. It creates the possibility of pointing at what is observed through the objectification experiment and giving it a name. Therefore, after the objectification of entities, the meaning of scientific terms which stand for those entities is no longer determined by theory. The term now has a fixed reference determined by objectification experiments.

This is a reason why the reality of phlogiston was mostly determined by theory, but the reality of the electron was not bound by any particular theory. Thomson's experiments provided the possibility for the electron to be dubbed by ostension, and from that point on, the reality of the electron was to a large extent freed from theory. After Thomson's experiments, the term 'electron' refers to the same type of entities despite the fact that the atomic theory has undergone revolutionary changes. This reference is fixed by experimental observations.

Objectifying technologies, therefore, provide the possibility for unobservable entities to be named by ostension, which is a significant step towards securing the reality of an entity. If an entity remains non-ostensible, its reality remains largely dependent on the theory in which it is embedded.

Interestingly, the atom itself used to be an unobservable, non-ostensible entity for millennia. The term 'atom' was purportedly coined by the ancient Greek philosopher Democritus who suggested that material objects are composed of unbreakable particles which he called '*a*-toms'. The term was then used by others but remained a theoretical term referring to non-ostensible entities. Then, experiments in the nineteenth and twentieth century gave scientists empirical access to electrons, protons and neutrons, which physicists believe to constitute atoms. Up to the nineteenth century, then, the reality of the atom was mostly shaped by theoretical descriptions, and indeed different atomic theories could be said to have been theories of different entities altogether. Entities which are currently considered to be atoms are not the same atoms that Democritus talked about, simply because modern atoms are not unbreakable particles. The reality of Democritus's atoms is restricted to his theoretical descriptions, whereas the reality of the components of modern atoms is primarily determined by experimental observations. Given that these components are objectified and named by ostension, any future theory of the electron, proton and neutron will be about the same entities, namely, the electron, proton and neutron.

Having perceptual access to an object, therefore, makes that object ostensible and changes its reality. In the case of many observable entities, this perception is direct, but in the case of unobservable entities, the perception is made through objectifying technologies. Michael Devitt (1981) refers to this type of perception as 'quasi perception':

> Our problem with a theoretical term is that its referent cannot be perceived. We need some substitute for perception in our adaptation. . . . Our substitute must

be *very like* perception: quasi perception. I suggest that what we seek here is a relation consisting of an instrument 'perceiving' the referent and our 'reading' of the instrument: we are 'perceiving the referent through the instrument'. It would, of course, be difficult to fill out the details of this suggestion. I shall not attempt to do so. (Devitt, 1981, 200–201, italic in the original)

Devitt proposes his notion of quasi perception to demonstrate how causal theories of reference apply to unobservable entities. Without getting into details, he also acknowledges the role that technological instruments play in enabling this perception. This chapter can clarify some of the details that Devitt did not attempt to fill out.

After experimental observations of an unobservable entity, theoretical descriptions become almost irrelevant in the *acceptance* of the reality of the entity; they only *enrich* the entity's scientific reality. In this way, objectifying experiments liberate entities from their theoretical bounds and anchor them in scientific reality. When an entity like the electron is objectified, it becomes much harder to neglect its reality. Scientists may one day come to the conclusion that electrons are not elementary particles, and that they are composed of other elementary particles. But such theories will not easily lead scientists to abandon the reality of the electron as it was accepted back in the nineteenth and early twentieth century. As long as scientists believe in the reality of electron-objectifying experiments and refer to what they can point at on the screen of electron-objectifying technologies as 'effects of streams of electrons', electrons will remain secure in scientific reality.

Of course, it is not the case that the reality of objectified entities is not constituted by theoretical descriptions or by practical application *at all*. A part of the reality of objectified entities is still derived from the theories in which they are embedded and activities that involve their manipulation. However, compared to the other activities, experimental observations play a more dominant role in shaping the reality of unobservable entities.

CONSERVATISM AND DEGREES OF THE TECHNOLOGY-DEPENDENCE OF SCIENCES

One of the conclusions drawn from the discussions of the previous section is that the extent to which a particular activity shapes the reality of an entity depends also on other activities which shape the reality of the entity. When experimental observations of an entity are available, the extent to which theoretical descriptions shape the reality of scientific entities dwindles. This section builds upon this conclusion to argue that the technology-dependence of scientific entities is not limited to the sciences of unobservable entities.

Nevertheless, this technology-dependence is a matter of degree, and this degree is at its maximum in the case of sciences of unobservable entities.

Unlike other technologies used in scientific experiments, objectifying technologies do not measure or detect entities that are *non-scientifically* real. Entities can be non-scientifically real if they enter people's everyday activities outside scientific theories and experiments. Household objects, for example, can be non-scientifically real because we can perceive them, describe them and use them in different activities without requiring any specialist scientific knowledge about them. Some scientific entities can also be non-scientifically real. For example, distance and speed are two basic concepts in physics. But distance and speed are also non-scientifically real because we do not need to be scientists to be able to talk about distance and speed or use them in our decision making. Unobservable entities, however, have very thin realities outside their scientific realities. They do not play many roles in people's everyday activities. The reality of unobservable entities is to a large extent confined within the boundary of theoretical descriptions and laboratory experiments.

As an example, consider Cloud Chambers, on the one hand, and measuring tapes and speedometers, on the other. What Cloud Chambers reveal is not the same level of reality as that of speedometers or measuring tapes. A perceptual understanding of distance and speed could be achieved independently of Newtonian mechanics, the theory of relativity or any other scientific theory which in one way or another deals with distance and speed. The reality of distance and speed is also to a great extent independent of the function of measuring tapes, speedometers or any other instrument used to measure the distance between or the speed of objects. For millennia, distance and speed have been real for humans who needed to assess the urgency of the threats coming at them or the amount of force they needed to put into objects to throw them at different targets. What measuring tapes and speedometers have done to the reality of distance and speed, in other words, have only been adding a few more activities to a multitude of existing activities from which distance and speed have been acquiring their realities. Therefore, measuring tapes and speedometers, on the one hand, and Newtonian mechanics and theory of relativity, on the other, have not significantly altered the reality of distance and speed as we experience in our everyday activities.

This also means that distance and speed are already so real that it is up to the quantities that we read via measuring tapes and speedometers to match our non-scientific understandings of distance and speed, and not the other way around. If a measuring tape shows the thickness of a road bike wheel wider than that of a mountain bike wheel, or if a speedometer measures the average speed of a runner higher than that of a racing car, we would not redefine our conceptions of distance and speed; instead, we would discard those objects as faulty measuring tapes and speedometers.

Similar points can be made about scientific theories that provide descriptions of observable entities. Most of the time, observable entities already have an established reality before new scientific theories are proposed to describe them. It is often up to the technical definitions of scientific terms derived from new scientific theories to be consistent with the prior reality of observable entities, not the other way around. If, for example, a theory defines distance and speed in a way that the new definitions are radically inconsistent with the non-scientific reality of distance and speed, then there is at least one reason not to accept the theory.

Nevertheless, if the new scientific definitions are considerably inconsistent with the prior reality of an entity, one way to 'save' the scientific theory is to rename its technical terms. For instance, instead of saying that the new theory is about distance and speed, scientists can claim that the new theory is about 'fistance' and 'fespeed'. By doing so, scientists can maintain their hypotheses, because if fistance and fespeed do not have any prior realities, then there is nothing which the new scientific definitions of these terms can contradict with. But obviously, if scientists take this route, then the new theory would not be about distance and speed anymore.

All in all, the prior realities of entities influence the acceptance of proposed scientific theories about those entities. This point can be interpreted as 'the tyranny of the status quo': what is the case demands any alternative future to fall within its acceptable boundaries. From the viewpoint of theory choice, this can be interpreted as a virtue which new hypotheses must possess in order to increase their chance of acceptance. Willard van Orman Quine and Joseph Ullian refer to this virtue as 'conservatism':

> In order to explain the happenings that we are inventing it to explain, the hypothesis may have to conflict with some of our previous beliefs; but the fewer the better. Acceptance of a hypothesis is of course like acceptance of any belief in that it demands rejection of whatever conflicts with it. The less rejection of prior beliefs required, the more plausible the hypothesis – other things being equal. (Quine & Ullian, 1978, 44)

One point that can be added here is that the significance of matching our prior beliefs – the importance of conservatism – is more applicable to theories that deal with observable entities than those that deal with unobservable entities. This is because observable entities can already have established realities, and it is those realities with which new theories must be consistent. If someone presents a new theory about distance and speed, they must be careful about how distance and speed are defined in their theory, because of the present reality of distance and speed. Otherwise, the definitions that their theory provides may create resistance against the acceptance of the theory. However, the restrictions of our prior beliefs in relation to new hypotheses about *un*observable entities are similar to the restrictions of our prior beliefs in relation to hypotheses about fistance and fespeed. In both cases, inconsistency with our prior beliefs is almost impossible to occur. The virtue of conservatism is less significant in relation to how a newly accepted unobservable entity is conceptualised, as unobservable entities do not have rich realities.

Interestingly, in the case of observable entities, too, we can act less conservatively if new theoretical claims are on a scale which is outside the reality of our everyday activities. Quantum physics and the theory of relativity, for example, have challenged our prior conceptions of space, time and speed. However, both quantum physics and the theory of relativity deal with scales which are outside our everyday activities. Thus, we can accept their conclusions. We can accept that at extremely high relative speeds, the length of an object contracts, or that at the subatomic level, time and space are not continuous. If these claims were meant to apply on an observable scale, they would have been markedly contradictory to our everyday experiences and perceptions of length, time and space. But the apparent inconsistencies occur at scales which are not very real to us. They do not challenge our reality. As Wittgenstein rhetorically asked in his discussions around Godel's incompleteness theorem: 'there is a contradiction here. Does it do any harm here?' (Wittgenstein, 1978, 119). So even if there is an inconsistency between the definitions of a new hypothesis and our prior beliefs, if that inconsistency occurs on a scale outside our everyday activities, it would not be that 'harmful'. Extreme scales are not very real. In the case of unobservable entities, we are always dealing with scales outside the domain of everyday activities.

It should be clear by now why the technology-dependence of sciences comes in different degrees, and this degree is at its maximum in the case of the sciences of unobservable entities. Other sciences are technology-dependent too, only to a lesser degree. Consider these examples: (1) using a Cloud Chamber to observe the traces of the movements of positrons, (2) using a microscope to study viruses, (3) observing the surface of the planet Mars via a telescope and (4) measuring the circumference of a tree trunk with a measuring tape. These examples show a spectrum of cases in which the reality of the objects of the scientific experiments becomes less and less dependent on technologies, because they have richer and richer non-scientific realities.

When technologies are used to provide a new scientific description, observation or application of an entity, that entity's scientific reality becomes more technology-dependent. The more the reality of the objects of scientific inquiry depends on technologies, the more the respective sciences will be technology-dependent. In the case of unobservable entities, because most of the entities' descriptions, observations and applications require using technologies, then their scientific reality is to a large extent technology-dependent. In the case of observable entities, when many non-scientific descriptions, observations and applications of an entity are available, the scientific reality of the entity becomes less technology-dependent. The less the reality of the objects of scientific inquiry depends on technologies, the less the respective sciences will be technology-dependent, and the more conservative we should be in suggesting new hypotheses about the objects.

SUMMARY

Different bodies of human knowledge, broadly understood, are intertwined with different realities. And each of these realities perpetuates the reality of different entities. Some religious systems, for example, perpetuate the reality of angels or demons, and some fantasy novels perpetuate the reality of mermaids or vampires. Different sciences, too, perpetuate the reality of different entities. Entities which are claimed by sciences to play fundamental causal roles are called scientific entities.

In general, three main types of activities shape the reality of scientific entities: theoretical descriptions, experimental observations and practical applications. Of these three activities, experimental observations play a more significant role in shaping the reality of entities and securing their place in scientific reality than the other two.

Technologies shape the scientific reality of entities by playing roles in their observations, descriptions or manipulations. Scientific entities, and their respective scientific theories, can become more and more technology-dependent when most of their realities are derived from activities which require the use of technologies. The level of the technology-dependence of sciences is at its extreme in the case of the sciences of unobservable entities.

When an entity is more real than another entity, it means that revolutions that may happen in the science of the former would be more significant than revolutions that may happen in the science of the latter. The more real an entity, the more conservative scientists need to be in proposing new theories about that entity, and the harder it is to accept new theories about that entity. Observable entities are more real than unobservable entities. Hence, scientific theories of observable entities need to be more conservative, and it is harder to successfully propose new scientific theories about observable entities.

Chapter 12

The Human, the Technological and the Limitations of Autonomous Systems

In what type of activities can autonomous systems replace humans? Autonomous systems can be defined as systems which are capable of acting upon the world independently of real-time human control, such as autonomous vehicles or autonomous military robots, which are both still in the development phase. The suitability of the term 'autonomous' to refer to artificial systems of course can be questioned. This is because current machines are not autonomous in the sense in which the term is used in political and moral philosophy; that is, they do not have the capacity to reflect on and understand reasons for actions (Purves et al., 2015; Nyholm, 2018). Nevertheless, this chapter does not engage with the debate on whether artificial systems are autonomous in any meaningful way. Such a debate requires a metaphysical understanding of autonomy. As discussed in chapters 6 and 10, however, a distinction can be made between a metaphysical understanding and a linguistic understanding of technologies. A linguistic understanding is concerned with the way a term works in language. And this is the approach taken towards 'autonomous systems' here. The phrase 'autonomous systems' has been used in its broad sense as an umbrella phrase to refer to a range of systems that can operate independently of direct human control. It does not carry any metaphysical assumptions about the intrinsic properties of the systems in question. Whether such systems are *truly* autonomous or not does not affect the conclusions of this chapter.

One of the central questions which has guided the research into autonomous systems is whether these systems can replace humans in their activities. Currently most works which address the replaceability of humans by autonomous systems do so by focusing on the normative question of whether the performance of certain human activities *should* be delegated to autonomous systems; whether there are any decisions or actions which, for moral or legal reasons, should be made or performed only by humans. For instance, some have argued that autonomous systems are likely to lead to responsibility or retribution gaps, and as such, it is morally wrong to introduce autonomous vehicles and autonomous weapon systems into society which will inevitably need to make morally significant choices (Danaher, 2016; de Jong, 2019; Matthias, 2004; Roff, 2014; Sparrow, 2007, 2016). Some others have argued that autonomous systems are likely to cause less harm than humans, and that autonomous systems should not be held to higher standards than their human counterparts (Schulzke, 2011; Strawser, 2010).

Here, however, the replaceability of humans by autonomous systems is addressed from a different perspective. The question is not whether autonomous systems *should* but *are able to* replace humans in their activities. This chapter provides an analysis of different types of human activities to illustrate specific epistemic and logical conditions which need to be fulfilled in order for autonomous systems to be able to replace humans in their activities. It will be argued that autonomous systems can only replace humans in problem-solving, or in other words, technological activities. Using examples taken mostly from activities in which vehicles are used, this chapter offers a philosophically rich analysis of activities in which autonomous systems can and cannot replace humans. The final section discusses some implications of this analysis for the design and regulation of autonomous systems.

ACTIVITY REALISM AND AUTONOMOUS SYSTEMS

As extensively argued in the first and second parts of this book, objects and systems can be used in different types of activities and acquire different functional identities. A paper bag, for instance, can be used as a rubbish bin, a sick bag or wrapping paper. Different software and applications create even further functional possibilities for digital and complex systems, such as modern TVs, robots and smart phones. This means that modern technologies are often more versatile and used in more varied activities.

In activity realism, the evaluation of objects and systems must be preceded by the study of human activities. Since normative evaluations of an object are activity-dependent, the adjustments required to improve an object for the performance of one activity may or may not improve the performance of a different activity. To make a paper bag a better bin bag, for example, it may need to become water resistant and tough. However, the first adjustment is unnecessary for a paper bag to be used as wrapping paper, and the second might only make the paper bag worse as wrapping paper, as fine wrapping papers may be more appealing.

One of the adjustments made to modern systems is adding autonomous features to them. Autonomous features are often added to pre-existing systems in order to improve their performance. Autonomous cars, for example, are meant to be an improved version of normal cars, which are already widely used in society.

As systems become more autonomous, more tasks are delegated from humans to machines. For example, some modern vehicles are equipped with smart wipers which would automatically run when the sensors detect liquid dropping on the vehicle's windscreen. This means that to achieve the goal of cleaning the windscreen from rain water, the driver does not need to perform any actions. All required actions are performed by the smart wipers.

As the performance of certain actions is taken away from humans and delegated to autonomous systems, the nature of user engagement may change. This change may in some cases be desirable as users will be able to focus on other tasks. In fact, one of the marketing features of autonomous vehicles will be that they allow users to engage in other activities, such as reading books or checking their mobile phones, while the vehicle performs the task of driving.

However, removing the possibility of user engagement may also limit the activities in which the system can be used, as autonomous systems may not be able to replace humans in some activities. As such, it is imperative to study the conditions which need to be met in order for autonomous systems to be able to replace humans. This chapter highlights the types of activities which autonomous systems can and cannot perform. In order to do so, human activities are first examined in more detail.

NORMS AND GOALS OF ACTIVITIES

First, a distinction can be made between *engagement* in an activity and *performing* actions which are required to achieve the goal of an activity. One can be engaged in the activity of using a vehicle to go from a particular place to a destination by performing the act of driving oneself, or by delegating the act of driving to another driver, be it a human taxi driver or an intelligent artificial system. One who is engaged in the activity of going from home to work is the passenger, not the taxi driver or the vehicle. One who performs the act of driving the vehicle is the one who needs to have the required skill and knowledge to be able to drive a vehicle from the passenger's home to their work. Although autonomous systems can perform a series of actions, the entity who is engaged in the activity is the human user.

Activities can be studied through the general norms governing them, their goals and the actions required to bring about the goals. To perform an activity, a person considers a series of *general norms* which govern the activity. Road rules are an example of general norms. Regardless of why a person is using their vehicle on a public road, their driving style, the routes which they follow or the model of their vehicle, they should stop at red lights or drive on the correct side of the road.

General norms are often prescribed by authorities. Health and safety regulations, legal rules and moral codes are examples of general norms set by authorities. These general norms are context-sensitive. Whether one is required to drive on the left or right side of the road, for example, is prescribed by authorities of the country in which they are driving.

However, not all general norms are decided by authorities. Some general norms may be conventional or personal. Consider a car user who has a strong sense of environmental responsibility and wishes to minimise their greenhouse gas emissions on every trip. Minimising greenhouse gas emissions is a personal value, as other users may not value it. But it may be upheld over a wide range of contexts and work as a general norm for that particular user. As another example, consider a user who wishes to exhibit altruistic character traits while driving their car. They may do so by slowing down their car to allow other cars to join the traffic, or change lanes. Showing altruistic character traits while driving is also a personal norm, but it may be upheld over a wide range of contexts by a user and work as a general norm for them.

Therefore, what makes something a general norm for a specific user is the fact that the user considers that norm in decisions which they make over a wide range of activities. General norms, therefore, are frameworks through which goals are achieved. They work in the background and govern activities.

Activity-dependent goals are the reasons which motivate engagement in activities. In the context of using a vehicle, for instance, a user may want to use their vehicle in a purely problem-solving activity, as a technological means to go from home to work or to look for their escaped dog. Or they may want to use the vehicle in an entertainment activity to perform a burnout, or rather aimlessly go for a leisurely drive. Each of these goals is an activity-dependent goal as they motivate engagement in a particular activity. These goals vary from one individual to another, and can dynamically change for one individual.

Successful completion of an activity requires the achievement of the goal of the activity. The activity of going from home to work, for instance, is successfully completed when the user arrives at work. The activity of leisurely driving is successfully completed when the user has had an enjoyable drive.

Activity-dependent goals are often set by users. Users have the freedom to decide which activities they wish to engage in. However, authorities may also regulate and restrict certain activities. For example, users are not allowed to use their vehicle to purposefully inflict harm on others. Engaging in an activity to pursue such goals is prohibited.

Nevertheless, a user cannot follow their general norms or achieve activity-dependent goals simply by sitting and waiting for the norms and goals to realise. More specific intermediate steps need to be set in order for general norms and activity-dependent goals to be realised. These intermediate steps, which can be called *momentary goals*, shape the momentary actions which are taken by the user. For example, when a user aims to go from home to work, they will need to take many momentary actions which jointly contribute to the achievement of the general norms and activity-dependent goals. At each intersection, they need to decide to turn left, right or go straight in order to arrive at work rather than at another location. They need to decide which route to take, and dynamically adjust the route in case of traffic congestion or road closures. They also need to constantly decide if and when to overtake other vehicles on the road, when to accelerate, push the brakes, change the gears or give way to other vehicles to join the traffic on a busy road. Finally, they need to consider general norms, such as road rules, and make momentary decisions which are consistent with these norms. Momentary goals, therefore, are dynamic and short-lived.

Momentary goals also have action-guiding roles. By setting momentary goals, general norms and activity-dependent goals can be broken into smaller, achievable steps so that the achievement of these smaller steps leads to the achievement of general norms and activity-dependent goals. Momentary goals, in other words, can reveal *how* to perform an activity.

Momentary goals are meant to contribute to, and need to be justified by, general norms and activity-dependent goals. Different activities require different momentary goals, and while a momentary goal may be justified in one activity, it may not be justified in another. For instance, if the activity in which the user wants to engage is to go for a leisurely drive, they can justifiably slow down to look at the houses which are recently constructed, or make a sudden stop to purchase an ice cream. However, these momentary decisions would not be justified if the user wants to go from home to work as quickly as possible.

Performing an activity requires taking intermediate steps (achieving momentary goals) which contribute to the completion of the activity. But the way momentary goals support activity-dependent goals can vary. Depending on the activity, momentary goals may be *instrumental* or *constitutive* of the activity. This point can be clarified with two examples.

The first activity to consider is using a vehicle to go from home to work. The goal of this activity is to bring about a particular state of affairs: the state of affairs in which the user has arrived at work. This state of affairs, which represents the successful completion of the activity, is defined prior to the engagement in the activity. Before using the vehicle, the user knows what the world would be like upon the completion of the activity. The success or failure of the activity can also be assessed solely by the changes made to the outside world, that is, the whereabouts of the user at the end of the activity.

What defines the activity of using a vehicle to drive from home to work is the initial and the final states of affairs. The activity is defined by the changes which are made to the outside world. One is engaged in the activity of going from home to work if one is going from home to work. It does not matter if the person goes fast or slow. It does not matter if the person shows respect to other drivers or not. It does not matter which route is taken. In a nutshell, as long as the person gets to the work, it does not matter which or how momentary goals are set and followed in order to bring about the final state of affairs. This is because this activity is not defined by momentary goals, but by the initial and final states of affairs. Therefore, in the activity of driving from home to work, the momentary goals which are set are *instrumental* for the realisation of the activity-dependent goal. From here on, activities such as this, where momentary goals are instrumental, are referred to as Type 1 activities.

Now consider the activity of leisurely driving. In the activity of leisurely driving, momentary goals play a *constitutive* role. This is because the goal of this activity is about the quality of the experience of driving; it is not about bringing about a particular state of affairs. What defines the activity of leisurely driving is shown through the way momentary goals are set and followed. One is engaged in the activity of leisurely driving when one makes relaxed and perhaps unpredictable decisions which are triggered by spur-of-the-moment feelings and curiosities. These relaxed and unpredictable momentary decisions constitute the activity of leisurely driving.

The constitutive role of momentary goals in activities such as leisurely driving means that if momentary goals are set differently, the nature of the activity can change. When relaxed decisions which are triggered by spur-of-the-moment feelings and curiosities are taken away from an activity, and are replaced by constant accelerations, brakes and turns of the steering wheel, the activity of leisurely driving may turn into a different activity, such as the activity of torturing the passengers. In activities such as leisurely driving and torturing the passengers, therefore, whether one is successfully engaged in the activity depends on the way momentary goals are formed and pursued. From here on, this second group of activities are referred to as Type 2 activities.

REPLACEABLE ACTIVITIES

In the previous section, two examples demonstrated two different relations that momentary goals can have to activity-dependent goals. In this section and the next, the distinction between Type 1 and Type 2 activities is used to argue that Type 1 activities can, and Type 2 activities cannot, be replaced and performed by autonomous systems. First, further clarifications need to be made about what is required to perform an activity.

What does it mean to perform an activity? And what does it require for an entity, be it human, animal or an autonomous system, to be able to perform an activity? The performance of an activity can be defined as taking a number of intermediate steps which can jointly bring about the goal of the activity. The activity of changing a lightbulb, for example, requires separating the old bulb from the socket, grabbing the new bulb, and screwing the new bulb in. Each of these steps needs to be broken into yet smaller steps. For example, to open the broken bulb, one may need to first bring a chair, stand on top of the chair, raise one of their arms, grab the bulb and twist the bulb counter-clockwise until the bulb is separated from the socket. Each of these smaller steps works as a momentary goal which is set in order for the activity-dependent goal of changing the lightbulb to realise. These momentary goals jointly make up the *plan of action* for changing the lightbulb.

Here it is worth clarifying that the activity of changing a lightbulb is a Type 1 activity, similar to the activity of using a vehicle to go from home to work. The goal of the activity of changing a lightbulb is to make changes to the outside world (i.e. to replace the old bulb with the new bulb). Also, in this activity the intermediate steps which are taken to perform the activity are instrumental for the realisation of the goal of the activity. It does not matter what or how momentary goals are set, as long as they contribute to the completion of the activity. For example, it does not matter which stool or chair is used to reach the bulb, who changes the bulb or how quickly the old bulb is unscrewed from the socket.

Overall, at least three conditions need to be met for an entity, such as an autonomous system, to be able to perform an activity: physical, epistemic and logical conditions.

The first condition is for the entity to have the right physical capacities. In the case of autonomous systems, this condition is met when systems are designed with physical features which can be used to perform the task. To be able to change a lightbulb which is installed on a ceiling, a robot, for example, needs to be able to physically reach the lightbulb. One which is only 20 cm tall and is unable to expand or to fly, or to climb the walls or other furniture, cannot perform the function of changing a lightbulb, because it does not have the physical capacities to do so. Autonomous systems' physical capacities are restricted by available materials and production techniques. However, machines can sometimes far exceed humans in this respect. Machines can be designed to reach places where humans cannot reach, or function in environments which are too dangerous for humans. So autonomous systems' physical capacities will not always hinder them from replacing humans in performing different activities.

The second condition which needs to be met for an entity to be able to perform an activity is an epistemic condition. To be able to perform an activity, the entity needs to have a plan of action for the performance of the activity. Having a plan of action is important because, as discussed earlier, the goals of an activity do not magically realise out of the blue. A number of intermediate steps, or momentary goals, are required to be taken for the activity-dependent goals to realise. Having a plan of action means being endowed with, or being able to devise, momentary goals whose realisations would lead to the realisation of the activity-dependent goals. In the example of changing a lightbulb, it means knowing that changing a lightbulb requires smaller steps, such as unscrewing the broken bulb and screwing in the new one.

For autonomous systems to be able to replace humans, they need to have plans of action. So, for what types of activities can autonomous systems have plans of action? The answer to this question depends on the status of the intermediate steps required to perform the activity. It is feasible for autonomous systems to have a plan of action for an activity when the intermediate steps are objectively identifiable. Objectively identifiable here means something which can be referred to or perceived by sensory organs.

Objectively identifiable intermediate steps can be taught to autonomous systems. This is because autonomous systems can be equipped with sensors which can scan the environment, get feedback about their performance and make the necessary adjustments in order to successfully perform the intermediate steps. In fact, artificial sensors can surpass human sensory organs in the range of data that they can gather from the environment. Therefore, if the performance of an activity can be broken down into objectively identifiable steps, then autonomous systems can learn how to perform that activity.

Now the question is, what types of activities can be performed by following objectively identifiable intermediate steps? The intermediate steps required to perform Type 1 activities are objectively identifiable. This is because Type 1 activities are aimed at making changes to the objective world, and making changes to the objective world require reliance on *causal* forces. In Type 1 activities, intermediate steps causally link the initial state of affairs to the final state of affairs. In other words, in these activities, intermediate steps, if followed correctly, would *cause* the achievement of the activity-dependent goals. That is why the momentary steps required to achieve the goal of a Type 1 activity can be derived from activity-dependent goals. For example, using a step or flying can help to reach a lightbulb which is installed on the ceiling. Grabbing a lightbulb and twisting it counter-clockwise results in the separation of the bulb from the socket. In Type 1 activities, the intermediate steps are objectively identifiable as they cause the states of affairs which represent the completion of these activities.

The fact that the intermediate steps required to perform Type 1 activities are objectively identifiable makes it possible for autonomous systems to have plans of action for these activities. In the activity of using a vehicle to go from home to work, for example, the intermediate steps which need to be set in order to bring about the activity-dependent goal can be objectively defined as following one of the routes which take the user from home to work. The autonomous vehicle which is used to perform this activity can get dynamic feedback about its position in relation to the destination, use the accelerator, brakes, gears and the steering wheel to navigate itself, and follow the routes which would lead to the destination. All of these steps are objectively identifiable, and if they are followed, the activity will be successfully completed.

The third condition which needs to be met for an entity to be able to perform an activity is the logical requirement for engagement in the activity. As mentioned earlier, autonomous systems are meant to contribute to *human* activities. Even though they perform certain tasks for humans, the only entity who is engaged in an activity is the human user. The logical requirement stipulates that the definition of the activity should allow the transfer of the performance of the activity to others. To be able to perform an activity for a user, an autonomous system needs to preserve the activity in the logical sense so that the user remains engaged in that particular activity. Preserving the activity here means not spoiling the activity by ceasing it or turning it into a different activity. An example can clarify this point.

The religious activity of worshiping a deity is typically a human activity. The performance of this activity, say, in terms of hand gestures or words which need to be uttered, may be objectively identifiable. As such, autonomous systems can learn how to perform the hand gestures and utterances. However, some religions do not allow the activity of worshiping to be delegated to others. In these religions, one needs to worship the deity oneself. Therefore, from a religious point of view, as soon as an autonomous system replaces a human in the performance of the activity of worshiping, the human will not be engaged in the activity of worshiping the deity anymore. In other words, autonomous systems cannot replace the performance of the activity of worshiping for humans, because as soon as they do so, the activity of worshiping ceases and is replaced, say, by an entertainment activity or show business. The active participation of the human subject, therefore, is a logical requirement for engagement in the activity of worshiping. To be engaged in the activity, one needs to actively perform it.

However, unlike the activity of worshiping, Type 1 activities are solely defined by the changes which need to be made to the world. In Type 1 activities, the momentary goals are only instrumental: it does not matter *who* performs the momentary goals or *what* momentary goals are achieved. As long as the final states of affairs are realised, the activity is successfully completed.

As such, in Type 1 activities, delegating the performance of the intermediate steps to others does not spoil the activity. The activity of changing a lightbulb or that of driving from home to work, for example, can be delegated to others, such as friends, family members, taxi drivers, robots or autonomous vehicles. One can still achieve the goal of getting a lightbulb changed or going from home to work without performing the acts of changing the lightbulb or driving a vehicle oneself. Delegating these activities to other entities does not spoil them.

To conclude this section, autonomous systems can fulfil the three conditions which are required for them to replace humans in the performance of Type 1 activities. The first condition is the physical condition. This condition can be met by designing systems with physical capacities appropriate for the task. The second condition is the epistemic condition. Autonomous systems can be equipped with the plan of action to perform Type 1 activities because performing these activities can be expressed in terms of objectively identifiable intermediate steps. The third condition is the logical condition. Autonomous systems can replace humans in the performance of the intermediate steps required for Type 1 activities without spoiling the logic of these activities.

IRREPLACEABLE ACTIVITIES

The above conclusions cannot be generalised to Type 2 activities, such as leisurely driving, where the quality of the experience of engaging in an activity is also important. In the case of Type 2 activities, there are epistemic challenges in replacing the human performance of the activity by an autonomous system. Replacing human performance of the activity may also violate the logical requirement for engagement in these activities.

The Epistemic Condition of Performance

One of the epistemic challenges in using autonomous systems to perform Type 2 activities is that it is hard, if not impossible, to supply autonomous systems with plans of action which can be used to bring about activity-dependent goals. This is a challenge because there is no objective recipe for performing Type 2 activities.

Consider the activity of leisurely driving. There cannot be an objective plan for performing this activity. This activity cannot be broken down into smaller steps which would necessarily bring about the achievement of the activity-dependent goal of leisurely driving, which is enjoying the ride. First, there are always individual differences in what makes a drive a leisurely one.

While some may enjoy driving fast on highways, some others may prefer to drive around national parks and others around the city centre. Second, even the person who wants to go for a leisurely drive may not know in advance what momentary decisions they will make to perform this activity. This is because a person's preferences can dynamically change in one trip. The person may begin by driving towards a quiet leafy suburb, but before reaching there they may decide to follow their curiosity and drive towards some newly built apartments, only to notice an ice cream store on the way to the apartments, stop, have an ice cream and directly return home without going to the quiet leafy suburb or visiting the new apartments. Despite these dynamic changes and not going to places where they initially wanted to go, the person can still enjoy a leisurely drive. In fact, following the initial plan might have resulted in a boring ride.

The above-mentioned epistemic challenge is due to the fact that in Type 2 activities, the realisation of the goal of the activity cannot be assessed by the changes made to the outside world. Whether one has enjoyed what is meant to be a leisurely drive cannot be assessed by the changes made to the position of the vehicle during the activity of leisurely driving. Rather, the realisation of the goals of Type 2 activities can only be subjectively assessed by the individual who is engaged in the activity.

Since the goals of Type 2 activities are not to make specific changes to the outside world, one also cannot rely on objectively identifiable intermediate steps to fulfil these goals. No particular worldly intervention can necessarily lead to the fulfilment of the goals of Type 2 activities. Consider leisurely driving again. Leisurely driving involves momentary, unpredictable decisions made in reaction to surrounding distractions. A mathematically infinite number of distractions can trigger a mathematically infinite number of unpredictable reactions. The challenge here is that, depending on the preference of the individual, any of these distractions may be justifiably pursued. So there are no defined sets of objective steps which can cause the realisation of the goal of the activity. In Type 2 activities, there is a non-causal and subjective connection between momentary goals and activity-dependent goals.

The subjective aspect of the performance of Type 2 activities has other ramifications as well. One of these ramifications is that from a third person perspective, it can be impossible to distinguish between an activity which is performed to bring about a predefined state of affairs (a Type 1 activity), and an activity in which forming and performing momentary objectives are constitutive of the activity (a Type 2 activity). Imagine a person, who after finishing work, enters their car, takes a particular route and stops at a cafe to order a drink. What was the activity in which the person was engaged? Although from an objective point of view, everything about the movement of the vehicle may be known, this knowledge is insufficient to determine the type of activity in which the person was engaged. The person might have been engaged in the activity of going to a predetermined cafe (Type 1), say, to meet with someone. Or they might have been engaged in the activity of leisurely driving (Type 2). It is possible that the random decisions which the person makes during the activity of leisurely driving guide the vehicle through the exact same route as purposeful decisions which need to be made in order to take the person to a particular location. Objective knowledge is not sufficient to distinguish between a Type 2 and a Type 1 activity.

The above point highlights the contrast between Type 1 and Type 2 activities. Type 1 activities can be objectively distinguished from each other because each Type 1 activity is defined by changes which are made to the outside world. Type 2 activities, however, cannot objectively be distinguished from Type 1 activities or from other Type 2 activities because performing these activities cannot be described by reference to a series of objective changes made to the outside world. A drive which may objectively seem to represent an activity in which the user goes from a particular point to a destination may be a leisurely drive, a curious drive, a funny drive or a drive to frighten or torture the passenger (Type 2).

The inherent subjectivity of Type 2 activities, therefore, poses an epistemic challenge for autonomous systems to replace the performance of Type 2 activities on behalf of their users. No other entity, even another human, may be able to perform these activities for someone else.

Here it should be acknowledged that some people may indeed take pleasure from delegating the task of leisurely driving to others. In fact, in some countries, one can ask a taxi driver to simply 'take them for a drive'. The taxi driver may not even know the person, but the passenger may still enjoy the drive. Similarly, some people may willingly let autonomous vehicles take them for leisurely drives, in the same way that some people happily let algorithms stream random music for them on online platforms. However, this does not affect the epistemic argument made in this section. The argument does not rely on the premise that *no one* would be willing to allow autonomous systems or other humans to perform Type 2 activities for them. Rather, the argument is that individuals vary in how they would perform Type 2 activities, and there is no way of knowing in advance how a person would like to perform these activities.

Nevertheless, in addition to epistemic challenges, there are also logical limitations which can restrict other entities from performing Type 2 activities on behalf of others.

The Logical Condition of Engagement

According to the logical condition of engagement, activities which by definition require active subject participation cannot be delegated to autonomous systems. A defining feature of Type 2 activities is that what determines engagement in these activities is the individuals' quality of experience. What constitutes the quality of an experience varies for different people. However, for some individuals, the quality of an experience can be constituted by actively performing the activity by setting and performing the momentary goals. For example, for some people, the joyful experience of leisurely driving is not about where or how they go; it is in the very act of driving. When they are not driving a vehicle, they cannot be engaged in the activity of leisurely driving.

There are various activities in which it is necessary for one to actively perform the activity in order to be engaged in the activity. This necessity can have at least three different sources. In some cases, this necessity may be a personal preference. This is the case with the activity of leisurely driving. While some people require to actively drive a vehicle to take pleasure, some others may be happy for others to take them for a drive. In some other cases, this necessity may be imposed by authorities who determine the conditions of performing the activity. This is the case with the example of worshiping a deity which was given in the previous section. Whether one needs to personally perform certain actions in order to be engaged in the activity of worshiping is a matter which is determined by religious authorities. In some other activities, such as playing a board game, performing in improvised theatre, partying, moaning, respecting others or listening to music, this necessity may be in the logic of engagement in the activity. It is logically contradictory for a person to be engaged in these activities without personally performing them. A person cannot engage in the activity of playing a board game, performing an improvised theatre, partying, moaning, respecting others or listening to music, by sitting aside and delegating the performance of these activities to others.

In any case, when being engaged in an activity requires actively performing the activity, the activity cannot be delegated to any other person or autonomous system. No entity, be it a human or an autonomous system, can perform such activities on behalf of others. As soon as these activities are delegated to other entities, they cease to be what they are. These activities, therefore, set a logical limit to human activities that autonomous systems can replace.

Before discussing the ramifications of this analysis for the design and regulation of autonomous systems, two further points need to be mentioned.

First, it is worth noting that the epistemic condition of performance and the logical condition of engagement divide activities into four types: those which satisfy one condition but not the other, those which satisfy both and those which satisfy neither. For brevity of analysis, Type 1 and Type 2 activities were chosen as two extreme cases where, respectively, both and neither of the conditions are satisfied. But there can be activities where the epistemic condition of performance can be met, but the logical condition of engagement cannot be met. Worshiping a deity can be an example here. Uttering certain words and using specific hand gestures to worship a deity can be taught to autonomous systems, as these are objectively identifiable actions. However, engagement of the subject can be a necessary condition for this activity. And when religious authorities require the subject's active engagement, the worshippers cannot remain engaged in the activity when they delegate the performance of the activity to other entities.

There can also be activities where the logical condition of engagement can be met, but the epistemic condition of performance can pose a challenge. Decorating a house according to a person's taste is an example of such activities. House decoration does not necessarily require the subject's engagement. It involves moving the house furniture around and perhaps repainting the walls or hanging new pictures. The person who wants their house to be redecorated is not logically required to perform these actions to have their house decorated. But people decorate their houses differently, and there is not universal way of decorating a house. To perform the activity of decorating a house for someone else, one needs to know their preferences. Therefore, the activity of house decoration cannot be reliably taught to machines as it requires access to subjective knowledge.

Second, the distinctions made between different activities are not meant to be exclusive, as one person may be simultaneously engaged in two activities of different types by performing one set of actions. For example, a person may want to use a vehicle to go from one point to another, but they may also want to enjoy the drive. In this case, although the momentary goals must jointly contribute to the realisation of the Type 1 activity of going from one place to another, they would not be purely instrumental, as in this case, the quality of the drive also matters. In such activities, the way momentary objectives are set and followed is constitutive of some of the objectives of the activity; thus, these activities fall outside the realm of activities which autonomous systems can perform.

Autonomous systems can replace humans in the performance of Type 1 activities where they would play purely instrumental roles. Type 1 activities are those which are performed solely to make changes to the states of affairs; they are practical problem-solving activities. As discussed in the first part of this book, practical problem-solving activities are those which give technological identities to objects and systems. Hence, autonomous features can make systems to be better *technological* systems. In other words, autonomous features can be safely used only when artificial systems are employed purely in their technological, problem-solving capacities.

In cases where systems play other roles, such as religious, artistic or entertainment roles, using autonomous features can spoil the activity, as these features may violate the epistemic condition of performance or the logical condition of engagement. This does not mean that it is impossible for autonomous systems to replace humans in the performance of any non-technological activity. There may be people who enjoy delegating the performance of the activity of leisurely driving or decorating their house to others, including autonomous systems, and still enjoy the driving or decorating decisions made. Also, it may not be necessary for some people to actively perform the act of driving to be able to enjoy the drive. There may be some religions which allow their followers to delegate the performance of worshiping the deity to others. But none of these scenarios can be assumed, and autonomous systems can at best only *sometimes* replace humans in the performance of non-technological activities. On the one hand, individual differences imply that autonomous systems cannot necessarily fulfil the epistemic condition of performance, and hence, autonomous features do not necessarily improve the performance of systems. On the other hand, the active performance of certain activities, such as partying, playing board games, performing a burnout or worshiping a deity (in religions which do not allow the performance of worshiping to be delegated to others), remains a logical condition of engagement which is impossible for autonomous systems to fulfil.

DESIGN RAMIFICATIONS

Why is it important to clarify the type of activities which necessarily need to be performed by humans and cannot be delegated to autonomous systems? In addition to helping us further understand the epistemic and logical requirements of different activities, such an analysis also has ramifications for the ethical design and regulation of autonomous systems.

Consider autonomous vehicles as an example again. Some have argued that if, in the future, autonomous vehicles prove to be safer than human drivers, then it should become illegal for humans to drive vehicles (Müller & Gogoll, 2020; Sparrow & Howard, 2017). Müller and Gogoll describe such a future with the phrase 'the angel car scenario', and Robert Sparrow and Mark Howard compare human drivers of that future to 'drunk robots'. Placing a ban on human driving in such a future would be to reduce the risks of human drivers endangering the lives of themselves and others due to being fatigued, anxious, fearful, distracted or under the influence of drugs or alcohol. From the harm-reduction, consequentialist point of view, which Sparrow and Howard explicitly adopt (Sparrow & Howard, 2017, 210), this is a valid point. If society's only concern is to make roads safer, then humans should not be allowed to drive vehicles when driving vehicles will result in more road casualties than autonomous driving.

The argument to ban manual driving when autonomous vehicles become safer than humans is valid when Type 1 activities are concerned, which are problem-solving activities in which vehicles are employed in their technological capacities as means to ends. As discussed, in Type 1 activities, momentary goals are only instrumental to the achievement of activity-dependent goals. What matters in these activities are the changes made to the outside world. This aspect of Type 1 activities makes consequentialism the only relevant ethical theory. Other theories, such as deontology or virtue ethics, will be irrelevant in Type 1 activities. This is because in these activities no intrinsic value is attached to user participation or to the way momentary goals are set; the only things which matter are the consequences. This is how Type 1 activities are defined.

However, vehicles are not used only in Type 1 activities, such as taking the passengers from one place to another, where they play purely instrumental roles. Vehicles can be used in other activities in which user participation and momentary goals can be intrinsically valuable, such as going for a leisurely, curious, funny or frightening drive, or performing a burnout. In such activities, the ethics of performing driving tasks cannot be reduced to consequentialist arguments which only consider the impacts of driving vehicles on society at large.

Therefore, there is more to consider in the ethical design and regulation of autonomous vehicles than making roads safer. The consequentialist policy of forbidding driving a car by humans clashes with the duty to respect user autonomy by allowing them to engage in activities which contribute to their personal fulfilment, and possibly their personal identity. Autonomy is here understood as 'the authority to make decisions of practical importance to one's life' (Mackenzie, 2008, 512). Respecting others' autonomy is an important moral principle (Beauchamp & Childress, 2001; Gillon & Lloyd, 1994; Gillon, 2003), and is regarded as an important value in the design of autonomous systems (Verdiesen, 2017). In the context of designing and regulating the use of vehicles, respecting others' autonomy requires allowing people to engage in various activities by using their vehicle.

What this means is that autonomous vehicles can operate as taxis, trams, delivery vehicles, bin collectors or in general, for transferring goods and passengers from a starting point to a destination. When vehicles are used as modes of transport, then their roles are only instrumental. These activities do not require users' active performance, and hence, user autonomy is not violated when they are deprived from actually driving vehicles. In these activities, the consequentialist argument of increasing road safety can be used to ban driving because no strong counter-argument stands against it. However, unless a user specifically requests otherwise, privately owned autonomous vehicles should always have the option for the user to switch to manual driving mode. This is a way for designers and regulators to respect users' autonomy.

Here it should also be noted that allowing humans to drive their vehicles does not necessarily open the door to avoidable road fatalities caused by careless driving or intentionally harmful acts. These risks can be mitigated by designing safety mechanisms into vehicles that would automatically trigger to prevent harmful outcomes. In the same way that some modern vehicles are equipped with autonomous emergency braking systems which stop the vehicle when it is about to hit an obstacle, autonomous vehicles can have further mechanisms which activate the brakes or take control over the steering wheel to prevent unnecessary harm. Such mechanisms can increase the safety of passengers and other road users by allowing 'AI-supervised human driving' (Müller & Gogoll, 2020). Through AI-supervised human driving, the outcome of reducing road fatalities can be achieved by autonomous safety mechanisms which trigger in circumstances when avoidable crashes are about to occur.

The conclusion made here about the design of autonomous vehicles can be generalised to other autonomous systems. Autonomous systems can operate in Type 1 activities where their role is purely technological. This includes activities such as changing a lightbulb, vacuum cleaning a house, deactivating a landmine, digging wells and painting objects on an assembly line. Those artificial systems which may be used in activities where they would play non-instrumental roles need to be designed with a manual control option.

SUMMARY

According to activity realism, objects and systems cannot be optimised without regard to the activities in which they are used. What should be optimised are the activities in which a system is used, and that *may* be achieved by making adjustments to the system. Each object or system can be used in different activities, and adjustments made to the object or system to optimise one activity may spoil others.

Autonomous features may optimise a system in the performance of some activities, but spoil other activities. Autonomous features can optimise artificial systems only when these systems are purely used as technological systems. This includes practical problem-solving activities. These activities are aimed at making changes to the outside world, and the means, methods and intermediate steps taken are only instrumental for the realisation of their goals. Other activities which require active user engagement or those whose performance cannot be broken down into objectively identifiable steps set a limit to what autonomous systems can do. Artificial systems used in non-technological activities need to be designed with a manual control option.

References

American Humanist Association. (1973a, originally written in 1933). Humanist Manifesto I. *The Humanist, 33* (5), 1–3.

American Humanist Association. (1973b). Humanist Manifesto II. *The Humanist, 33*(5), 4–9.

American Humanist Association. (2003). Humanism and Its Aspirations: Humanist Manifesto III, a successor to the Humanist Manifesto 1933. *The Humanist, 63*(3), 13–14.

Baird, D. (2004). *Thing Knowledge: A Philosophy of Scientific Instruments*. US: University of California Press.

Baker, L. R. (2004). The Ontology of Artifacts. *Philosophical Explorations, 7*(2), 99–111.

Baker, L. R. (2008). The Shrinking Difference between Artifacts and Natural Objects. In P. Boltuc (Ed.), *Newsletter on Philosophy and Computers, vol. 2*. American Philosophical Association Newsletters 07(2).

Bargh, J. A., & Chartrand T. L. (1999). The Unbearable Automaticity of Being. *American Psychologist, 54*(7), 462–479.

Beauchamp, T., & Childress, J. (2001). *Principles of biomedical ethics*. New York: Oxford University Press.

Beck, B. B. (1980). *Animal tool behavior: The use and manufacture of tools by animals*. Garland STPM Press.

Bloom, P. (1998). Theories of Artefact Categorization. *Cognition, 66*, 87–93.

Bloom, P. (2007a). More than Words: A Reply to Malt and Sloman. *Cognition, 105*(3), 649–655.

Bloom, P. (2007b). Water as an Artifact Kind. In E. Margolis, & S. Laurence (Eds.), *Creations of the mind: Theories of artifacts and their representation* (150–156). Oxford: Oxford University Press.

Bogen, J., & Woodward, J. (1992). Observations, Theories, and the Evolution of the Human Spirit. *Philosophy of Science, 59*, 590–611.

Boorse, C. (1976). Wright on Functions. *Philosophical Review, 85*(1), 70–86.

Brey, P. (2010). Philosophy of Technology after the Empirical Turn. *Techne, 14*(1), 36–48.

Brey, P. (2014). From Moral Agents to Moral Factors: The Structural Ethics Approach. In P. Kroes, & P. P. Verbeek (Eds.), *The Moral Status of Technical Artifacts* (124–142). Springer.

Briggle, A. (2016) The Policy Turn in the Philosophy of Technology. In M. Franssen, P. Vermaas, P. Kroes, & A. Meijers (Eds.), *Philosophy of technology after the empirical turn. Philosophy of engineering and technology, vol 23*. Cham: Springer.

Clark, A., & Chalmers, D. (1998). The Extended Mind. *Analysis, 58*, 7–19.

Cummins, R. (1975). Functional Analysis. *The Journal of Philosophy, 72*, 741–765.

Cummins, R. (2002). Neo-Teleology. In A. Ariew, R. Cummins, & M. Perlman (Eds.), *Functions: New essays in the philosophy of psychology and biology* (164–174). New York: Oxford University Press.

Danaher, J. (2016). Robots, Law and the Retribution Gap. *Ethics and Information Technology, 18*(4), 299–309.

de Jong, R. (2019). The Retribution-Gap and Responsibility-Loci Related to Robots and Automated Technologies: A Reply to Nyholm. *Science and Engineering Ethics, 26*, 727–735.

Devereux, D. (1977). Artifacts, Natural Objects, and Works of Art. *Analysis, 37*, 134–136.

Devitt, M. (1981). *Designation*. New York: Columbia University Press.

Dewey, J. (1905). The Postulate of Immediate Empiricism. *The Journal of Philosophy, Psychology and Scientific Methods, 2*(15), 393–399.

Dickie, G. (2004). Defining Art: Intention and Extension. In P. Kirvy (Ed.), *The Blackwell Guide to Aesthetics* (45–63). Oxford, United Kingdom: Blackwell Publishing Ltd.

Dipert, R. (1993). *Artifacts, Art Works, and Agency*. Temple University Press.

Douglas, H. (2004). The Irreducible Complexity of Objectivity. *Synthese, 138*(3), 453–473.

Duchamp, M. (1913). *Bicycle Wheel*. Canberra, National Gallery of Australia, no. 1973.817.

Duchamp, M. (1917). *Fountain*. San Francisco, San Francisco Museum of Modern Art, no. 98.29.

Elder, C. (1989). Realism, Naturalism, and Culturally Generated Kinds. *Philosophical Quarterly, 39*, 425–444.

Elder, C. (2007). On the Place of Artifacts in Ontology. In E. Margolis, & S. Laurence (Eds.), *Creations of the mind: Theories of artifacts and their representation* (33–51). Oxford: Oxford University Press.

Ellul, J. (1964). *The technological society* (J. Wilkinson, Trans.). New York: Knopf Doubleday Publishing Group.

Floridi, L., & Sanders, J. W. (2004). On the Morality of Artificial Agents. *Minds and Machines, 93*, 349–379.

Franssen, M. (2006). The Normativity of Artifacts. *Studies in History and Philosophy of Science, 37*, 42–57.

Franssen, M. (2008). Design, Use, and the Physical and Intentional Aspects of Technical Artifacts. In P. Kroes, P. E. Vermaas, A. Light, & S. A. Moore (Eds.), *Philosophy and design* (21–35). Dordrecht: Springer.

Franssen, M., Kroes, P., Reydon, T., & Vermaas, P. (Eds.). (2014). *Artefact kinds: Ontology and human-made world*. Switzerland: Springer.

Franssen, M., Vermaas, P., Kroes, P., & Meijers, A. (Eds.). (2016). *Philosophy of technology after the empirical turn*. Switzerland: Springer.

Franssen, M., Lokhorst, G.J., & van de Poel, I. (2018). Philosophy of Technology. *The Stanford Encyclopedia of Philosophy*, E. N. Zalta (Ed.).

Gillett, A. J., & Heersmink, R. (2019). How Navigation Systems Transform Epistemic Virtues: Knowledge, Issues and Solutions. *Cognitive Systems Research, 56*, 36–49.

Gillon, R. (2003). Ethics Needs Principles—Four Can Encompass the Rest—and Respect for Autonomy Should Be "First among Equals". *Journal of Medical Ethics, 29*, 307–312.

Gillon, R., & Lloyd, A. (Eds.). (1994). *The principles of health ethics*. Chichester: John Wiley & Sons Ltd.

Godfrey-Smith, P. (1994). A Modern History Theory of Functions. *Nous, 28*(3), 344–362.

Goleman, D. (2006). *Social intelligence: The new science of human relationships*. New York: Bantam.

Hacking, I. (1983). *Representing and intervening*. Cambridge: Cambridge University Press.

Hacking, I. (1984). Experimentation and Scientific Realism. In J. Leplin (Ed.), *Scientific realism* (154–172). Berkeley: University of California Press.

Hacking, I. (1988). The Participant Irrealist at Large in the Laboratory. *British Journal for the Philosophy of Science, 39*(3), 277–294.

Haidt, J. (2001). The Emotional Dog and Its Rational Tail: A Social Intuitionist Approach to Moral Judgment. *Psychological Review, 108*, 814–834.

Hauser, M. D. (2006). *Moral minds*. New York: Harper Collins.

Heersmink, R. (2013). A Taxonomy of Cognitive Artifacts: Function, Information, and Categories. *Review of Philosophy and Psychology, 4*(3), 465–481.

Heersmink, R. (2015). Dimensions of Integration in Embedded and Extended Cognitive Systems. *Phenomenology and the Cognitive Sciences, 14*, 577–598.

Heidegger, M. (1977). *The question concerning technology and other essays* (W. Lovitt Trans.). New York: Harper & Row.

Hickman, L. (2001). *Philosophical tools for technological culture: Putting pragmatism to work*. Bloomington: Indiana University Press.

Hickman, L. (2008). Postphenomenology and Pragmatism: Closer Than You Might Think? *Techné, 12*(2), 99–104.

Hillerbrand R., Roeser S. (2016) Towards a Third 'Practice Turn': An Inclusive and Empirically Informed Perspective on Risk. In M. Franssen, P. Vermaas, P. Kroes, & A. Meijers (Eds.), *Philosophy of technology after the empirical turn. Philosophy of engineering and technology, vol 23*. Cham: Springer.

Hilpinen, R. (1993). Authors and Artifacts. *Proceedings of the Aristotelian Society, 93*, 158–178.

Hilpinen, R. (2011). Artifact. *The Stanford Encyclopedia of Philosophy (Winter 2011 Edition)*, E. N. Zalta (Ed.).

Himma, K. (2009). Artificial Agency, Consciousness, and the Criteria for Moral Agency: What Properties Must an Artificial Agent Have to Be a Moral Agent? *Ethics and Information Technology, 11*, 19–29.

Holvast, J. (2009). History of Privacy. *IFIP Advances in Information and Communication Technology, 298*, 13–42.

Houkes, W., & Meijers, A. (2006). The Ontology of Artifacts: The Hard Problem. *Studies in History and Philosophy of Science, 37*(1), 118–131.

Houkes, W., & Vermaas, P. (2004). Actions Versus Functions: A Plea for an Alternative Metaphysics of Artifacts. *The Monist, 87*(1), 52–71.

Houkes, W., & Vermaas, P. (Eds.). (2009a). Artefacts in Analytic Metaphysics. *Techné: Research in Philosophy and Technology, 13*(2).

Houkes, W., & Vermaas, P. (2009b). Artefacts in Analytic Metaphysics: Introduction. *Techné: Research in Philosophy and Technology, 13*(2), 74–81.

Houkes, W., & Vermaas, P. (2010). *Technical functions: On the use and design of artefacts*. Springer.

Hughes, J. (2009). An Artefact Is to Use: An Introduction to Instrumental Functions. *Synthese, 168*, 179–199.

Ihde, D. (1979). *Technics and praxis: A philosophy of technology*. Netherlands: Springer.

Ihde, D. (1991). *Instrumental realism: The interface between philosophy of science and philosophy of technology*. Bloomington: Indiana University Press.

James. W. (1981). *The principles of psychology*. Harvard University Press. Originally published in 1890.

Johnson, D., & Powers, T. (2008). Computers as Surrogate Agents. In J. van den Hoven, & J. Weckert (Eds.), *Information technology and moral philosophy* (251–269). Cambridge University Press.

Jones, O., & Cloke, P. (2008). Non-Human Agencies: Trees in Place and Time. In C. Knappett, & L. Malafouris (Eds.), *Material agency: Towards a non-anthropocentric approach* (79–96). Springer.

Joerges, B. (1999). Do Politics Have Artefacts? *Social Studies of Science, 29*(3), 411–431.

Keulartz, J., Schermer, M., Korthals, M., & Swierstra, T. (2004). Ethics in Technological Culture: A Programmatic Proposal for a Pragmatist Approach. *Science, Technology and Human Values, 29*(1), 3–29.

Kirsh, D., & Maglio, P. (1994). On Distinguishing Epistemic from Pragmatic Action. *Cognitive Science, 18*, 513–549.

Kornblith, H. (2007). How to Refer to Artifacts. In E. Margolis, & S. Laurence (Eds.), *Creations of the mind: Theories of artifacts and their representation* (138–149). Oxford: Oxford University Press.

Kripke, S. (1980). *Naming and necessity*. Cambridge, MA: Harvard University Press.

Kroes, P. (2001). Technical Functions as Dispositions: A Critical Assessment. *Techné, 5*(3): 1–16.

Kroes, P. (2012). *Technical artifacts: Creations of mind and matter*. Netherlands: Springer.

Kroes, P., & Meijers. A. (2006). The Dual Nature of Technical Artifacts. *Studies in History and Philosophy of Science*, *37*(1).

Kroes P., & Meijers, A.W.M. (2016). Toward an Axiological Turn in the Philosophy of Technology. In M. Franssen, P. Vermaas, P. Kroes, & A. Meijers (Eds.), *Philosophy of technology after the empirical turn. Philosophy of engineering and technology, vol 23*. Switzerland: Springer.

Kroes, P., & Verbeek, P. P. (Eds.). (2014). *The moral status of technical artifacts*. Springer.

Kuhn, T. (1962). *The structure of scientific revolutions*. Chicago: University of Chicago Press.

Latour, B. (1992). Where Are the Missing Masses? The Sociology of a Few Mundane Artifacts. In W. E. Bijker (Ed.), *Shaping technology-building society: Studies in sociotechnical change* (225–258). Cambridge: MIT Press.

Latour, B. (1993). *We have never been modern* (C. Porter, Trans.). Cambridge, MA: Harvard University Press.

Latour, B., & Couze, V. (2002). Morality and Technology: The End of the Means. *Theory, Culture & Society*, *19*(5–6), 247–260.

Law, J., & Mol, A. (2008). The Actor-Enacted: Cumbrian Sheep in 2011. In C. Knappett, & Malafouris (Eds.), *Material Agency: towards a non-anthropocentric approach* (57–77). Switzerland: Springer.

Mackenzie, C. (2008). Relational Autonomy, Normative Authority and Perfectionism. *Journal of Social Philosophy*, *39*(4), 512–533.

Malafouris, L. (2008). At the Potter's Wheel: An Argument *for* Material Agency. In C. Knappett, & Malafouris (Eds.), *Material Agency: towards a non-anthropocentric approach* (19–36). Switzerland: Springer.

Malt, B., & Sloman, S. (2007). More than words, but still not categorization. *Cognition*, *105*(3), 656–657.

Matthias, A. (2004). The Responsibility Gap in Ascribing Responsibility for the Actions of Automata. *Ethics and Information Technology*, *6*, 175–183.

McLaughlin, P. (2001). *What functions explain: Functional explanation and self-reproducing systems*. Cambridge: Cambridge University Press.

McLaughlin, P. (2002). Functional Explanation. In R. Mayntz (Hg.), *Akteure – Mechanismen – Modelle: Zur Theoriefähigkeit makro-sozialer Analysen* (196–212). Campus Frankfurt a.M.

Meijers, A. (Ed.). (2009). *Philosophy of technology and engineering sciences, vol 9*. Elsevier.

Merricks, T. (2001). *Objects and persons*. Oxford: Clarendon Press.

Millikan, R. G. (1984). *Language, thought and other biological categories*. Cambridge, MA: MIT Press.

Millikan, R. G. (1989). In Defense of Proper Functions. *Philosophy of Science*, *56*(2), 288–302.

Millikan, R. G. (1999). Spoons, Pills, and Quills: A Pluralist Theory of Function. *Journal of Philosophy*, *96*(4), 191–206.

Müller, J., & Gogoll, J. (2020). Should Manual Driving be (Eventually) Outlawed? *Science and Engineering Ethics, 26*, 1549–1567.

Neander, K. (1991). Functions as Selected Effects: The Conceptual Analyst's Defense. *Philosophy of Science, 58*(2), 168–206.

Norman, D. A. (1991). Cognitive Artifacts. In J. M. Carroll (Ed.), *Designing interaction: Psychology at the human-computer interface* (17–38). Cambridge, UK: Cambridge University Press.

Nyholm, S. (2018). Attributing Agency to Automated Systems: Reflections on Human–Robot Collaborations and Responsibility-Loci. *Science and Engineering Ethics, 24*, 1201–1219.

Ortega y Gasset, J. (1961). *History as a system and other essays: Towards a philosophy of history* (H. Weyl, Trans.). US: Norton.

Oderberg, D. (2012). No Potency without Actuality: The Case of Graph Theory. In T. Tahko (Ed.), *Contemporary Aristotelian metaphysics* (207–228). Cambridge: Cambridge University Press.

Perlman, M. (2004). The Modern Philosophical Resurrection of Teleology. *The Monist, 87*(1), 3–51.

Preston, B. (1998). Cognition and Tool Use. *Mind & Language, 13*(4), 513–547.

Preston, B. (2009). Philosophical Theories of Artifact Function. In A. Meijers (Ed.), *Philosophy of technology and engineering sciences: volume 9* (213–233). Elsevier.

Preston, B. (2013). *A philosophy of material culture: Action, function, and mind*. Routledge.

Preston, B. (2018). Artifact. *The Stanford Encyclopedia of Philosophy*, Edward N. Zalta (Ed.).

Purves, D., Jenkins, R., & Strawser, B. (2015). Autonomous Machines, Moral Judgment, and Acting for the Right Reasons. *Ethical Theory and Moral Practice, 18*, 851–872.

Putnam, H. (1975). *Mind, language, and reality: Philosophical papers, vol. 2*. Cambridge, UK: Cambridge University Press.

Quine, W. V. O., & Ullian, J. S. (1978). *The web of belief*. US: McGraw-Hill Education.

Roff, H. (2014). The Strategic Robot Problem. *Journal of Military Ethics, 13*(3), 211–227.

Roque, X. (1997). The Manufacture of the Positron. *Studies in History and Philosophy of Modern Physics, 28*(1), 73–129.

Salmon, N. U. (1979). How *not* to Derive Essentialism from the Theory of Reference. *Journal of Philosophy, 76*(12), 703–725.

Salmon, N. (1982). *Reference and essence*. Oxford: Basil Blackwell.

Schmidt, J. C. (2011). What is a Problem? On Problem-oriented Interdisciplinarity. *Poeisis Prax, 7*, 249–274.

Schulzke, M. (2011). Robots as Weapons in Just Wars. *Philosophy & Technology, 24*, 293–306.

Schyfter, P. (2009). The Bootstrapped Artefact: A Collectivist Account of Technological Ontology, Functions, and Normativity. *Studies in History and Philosophy of Science, 40*, 102–111.

Shumaker, R. W., Walkup, K. R., & Beck, B. B. (2011). *The animal tool behavior: The use and manufacture of tools by animals*. The John Hopkins University Press.

Searle, J. (1995). *The construction of social reality*. The Free Press.

Searle, J. (2007). Social Ontology and the Philosophy of Society. In E. Margolis, & S. Laurence (Eds.), *Creations of the mind: Theories of artifacts and their representation* (3–17). Oxford: Oxford University Press.

Smythe, T. W., & Evans, T. G. (2007). Intuition as a basic source of moral knowledge. *Philosophia, 35*, 233–247.

Soltanzadeh, S. (2015). Humanist and Nonhumanist Aspects of Technologies as Problem Solving Physical Instruments. *Philosophy and Technology, 28*(1), 139–156.

Soltanzadeh, S. (2016). Questioning Two Assumptions in the Metaphysics of Technological Objects. *Philosophy and Technology, 29*(2), 127–135.

Soltanzadeh, S. (2019). A Practically Useful Metaphysics of Technology. *Techné, 23*(2), 232–250.

Soltanzadeh, S. (2021). Strictly Human: Limitations of Autonomous Systems. *Minds and Machines*. https://doi.org/10.1007/s11023-021-09582-7

Soltanzadeh, S., Galliott, J., & Jevglevskaja, N. (2020). Customizable Ethics Settings for Building Resilience and Narrowing the Responsibility Gap: Case Studies in the Socio-Ethical Engineering of Autonomous Systems. *Science and Engineering Ethics 26*, 2693–2708.

Sparrow, R. (2007). Killer Robots. *Journal of Applied Philosophy, 24*(1), 62–77.

Sparrow, R. (2016). Robot and Respect: Assessing the Case Against Autonomous Weapon Systems. *Ethics & International Affairs, 30*(1), 93–116.

Sparrow, R., & Howard, M. (2017). When Human Beings Are Like Drunk Robots: Driverless Vehicles, Ethics, and the Future of Transport. *Transportation Research Part C: Emerging Technologies, 80*, 206–215.

Strawser, B. J. (2010). Moral Predators: The Duty to Employ Uninhabited Aerial Vehicles. *Journal of Military Ethics, 9*(4), 342–68.

Sutton, J. (2002). Porous Memory and the Cognitive Life of Things. In D. Tofts, A. Jonson, & A. Cavallero (Eds.), *Prefiguring cyberculture: An intellectual history* (130–141). MIT Press.

Sutton, J. (2008). Material Agency, Skills and History: Distributed Cognition and the Archaeology of Memory. In C. Knappett, & L. Malafouris (Eds.), *Material agency: Towards a non-anthropocentric approach* (37–55). Switzerland: Springer.

Thomasson, A. (2007). Artifacts and Human Concepts. In E. Margolis, & S. Laurence (Eds.), *Creations of the mind: Theories of artifacts and their representation* (52–73). Oxford: Oxford University Press.

Thomasson, A. (2009). Artifacts in Metaphysics. In A. Meijers (Ed.), *Philosophy of technology and engineering sciences: volume 9* (191–212). Elsevier.

van Inwagen, P. (1990). *Material beings*. US: Cornell University Press.

Vermaas. P., & Houkes, W. (2006). Technical Functions: A Drawbridge between the Intentional and the Structural Natures of Technical Artefacts. *Studies in History and Philosophy of Science*, 37, 5–18.

Verbeek, P. P. (2005). *What things do*. The Pennsylvania State University Press.

Verbeek, P. P. (2009). Cultivating Humanity: Towards a Non-humanist Ethics of Technology. In J. K. B. Oslen, E. Selinger, & S. Riis (Eds.), *New waves in philosophy of technology* (241–263). Palgrave macmillan.

Verbeek, P. P. (2010). Accompanying Technology: Philosophy of Technology after the Empirical Turn. *Techné, 14*(1), 49–54.

Verbeek, P. P. (2011). *Moralizing technology: Understanding and designing the morality of things*. Chicago, US: The University of Chicago Press.

Verdiesen, I. (2017). How Do We Ensure that We Remain in Control of our Autonomous Weapons? *AI Matters, 3*(3), 47–55.

Weckert, J. (1986). Putnam, Reference and Essentialism. *Dialogue, 25*, 509–521.

Weir, A., Chappell, J., & A. Kacelnik. (2002). Shaping of Hooks in New Caledonian Crows. *Science, 297*(5583), 981.

Whitehead, A. (1967). *Process and reality*. New Jersey: The Macmillan Company.

Winner, L. (1980). Do Artifacts Have Politics? *Daedalus, 109* (1), 121–136.

Winters, A. (2017). *Natural processes: Understanding metaphysics without substance*. Pennsylvania: Palgrave Macmillan.

Woolgar, S., & Cooper, G. (1999). Do Artifacts Have Ambivalence? *Social Studies of Science, 29*(3), 433–449.

Wright, L. (1973). Functions. *Philosophical Review, 82*(2), 139–168.

Wittgenstein, L. (1978). *Remarks on the foundations of mathematics* (G. E. M. Anscombe. Trans.), (G. H. von Wright, & R. Rhees (Eds.). US: The MIT Press.

Index

accidental discovery(ies), 162–63
accompanying technology, 3. *See also* Verbeek, Peter-Paul
action, theories of, 66
activity realism, 8–9, 33–35, 88–89. *See also* function theories, belief-based consequentialist; reality
agency, 58, 59
AI-supervised human driving, 189
algebra, 150
American Humanist Association, 57
animal(s), 26, 48, 53–54
anthropocentrism. *See* humanism, broad sense of
anthropology, 9–14. *See also* archaeology
anti-essentialism, 7–8
application(s) of scientific entities, 161
archaeology, 25–26
Archimedes, 123
art, 41–42. *See also* object(s), artistic
artefact(s), 21–25, 40; dual nature of, 23; existence of, 131–38; *vs.* non-artefact(s), 25–32, 40–44; study of, 5, 25–26; *vs.* technology(ies), 38–40
atom, 166
authenticity, 41
autonomous systems, 62, 173; limitations of, 182–87

autonomous vehicles, 187–89
autonomy, 48, 188
axiological turn, 4

Baird, Davis, 145–46, 163
Baker, Lynne, 23, 28, 95, 105, 136
Bargh, John, 13
Beethoven, 34
black box, 121–24
the Black Stone, 121–22, 124
Bloom, Paul, 86
Bohr, Niels, 164
Brey, Philip, 58
Briggle, Adam, 4

capacity: mental, 11, 53–54, 66–69, 71–73; physical. *See* function theories, capacity-based
categorisation, 20–21, 25, 134; general, 7–8, 19–20, 36, 40, 44, 47–48; particular, 8, 77–79
cathode ray experiment(s), 130, 161, 164–66
Chalmers, David, 69–70
change: internal, 22; natural, 23
Chartrand, Tanya, 13
Chopin, 34
Clark, Andy, 69–70
Cloud Chamber, 159, 163, 168

cognitive artefacts. *See* object(s), cognitive
complexity, 50
conditions of possibility, 55–56
consciousness, 13–14
consequentialism, 188
conservatism, scientific, 169–71
control (and use), 48, 65–66
Copernicus, 136
creative use, 87–88

demarcation. *See* categorisation, general
Democritus, 166
description(s), theoretical, 160–61, 163
design, 43–44, 187–89. *See also* intention condition
designer(s). *See* maker(s)
desire(s). *See* value(s)
Devereux, Daniel, 22
Devitt, Michael, 166–67
Dewey, John, 9, 143
Dickie, George, 47
Dipert, Randall, 23
Douglas, Heather, 158–59
Duchamp, Marcel, 36, 143

Elder, Crawford, 135
electron, 164–67
empirical turn, 2–4, 103
end(s). *See* goal(s)
engagement (in an activity), 175. *See also* logical condition of engagement
entity realism, 29–30, 44, 94–95, 130–31
environment, 12. *See also* function theories, causal-role; nature; state(s) of affairs
environmentalism, 57
epistemic action, 70
epistemic condition of performance, 180–84
essence, 2, 7–8, 30

essentialism, 2–3, 30, 101–2; function, 94–95. *See also* anti-essentialism; entity realism
ethics, 56–57, 62–63; of technology, 58
ethics setting(s), 62–63
evaluation, 46, 67–69, 71
existence, 9, 11, 130–31, 148–49
existence condition(s), 136–37; the formal, 137–38
extended mind thesis, 59, 69–70
externalist: function theories, 105–8, 124. *See also* problem–solving, strategies

facts, worldly. *See* state(s) of affairs
Faraday, Michael, 145–46
Farsi, 151–52
feeling(s), reality of, 145
fluidity. *See* property(ies), dynamic
Franssen, Maarten, 27, 133
function: accidental, 88; authentic, 99; conservative, 99; justification. *See* function theories, epistemological. *See also* categorisation, particular; intention condition
function, proper, 88. *See also* essentialism, function
function, system, 97; *vs.* proper function, 98–100
function kind(s). *See* kind(s), artefact
function theories: belief-based, 80, 108, 111–12; belief-based consequentialist, 112–24; capacity-based, 81–82, 95, 104–5, 111–12, 121–22; causal-role. *See* function theories, capacity-based; epistemological, 78–79, 84–85; evolutionary (etiological), 82–85, 90, 119–20; intentional, 79–81, 94–95, 105–8; linguistic, 78–79, 86–87; metaphysical, 78, 79

Index

Gillett, Alexander James, 69
goal(s), 10–11, 13, 31, 62–63; activity-dependent, 176; constitutive, 177–78; instrumental, 177–78; momentary, 177
goal-oriented activities, 10–11; habitual. *See* habit
Gogoll, Jan, 187, 189

habit, 10–11, 51–52
Hacking, Ian, 29, 157
Heersmink, Richard, 69
Heidegger, Martin, 3
Higgs boson, 161
Hillerbrand, Rafaela, 4
Hilpinen, Risto, 22–23
Himma, Kenneth, 66
historiography, 58
Hobbit(s), 138, 143–45, 149
Holvast, Jan, 62
Houkes, Wybo, 28, 52, 80, 85, 94, 114
Howard, Mark, 187
human (characteristics), purely, 56, 57, 59, 61–62
human(s), 9–14
humanism: broad sense of, 56–57; narrow sense of, 57; *vs.* non-humanism, 56–60; in philosophy of technology, 57–60, 63–69, 80
humanist manifesto(s). *See* American Humanist Association

ICE theory, 84–85, 122
identification, 40. *See also* activity realism; categorisation; entity realism; function theories
identity: fluid, 36–37; racial, 12–13; sexual, 12–13
identity, functional, 98–99. *See also* function theories
Ihde, Don, 157
impact, 30–32, 44. *See also* usefulness

intended impact(s), 113, 117
intention condition, 23–25, 38–39, 133
internalist: function theories, 104–5. *See also* problem-solving, strategies
isolation, 2, 11. *See also* entity realism

James, William, 9, 142

kind(s): artefact, 9, 88, 102, 133–34; copied, 132, 135; natural, 101, 103, 133–34
kirpan, 148, 152
Kirsh, David, 70
Kornblith, Hilary, 87, 89
Kripke, Saul, 89. *See also* reference, causal theory of
Kroes, Peter, 4, 23, 82, 88, 106, 114
Kuhn, Thomas, 103

language, 145, 150–52
Large Hadron Collider, 161, 162
Latour, Bruno, 59
logical condition of engagement, 181–82, 184–85

Maglio, Paul, 70
maker(s), 23, 24, 43–44, 94–95, 105
malfunction, 106–7
Malt, Barbara, 86
manipulation. *See* application(s) of scientific entities
means, 10–11
Meijers, Anthonie, 4, 23, 114
metaphysics, substance, 29–30
metaphysics of technology, 19, 21, 59–60; subfields of, 6–9
mind-dependence, 11, 35, 61, 129–30, 133–34, 136–37
modification condition, 21–23, 39–40, 132–33
morality. *See* ethics; values
Müller, Julian, 187, 189

multi-functionality. *See* multiple utilisability
multiple realisability, 114–15
multiple utilisability, 114–16
music, 33–34, 37

naming, 165–67
nature, 41. *See also* animal(s); object(s), natural
naturefact(s), 22
non-humanism, 56–57; in philosophy of technology, 57–63, 81–82
Norman, Donald, 69
norms, general, 176

object(s): artistic, 40, 42, 47, 143, 147–48; cognitive, 69–70; educational, 40, 42; entertainment, 40, 42, 47, 147–48; natural, 52–53, 136; religious, 40, 42, 47, 121–22, 124, 143, 147–48; technological. *See* technology
objectifying technology(ies), 159
objectivity, 158–59, 180; instrumental, 163
observation(s), experimental, 160, 162–63
observational function ascription(s), 107–8
offspring, 2, 35
ontology, 9, 129–31
Ortega y Gasset, José, 13

perception, 11
performing (an activity), 175, 179. *See also* epistemic condition of performance
Perlman, Mark, 79, 115
philosophy of science, 7, 102–3
philosophy of technology, 1, 44, 103; history of, 2–4, 7, 103; practical relevance, 3–6, 32, 44; subfields of, 4–6; subject matter of, 5–7, 19, 32; trends in, 4–7. *See also* technology, essentialist theories of

phlogiston, 117–19, 143–44, 164–66
plan of action, 72, 179–81
policy turn, 4
practice turn, 4
pragmatic considerations, 99–100, 105, 106, 138–39, 141–42. *See also* artefact(s), *vs.* non-artefact(s); philosophy of technology, practical relevance
Preston, Beth, 95–98, 100, 114, 116, 120
privacy, 62
problem(s), 11, 67; identification of, 63–64, 71
problem-solving: activities, 9–14, 63–64; strategies, 11–13
process philosophy, 34
production history, 82–84
property(ies): dynamic, 34–35, 40; extrinsic, 2–3, 95; intrinsic, 2, 95; problem-solving, 49–50; technological, 40, 147

Quine, Willard van Orman, 103, 169

reality, 34, 142–46, 148–50; divine. *See* James, William; experienced. *See* Dewey, John; language and, 150–52; practical. *See* James, William; scientific, 162–67; technological, 146–47, 151
reference, causal theory of, 89–90, 101–2. *See also* naming
regulation(s), 83, 187–89
religion, 34, 36–37, 57. *See also* object(s), religious
responsibility, 62–63
robot(s), 65–66
Roeser, Sabine, 4
Roque, Xavier, 159
rule-setting activities, 10
Rutherford, Ernest, 164

Salmon, Nathan, 86–87
Santa Claus, 144–45

Schyfter, Pablo, 147
scientific entity(ies), 158
scientific revolution(s), 161–62
scientific term(s), 158; meanings of, 165–66
Searle, John, 60
Sloman, Steven, 86
social construction of technology, 58
sociology, 58
solution, 11, 49–50
solution-dependent, 51
Sparrow, Robert, 187
state(s) of affairs, 11–13
status, ontological. *See* ontology
stoicism, 12
subconsciousness, 13–14
subjectivity, 46, 143, 146, 182–84. *See also* mind-dependence

technological determinism, 58
technological-ness, degrees of, 48–51
technology(ies), 40, 45–48, 65, 146–47; conditions of possibility of, 2, 55–56, 61–69; essentialist theories of, 2–3. *See also* artefact(s), *vs.* technology(ies)
technology-dependence of sciences, 157, 162–64, 167–71
Thomasson, Amie, 23, 60, 84, 137–38, 144–45
Thomson, Joseph. *See* cathode ray experiment(s)

transcendentalism, 3
truth, 116–17

Ullian, Joseph Silbert, 103, 169
underdetermination. *See* multiple utilisability
unobservability, 159–60
unobservable entities, 162–64
use, 48, 52–53, 64–66, 72–73; context of, 43–44
usefulness, 20–21, 38

value(s), 12–13, 41, 56, 62–63; epistemic, 30. *See also* object(s), cognitive
van Gogh, Vincent, 132
van Inwagen, Peter, 133
Verbeek, Peter-Paul, 3, 62–63
Vermaas, Pieter, 28, 52, 80, 85, 94
Vivaldi, 33–34

Watt, James, 143, 164
weapon(s), 42–43
Weckert, John, 134
Whitehead, Alfred North, 34
Wittgenstein, Ludwig, 170
Wright, Larry, 117–18

X-ray, 161, 162

About the Author

Sadjad Soltanzadeh, PhD, is a researcher in philosophy of science and technology at the Asser Institute at the University of Amsterdam. Sadjad has a multidisciplinary background in philosophy, mechanical engineering and education, and has experienced diverse workplace and academic environments in Australia, Iran and the Netherlands.

Sadjad has developed a philosophical approach, named activity realism, for which he won the SPT 2019 Early Career Award. As an engineer, Sadjad contributed to several projects, including designing and building robots at the ARAS robotic group. Sadjad is also an experienced secondary schoolteacher and has jointly designed curriculum for four philosophy courses at the college level.

www.ingramcontent.com/pod-product-compliance
Lightning Source LLC
Chambersburg PA
CBHW062228300426
44115CB00012BA/2256